Unde[...] Constitution

The European Union's Constitutional Treaty has been much talked about, usually critically, by those who see it either as a blueprint for a centralized and protectionist superstate, or a triumph for Anglo-Saxon economics which will undermine the European social model and the institutions which support it. It has created great controversy throughout Europe and failed to gain popular approval in the French and Dutch referenda of 2005. Yet the actual text has been little read, notably in the United Kingdom, partly because it has not been widely circulated.

Understanding the European Constitution seeks to redress this imbalance and is one of the few books in English to give the reader an impartial and concise view of the Constitutional Treaty. An invaluable tool to understanding the Treaty, the book includes a full copy of its core Part I and a detailed and expert analysis of its main themes together with a brief introduction to the rest of the Treaty. The issues that are covered include:

- how and why the Treaty came about;
- how its content compares to the EU's existing treaties;
- why it has attracted so much controversy;
- the difficulties in trying to understand it, notably its dual status as treaty and constitution;
- how the Treaty is to be ratified and the issues which have figured in the ratification debates.

Understanding the European Constitution is written in uncomplicated language with explanatory tables and a glossary by two long-standing students of the treaties. It is essential reading for all students with interests in politics, the European Union and law.

Clive H. Church is Emeritus Jean Monnet Professor of European Studies at the University of Kent and a member of its Centre for Swiss Politics. His research interests continue to be in Swiss politics and the constitutional and democratic development of the EU. His most recent publications are *The Penguin Guide to the European Treaties* (Penguin, 2002), co-authored with David Phinnemore, and *The Politics and Government of Switzerland* (Palgrave, 2003).

David Phinnemore is Senior Lecturer in European Integration at Queen's University Belfast. His research interests include EU treaty reform, EU enlargement and EU–Romania relations. He is co-author with Clive H. Church of *The Penguin Guide to the European Treaties* (Penguin, 2002).

Understanding the European Constitution

An introduction to the EU Constitutional Treaty

Clive H. Church and David Phinnemore

LONDON AND NEW YORK

First published 2006
by Routledge
2 Park Square, Milton Park, Abingdon, Oxon OX14 4RN

Simultaneously published in the USA and Canada
by Routledge
270 Madison Ave, New York, NY 10016

Routledge is an imprint of the Taylor & Francis Group

Typeset in Baskerville with Helvetica by
Book Now Ltd
Printed and bound in Great Britain by
TJ International Ltd, Padstow, Cornwall, UK

British Library Cataloguing in Publication Data
A catalogue record for this book is available from the British Library

Library of Congress Cataloging in Publication Data
A catalog record for this book has been requested

ISBN10: 0–415–36339–X(hbk)
ISBN10: 0–415–36340–3 (pbk)

ISBN13: 9–78–0–415–36339–6 (hbk)
ISBN13: 9–78–0–415–36340–2 (pbk)

Contents

Illustrations

Figures

Tables

Boxes

Preface

What a difference a year (and the calling of a referendum) makes! In 2003 we sought to interest publishers in a booklet on the *Draft Treaty establishing a Constitution for Europe*, which had recently been produced by the European Convention, but to no avail. So, while over the next few months other countries were producing a crop of books, there were only two in the United Kingdom, despite the greater intensity of its, admittedly often superficial, debate. Even by the time the Referendum Bill was being initially debated, in early 2005, there were still no more than a handful of studies, despite the fact that calling a referendum was a real challenge for UK politics.

Hence we are very grateful to Craig Fowlie of Routledge for rapidly realizing the importance of the Constitutional Treaty in the post-referendum decision world. In approaching us he rightly sought a book with a wide general appeal. We are grateful for his encouragement and understanding and hope that this measures up to his expectations. We are equally grateful to Heidi Bagtazo, Harriet Brinton, Nadia Seemungal, Richard Cook, Frances Maher and their colleagues for helping to see the book through to completion.

Given this brief, what we have tried to provide in *Understanding the European Union Constitution Treaty* is something rather different from the style of book we have previously written on the EU's treaties. We are not offering a systematic line-by- line commentary, although we hope this will come in due course. Nor are we attempting a detailed study of the whole text of the Constitutional Treaty with its four Parts, multiple Protocols and innumerable Declarations. Nonetheless, this is more than ever a joint work. We also had to give up the idea of printing the whole text since this would have made the book unconscionably long and expensive. (The UK government's edition of the Constitutional Treaty retails at £47.00 as does the Foreign and Commonwealth Office's own 500-page commentary.)

Rather we are trying to introduce the basic elements of the Constitutional Treaty. We prefer to call it this because a constitutional treaty is what it is, and this name brings out its dual nature. Simply calling it a Constitution, as opponents prefer to do, is to give way to polemic. The official title is the *Treaty establishing a Constitution for Europe* though the UK referendum question (as opposed to the French one) talks – accurately and understandably but, in legal terms, imprecisely – of a 'Constitution for the European Union'. All the major players accepted this for the sake of clarity and perhaps also because the somewhat grandiose use of Europe reflects the title of the Convention. However, it could still cause confusion among unwary readers. However, all three usages refer to the same text.

Introducing the Constitutional Treaty requires printing Part I so that it is more easily available and more exposed to analysis of its main themes. The rest of the document we merely outline, even though much of it is important. We also try and put the Constitutional Treaty into its chronological, methodological and political contexts. In all this, in other words, we are trying to respond to calls for a full, well-informed account and explanation of the Constitutional Treaty, and one which comes to terms with its difficulties. For it is not as simple a thing as extreme opponents, and some supporters, maintain. It does take some understanding.

Obviously, with such a controversial subject, our account will not satisfy all contending parties, especially those who regard anything other than denunciation as mere propaganda. Nonetheless, it is based on what is actually in the many pages of the Constitutional Treaty. These are not perfect, far from it, and we point to such imperfections. Nonetheless, it seems to us to be a useful consolidation of the status quo, with some modest improvements. It may not be a text worth dying for, but neither is it one so bad as to demand a wholesale crisis through a rejection.

So we hope that, by analysing the document in terms of existing treaties and practices and exploring its own inherent difficulties, we can do something to dissipate the miasma of ignorance and exaggeration which so often surrounds British debates on the European Union. And, by doing it ahead of any UK referendum, we also hope that this will develop the debate and allow people to come to a more informed decision than presently seems likely. However, our assessments only really cover up to 9 April 2005 and do not properly take into account the dramatic events of late May and early June.

Acknowledgement

We would like to thank the *Official Journal of the European Union* (http:// europa.eu.int/eur-lex) for allowing us to reproduce the text of the Constitutional Treaty. Please note that only European Union legislation as printed in the *Official Journal of the European Union* is deemed to be authentic.

CHC and DP
April 2005

Abbreviations

CFI	Court of First Instance
CFR	Charter of Fundamental Rights
CFSP	Common foreign and security policy
COREPER	Committee of Permanent Representatives
CSDP	Common security and defence policy
EAEC	European Atomic Energy Community
EC	European Community
ECB	European Central Bank
ECHR	European Convention on Human Rights
ECJ	European Court of Justice
ECSC	European Coal and Steel Community
EEC	European Economic Community
EIB	European Investment Bank
EMU	Economic and Monetary Union
EP	European Parliament
ERRF	European Rapid Reaction Force
ESCB	European System of Central Banks
EU	European Union
Euratom	European Atomic Energy Community
IGC	Intergovernmental conference
MEP	Member of the European Parliament
NATO	North Atlantic Treaty Organization
OOPEC	Office of Official Publications of the European Community
QMV	Qualified majority voting
TA	Treaty of Amsterdam
TEC	Treaty establishing the European Community
TEU	Treaty on European Union
TN	Treaty of Nice
UK	United Kingdom
UKIP	United Kingdom Independence Party
UN	United Nations
VAT	Value Added Tax
WTO	World Trade Organization

1 Introduction

The British public is normally profoundly unconcerned about matters constitutional, especially when these involve the European Union (EU). Interviewers asking about the European Parliament (EP) elections were often told 'I am not interested'. And, when asked at an official reception about his views on the proposed referendum, pop star Peter Andre said 'Er, blimey, you really got me there mate'. Moreover, the British are more likely to think there is too much media coverage of the European Union rather than too little.

This explains why the United Kingdom records high levels of ignorance about the Union. The Constitutional Treaty is no exception. Only six per cent, half the EU average, of a 2004 Eurobarometer poll admitted to knowing a lot about it, whereas 44 per cent knew a little and 50 per cent nothing at all – a figure only exceeded by Cypriots. The EU averages were, respectively, 56 per cent and 33 per cent. Recent reports have shown that BBC journalists and business leaders are equally poorly informed. So it is unsurprising that many letters to newspapers refer to what someone else has said about the Constitutional Treaty and not to what is actually in the text.

Yet the United Kingdom was the only country where opponents of the Constitutional Treaty always outnumbered supporters, by 30 per cent to 20 per cent. In the European Union as a whole, 16 per cent were opposed and 49 per cent in favour, with 35 per cent having no opinion (50 per cent in the United Kingdom). Lack of knowledge is often adduced as a major reason for being opposed. This reflects the lack of publications on the Constitutional Treaty in the United Kingdom. For, although it was easily available on the EU website (and many copies of the draft were circulated by the Convention) and the government published the Convention's draft as a Command Paper in September 2003, there was nothing like the private-sector interest found elsewhere. Thus in France, where the text is also controversial, there appeared a dozen solid works, either printing the text or commenting on it from a variety of perspectives.

Contrary to previous treaties, even eurosceptic forces failed to publish the Constitutional Treaty until very late in the day. Initially, only *Prospect* magazine published the text of the draft and a fringe publisher produced a general booklet. None of the broadsheets chose to do more than publish potted summaries. The Command Paper containing the full text did not appear until Christmas 2004, with detailed commentary and brief guides following. Hence, even many members of the cabinet were said to be unfamiliar with the text. All this suggests that the contents of the document may not be the whole of the problem, which is why debate has focused on symbolism and major institutional and procedural changes, not on the whole package. So while, unusually, the Constitutional Treaty seems to be of concern to many people, this is not because it is familiar reading.

We hope to help change this by printing the core of the text so that it is more easily available. Equally, we would like to make it better understood. This we try to do by setting it in context and assessing its key elements. However, before looking at some of the questions thrown up by the Constitutional Treaty, we feel we should introduce the text itself. We hope this will enable readers to do what Commission President, José Manuel Barroso, urges: examine the text and not be swayed by national politics. For, although it seems to be at the centre of debate, this is not always the case. Because it is a long and complicated document, and reading it would normally be as attractive as a trip to the dentist for many people, attitudes to it are often based on wider and more political considerations. This leads to misunderstandings about its purpose and significance.

The Constitutional Treaty in brief

Summing up the Constitutional Treaty is difficult. Reducing it to a few key points can mean that a lot is left out, including the overall packaging. So our account is a little longer because this provides a better basis for considering its overall significance, its evolution and the way it needs to be approached. What we find is that, although we now have a single, clarified and consolidated text, it is not a fully integrated document. As Box 1.1 shows, we are dealing with a seven-section treaty. The first, and shortest, is the *Preamble*, a brief statement, found in many treaties, which tries to sum up the motivation and spirit of the new document.

Then comes the Constitutional Treaty itself, which, like many books, is made up of 'Parts' or subdivisions. Although *Part I*, unlike the other three, has no label because it sets out in relatively simple language the basic structures and principles of the new Union, what it can do and how, it is the nub of the whole Constitutional Treaty. Hence many talk of it as 'the Constitution'. If the reality is more complicated, Part I does constitute a new

Box 1.1 The Treaty establishing a Constitution for Europe: an outline

Preamble	
Part I	***Untitled*** 9 Titles containing Articles I-1 to I-60
Part II	**The Charter of Fundamental Rights** 7 Titles containing Articles II-61 to II-114
Part III	**The policies and functioning of the European Union** 7 Titles containing Articles III-115 to III-436
Part IV	**General and final provisions** Article IV-437 to Article IV-448
Protocols (36)	
Annexes (2)	
Final Act	
Declarations (50)	Concerning provisions of the Constitution (30) Concerning Protocols (11) By Member States (9)

Union, replacing the confusing division into 'Union' and 'Community', and confirms the European Union's existing institutions, upgrading the European Council and adding a permanent President of the European Council and a Union Minister for Foreign Affairs. However, the size and membership of many of the Brussels bodies are changed, while the European Parliament is given new powers, notably over the budget.

In terms of principles the Constitutional Treaty now makes it clear that the Union derives its powers from the member states through the principle of 'conferral'. And states can now go back on their original granting of power through the new right of secession. The Union has, moreover, to respect the identities of the member states. In turn, states are expected to live up to their obligations. Existing provisions for suspending the voting rights of member states who fail to live up to democratic standards continue.

However, the new Union has a dual legitimacy, resting on its peoples as well as it member states. This is underlined in several ways, notably by the repetition of present provisions on citizenship and the new right of popular initiative. At the same time, Part I lists the European Union's values, objectives and principles. Great stress is laid on liberty, democracy and rights.

The Constitutional Treaty also classifies the powers conferred by the member states in new ways: exclusive, shared, supporting, coordinating or complementary. It then goes on to specify the ways in which the Union should work. Decision making is to reflect, at a minimum, the majority of member states and the majority of the population when, as will happen on an increasing scale, decisions are made by what is known as 'qualified majority voting' (QMV). This means that one member state cannot block all progress as can happen under unanimity. Both the EP and, to some extent, national parliaments are now involved in these processes.

Furthermore, Part I gives a good deal of attention to special arrangements for external affairs and internal security. These are no longer in separate 'pillars' subject to member-state control, but intergovernmental decision making remains the norm in these fields. Through the solidarity clause there is now provision for member states to aid each other in case of attack or natural disaster. And there is a new commitment to the European Union's eastern neighbours.

Otherwise Part I does not really extend the European Union's own policy competences apart from aspects of civil protection, energy, public health, sport and tourism. Exclusive competences are restricted to competition, monetary policy (for eurozone countries), external trade, customs and fisheries. The Internal Market remains untouched, as does economic and monetary union, although the member states involved gain new coordinating powers. Common action will continue in areas such as agriculture, environment and transport. The Constitutional Treaty also allows for future changes in decision making, allowing the heads of government to agree to use QMV.

All this is done through 60 articles. Some of these are very long, especially those on the Commission (Article I-25), foreign policy (Article I-40) and enhanced cooperation (Article I-43). Few are real 'one liners', most being 'portmanteau' articles with several paragraphs or elements to them. The articles, which are numbered consecutively and grouped into subsections known as Titles, also have a Latin numeral prefix indicating the 'Part' where they are found.

Overall, Part I has 10,800 words in the 29 pages of the *Official Journal* version. This compares with 9,372 in the 61 articles of the existing Treaty on European Union. It provides an introduction to, and basis for, the rest of the Constitutional Treaty. The whole document is much longer, running to 448 articles in the Treaty proper with a further 450 or so articles in its 36 Protocols and 50 Declarations. In all there are 482 pages and some 155,000 words.

Part II is the 'Charter of Fundamental Rights', which sets out the political and social rights already enjoyed by EU citizens through earlier treaties. It was drafted in 1999–2000 by a Convention. This is why, confusingly, it has a Preamble of its own. Including the Charter here gives it more salience and more authority and allows it to be used before the courts in cases involving the application of EU law. It links to the commitment in Part I to signing up to the wider 1950 European Convention on the Protection of Human Rights. Doing this cannot give the Union extra powers or override national legislation.

Although there are problems with the Charter, it was left unaltered. However, additional elements have been tacked on at the insistence of the UK government to ensure that it cannot be used to allow the European Union into new areas of national life. In fact, it applies mainly to the institutions, and only affects member states when implementing EU rules. Other parts of the Constitutional Treaty contain further constraining provisions and notes. Moreover, it is made clear that rights have to be interpreted in the light of national views and do not affect member states' own 'rights' jurisdiction.

These understandings are contained in Title VII of Part II. They follow on six other Titles setting out rights in various fields: basic, economic, personal, social, political and judicial. The articles are much shorter than those in Part I. Very often they start with a statement of the basic principle and go on to give guidance on implementation.

Part III: The policies and functioning of the Union is by far the longest Part of the whole Constitutional Treaty, bringing together as it does all those other elements of the Treaty establishing the European Community (TEC) and the Treaty on European Union (TEU) which are still needed. The reason for this is that the Union's nature actually depends on the agreements which constitute it. To drop these would mean giving up the achievements and understandings of the past and would create confusion and instability. So Part III reformulates existing articles and partially brings them into line with Part I. Hence article order sometimes diverges from that in the existing treaties. Numbering is always different. More technical language is used although redundant or repeated elements are excised.

In some cases the way Part III develops and adapts ideas outlined in Part I brings out points of principle that are not made clear in the latter. And, in detailing how principles are to be applied, it further defines institutions and procedures. So Part III cannot be treated purely and simply as an exemplification of Part I. It has its own value and importance, being partly constitutive and not just derivative.

It is divided into seven Titles. The first two are short. Title I sets out considerations to be borne in mind when applying the Constitutional Treaty, including social inclusion, consistency and animal welfare. The next states the legal powers for taking and monitoring measures to prevent discrimination. It also lays down where specific decision-making procedures apply.

Title III is much longer since it deals with Internal Policies and Actions and it is subdivided into five chapters. The first, on the internal market, brings in the basic freedoms and competition policy and, again, specifies which instruments are to be used. There are new provisions on intellectual property rights. The chapter on economic and monetary policies includes new clauses on the running of the eurozone, while the rights of member states not using the euro are maintained. Chapter III covers employment and social policy. Agricultural policy remains and there are a few new provisions on, for example, energy. There is more change in the so-called 'area of freedom, security and justice'. New provisions for the European Council and national parliaments to play a part are included along with measures on solidarity, cross-border crime and the possible creation of an office to prosecute financial fraud against the Union. Harmonization of national criminal laws is ruled out. The final chapter deals with coordinating and supporting policies in other areas, including the new ones of civil protection and tourism.

Title IV is a somewhat dated set of provisions on relations between the Union and remaining colonial dependencies. The next Title, on external relations, is more significant, bringing together previously separated elements on external relations from the two main treaties. It maintains separate ways of working but updates them to take account of the new Minister for Foreign Affairs and the fact that groups of member states, along with the new diplomatic delegations and the European Defence Agency, can implement policies. The Court of Justice is largely excluded from this.

Title VI covers institutions, finance and 'enhanced cooperation', thus reformulating the detailed procedures for the functioning of the Union found in the existing treaties. There are very few institutional changes apart from new rules for the European Council, the European Union's administrative services and institutional cooperation. Equally, the financial provisions are little changed except that they write in the multi-annual framework and grant the EP a fuller role. Enhanced cooperation, as now, allows a group of member states to integrate further subject to tight safeguards. The final Title is relatively brief and mainly deals with the legal standing of staff, member states and the Union.

Part IV: General and final provisions is much the shortest Part of the Constitutional Treaty and has no subdivisions. It is a very traditional piece of treaty technology, dealing with five sets of questions: how the new Union links to the old Community and Union; the states and territories where it applies; the status of the various language versions and the protocols; when (and for how long) it is to come into force; and how it is to be revised. It makes clear that all previous decisions still apply even though many treaties are repealed. Equally it continues to establish that certain national territories are outside its influence.

All language versions are equally valid. Like its predecessors, the new Union is an ongoing body. The clauses on revision are new and allow, in certain instances, for less constraining ways of change. For historical reasons there is also an odd permissive reference to the Benelux Union.

Protocols and *Declarations*: Although all this is complex and detailed enough, there are further attachments. The most important and weighty of these are the Protocols, fully binding texts which are printed separately because they contain codes for specific bodies or detail which might otherwise overload the main treaty. Many refer either to individual articles and facets of the Constitutional Treaty or to specific national interests. Many, like the standing orders of bodies of the ECJ, the European Central Bank and the European Investment Bank, have been transferred from earlier agreements. Some are new, such as those which list the treaties being repealed and the elements of the accession treaties being retained. There is also a protocol on transitional arrangements for bringing the Constitutional Treaty into force.

Declarations are less authoritative texts which are not technically part of the Constitutional Treaty proper. They give guidance on how it will be understood and applied. Most of them relate to specific articles but others, inherited from the existing treaties, deal with the protocols. Most were accepted by all the member states. However, individual member states have added thoughts of their own. All this makes for a package which is still long and difficult, thanks in part to its own inconsistencies, and which does not greatly change the status quo.

Why all the fuss?

If this is so, why has the Constitutional Treaty caused so much excitement? It is primarily because the Constitutional Treaty has become caught up in an intensifying general campaign against 'Europe'. This included the question of how such changes should be approved in the United Kingdom. It is also because the meaning of the Constitutional Treaty is open to interpretation.

Essentially the Constitutional Treaty has become as much part of general political debate as a document in its own right. In fact, much of the tabloid press has long attacked all things to do with the Union in an attempt to shape policy. The Conservatives have also, since the late 1980s, become increasingly eurosceptic if not anti-European, egged on by the well-organized extra-parliamentary opposition to the Union. This reflects the way that politics has become both less parliamentary and more populist, focusing on single issues, such as the euro.

The Constitutional Treaty offers opponents of European integration a new target and one which, because so little was known about the treaties, served as a surrogate for the more basic question of membership. Hence, like most treaty amendments, the Constitutional Treaty has been attacked as creating a superstate. Indeed, in May 2003 an early draft was described by the *Daily Mail* as a 'blueprint for tyranny'. And much of the press, along with many letter writers, has taken this view. The Conservatives also condemned it root-and-branch as taking the Union in the wrong direction and threatening national independence, a view somewhat oddly supported by Gisela Stuart MP, a Labour member of the Convention.

Because of such views there was also a vigorous campaign, inspired by the right but supported by others, that there should be a referendum on its adoption. This developed a good head of steam because so many believed the Constitutional Treaty was more than the 'simple tidying-up exercise' that Jack Straw once rashly called it. 'Constitution' is understood as a big word which suggests sudden and major moves towards statehood and which cannot be seen as either evolutionary or a mere titivating. Hence it needed popular approval. So, on the 60th anniversary of D-Day, a copy of the Constitutional Treaty was ceremonially thrown into the Thames by a UKIP activist.

In March 2004 the Prime Minister conceded a referendum on the grounds that the issue was obscuring the actual merits of the case. Despite this, there was a new wave of bad-tempered comment at the time the final agreement was reached during the Brussels Summit in mid-June, with attacks on 'Blair the betrayer'. Although it somewhat dropped out of the headlines after the summer, there is no doubt that there is widespread opposition to the Constitutional Treaty. And this has been fed by the activism of root-and-branch opponents of the Union like the new UKIP MEPs.

The facts that supporters of the Union were much less active in putting contrary views across, while the government made its case in an intermittent and defensive manner, left the initiative with such opponents. This was particularly important given the calling of a referendum. This changed the political opportunity structure, allowing well-financed anti-European and eurosceptic movements more influence than parliament. Moreover, a referendum requires not just a response to an opinion poll but coming to an actual decision on a policy issue, something otherwise excluded in the UK system. It calls for different judgements than does an election, inviting different kinds of argument. It also allows other issues, such as views of the Blair government, to play a part. Underlying attitudes to European integration thus remain critical to the debate on the Constitutional Treaty.

So the second reason for concern, the actual contents of the Constitutional Treaty have played a secondary role. This explains both why so little use has been made of the many means of accessing it and why there is still so much ignorance and misinformation. Debate has continued to focus on the symbolism of the Constitutional Treaty and its main institutional and procedural changes, and not on the package as a whole. Because of this there have been many mistaken assumptions about what it is and does. The *Guardian* reported that 66 per cent of people believe it means the end of the United Kingdom's seat on the UN Security Council and 61 per cent that it will force the United Kingdom to change its trade union legislation. Neither is true, let alone to be found in the treaty. Equally, it is often believed that the Constitutional Treaty forces the United Kingdom to join the euro, takes away domestic powers of taxation and subjects the Queen to an elected executive President of Europe. It has even been said that it means that Napoleon will have to replace 'our Horatio' atop Nelson's column.

Given all this we try, in Box 1.2, to answer some of the major questions which seem to us to arise from the debate around the Constitutional Treaty. These summarize what we say about its changes, effects and prospects. Moreover, because the Constitutional Treaty is often seen as a malign plot against the United Kingdom, it is important to ask why it came about and what it was trying to do. Equally, what are we to make of its significance given the exaggerations of opponents and supporters?

Box 1.2 Frequently asked questions

Why a European Constitution? The idea of revising the treaties on which the Union is based has been on the agenda for several years. The European Union's leaders eventually agreed that this should be done at Laeken in December 2001. They believed that the Union was too complex and unwieldy to cope with more enlargement, too remote and too inclined to impose. They suggested that such a repackaging of the existing treaties might ultimately lead to a constitution. From the start the Convention set up to consider repackaging took a more constitutional approach so as to balance the economic integration with proper political structures. Yet, in form and legal status the Constitutional Treaty remains a treaty.

How was the Constitutional Treaty drafted? The bulk of the work was done by a Convention composed of representatives of governments, parliaments and EU institutions. Meeting in Brussels from February 2002 to July 2003 under the chairmanship of former French President Giscard d'Estaing, it considered proposals from its Praesidium and proceeded, through general discussion and working groups, to produce a document which revises and compresses the ground rules of the Union into one rather than many treaties.

How did the IGC respond? Because it involves treaty change, the existing rules require that the member states agree, and ratify, changes. Member states based their work on the Convention's proposals. They accepted the idea of a single document, but under Italian chairmanship they failed to resolve key questions on how the Council should vote and on the numbers of Commissioners and parliamentary seats. Then, under the patient chairmanship of the Irish, a deal was reached at the June 2004 Brussels European Council.

What does the Constitutional Treaty try to do, and how? It tries to set out, clearly, in one document, the principles, aims, powers, structures, and procedural rules

Box 1.2 Continued

of the Union plus the bases of its authority. It also seeks to simplify processes. It formally repeals all the existing treaties while preserving continuity by including their essential provisions.

How much does it differ from the existing treaties? It differs in structure, by moving from many treaties to one and by doing away with the confusing difference between the EC and the EU. Its Part I is clearer about principles and rights and these are developed in later Parts. In terms of content, the Constitutional Treaty retains 90 per cent of existing agreements and practices, making only limited – though sometimes significant – changes to structures and institutions. It is more manageable than the status quo.

What new powers does the Union get from it? The Union does not get vast new powers. It is clearly stated that, as has always been the case, where the member states have given the Union powers to act, its law takes precedence over contrary national legislation. It also bestows the right to negotiate treaties – technically known as 'legal personality' – on the Union as a whole and not just the Community as previously. It also makes the rights of citizens under EU law clearer by including the Charter of Fundamental Rights.

What institutional changes does it make? The existing structure remains much as it was. What changes are the respective powers of the institutions and the way they work. European Council meetings are made more organized and influential with their own President. The chairing of other Councils is also altered. And a Union Minister for Foreign Affairs, assisted by an 'External Action Service', is created from two existing posts. The powers of the EP are extended and, in the long term, the Commission will be smaller. An anti-fraud Public Prosecutor may also be appointed.

What new policies does it allow the Union? Very few, although administrative cooperation, energy, tourism, sport and space are given a new prominence. Changes are also made in asylum and migration policy. In foreign affairs further attempts to coordinate foreign policy are made while, in military matters, groups of member states may be allowed to act alone, although the position of NATO is respected.

Does it make the Union into a state? No. Although the new Union has a constitution, symbols and powers, the status quo is not much changed. The symbols were always there and have merely been written into a consolidated treaty of more constitutional style. The Union remains a compromise between the supranational and the intergovernmental. Its powers are clearly stated to be conferred by member states, which remain sovereign but which still have to implement all EU rules, though they are often able to adjust them to their own circumstances. But they have to work closely together in more cohesive political procedures.

Box 1.2 Continued

Will the Union be more democratic? This is the aim. Commitments to democracy are more emphatic than before while citizens' rights are spelt out more clearly. The EP, as the representative of the people, is given enhanced powers in the budget, nominations and policy making. In the name of subsidiarity, national parliaments gain new rights of information and intervention. And a million citizens can, for the first time, ask that new legislation be considered. Undemocratic states' voting rights can still be suspended.

Can the member states still block legislation? The Constitutional Treaty is committed to recognizing member states' identities and rights. In foreign affairs, social services and taxation they retain their vetoes, although the use of qualified majority voting (QMV) has been extended in less contentious areas. The new QMV procedures also recognize the demographic weight of member states. The latter can, for the first time, freely leave the Union if they so choose.

When will it come into operation? The final text of the treaty was signed on 29 October 2004. Two years are allowed for ratification. If this is delayed, entry into force will take place at the beginning of the second month following the presentation of the last instruments of ratification. Not all provisions of the treaty will come into effect at once, some being delayed until 2009 or 2014.

Who is in favour of it and who opposed? All governments, a majority of MEPs and Commissioners and many others support it, even if they feel it has not gone far enough in simplifying the Union and creating a viable political order. On the left, the United Kingdom is seen as having maintained too many rights for the member states, making the European Union too neo-liberal and anti-social. Eurosceptics on the right oppose the text as protectionist and centralizing, threatening the integrity and competitiveness of states. They believe that the Union should be stripped down to its economic essentials, that powers be given back to the member states and that all decisions be subjected to unanimous agreement.

What happens if it is not ratified? In theory, if the Constitutional Treaty is not ratified by all member states, it lapses and the European Union continues as now, with most things critics dislike still in place and with no legal means of withdrawal. The situation will have to be dealt with by the European Council. If a smaller member state rejects the Constitutional Treaty there could be pressure on it to try again, but if there is widespread opposition then some other solution will have to be found. This could involve activating all or part of the text, leaving rejecting member states in an uncertain position unless they chose to withdraw.

What will be its effects on ordinary people? Probably not a lot. But the workings of the Union will be more visible and transparent if people care to look. And they will have more rights and access.

What is the purpose of the Constitutional Treaty?

In the United Kingdom the Constitutional Treaty has often been attacked as a deliberate attempt to create a 'superstate' or 'a country called Europe', with its own citizenship, law and symbols. Gisela Stuart claims, less extravagantly, that the underlying motive was political deepening. The argument is that, because there was no need for a constitution, as there had been for the United States of America in 1787, the draft must have been an undemocratic attempt to gain power for the European Union. If so, it is odd that the document does not permit those things which a 'superstate' ought to be able to do: deciding on its own powers, having an autonomous army, wielding full financial powers and creating an overriding government with its own means of implementation.

The reality is more complicated. First, the process responded to outside circumstances. It looked to the future when the European Union will have 27 members, something which meant that it needed to become more efficient and less complex. Even with 15 members, difficulties had emerged and conventional wisdom argued that things would get worse with the planned expansion to Central and Eastern Europe. It was felt that the rules laid down for six member states in the 1950s could well produce gridlock, not to mention making the Union ineffective in world affairs, something much on peoples' minds after the divisions over Iraq. This reflected current thinking that the European Union should have more power and punch, which could only come from reform. Hence, more streamlined decision making was needed even if this meant reducing national vetoes. It was this which seems to have persuaded the United Kingdom government that a more regularized and constitutional approach was for the best.

The problem here is that doing this means more sharing of sovereignty. So, second, the aim was to clarify both the legal forms taken by EU legislation and who was responsible for what. This was demanded by the German *Länder* and others who felt that doing things at the EU level gave powers to the Federal government in Germany at the expense of their own authority. Limiting and specifying what could be done, and by whom, would help with this. It could also help make the European Union more democratically transparent. So the Constitutional Treaty was in part meant to be a limiting constitution and not simply one empowering the centre.

Third, the Constitutional Treaty responded to a growing awareness that the Union had lost something of its earlier support both from the public at large and from some member states. This demanded a new stress on democracy, transparency and the simplification of the arcane and distant structures and processes of the present European Union. Moreover, if the new deal could be a lasting and stable one, prevailing fears of continual (and threatening) institutional changes might be lessened.

The desire to simplify and democratize also extended to the text of the treaties. By consolidating the treaties – and some of the other sources of legislation such as the decisions of the Court of Justice – into one more approachable document, it might be possible for people to know what the European Union's rules actually are. This might give the rules more appeal and hence catalyse people into regarding the Union more favourably. Vaclav Havel called for a 'concise, clearly formulated and universally understandable constitution [which] would simply make it easier for the citizens of an integrating Europe to recognize what the European Union stands for; to understand it better; and, consequently, to identify with it'. So, if there were clear political intentions behind the Constitutional Treaty, they did not involve the creation of a superstate.

Assessing the significance of the Constitutional Treaty?

Having seen what is in the Constitutional Treaty and why, what are we to think of it? While this is a matter of interpretation, the Constitutional Treaty clearly makes important technical changes. As to their political meaning, opinions are divided. These range from seeing no political changes to the creation of a wholly new monolith. The reality is more mundane and middle of the road.

On one level the Constitutional Treaty is significant simply because the Convention and the intergovernmental conference (IGC) were able to agree on something so large scale. At times it often looked as if this might not be the case. More specifically, it is significant structurally because it creates a new European Union. For some this is frightening but for others it should make things clearer. Certainly it is in line with the way most people already talk about 'Europe', ignoring distinctions between Union and Communities.

Textually it is also a significant (rather than a mere tactical) piece of strategic consolidation and 'tidying up'. It takes a whole series of treaties and boils them down into one, admittedly long, text. This is now written in more comprehensible language, although the ghosts of the old treaties live on in the style. This helps to give it a new legal status although, as we shall see, whether it fully deserves the epithet of a full constitution given to it by defenders and detractors alike is open to question. It is a further stage in the constitutionalization of the European Union and not the end of the road. But it is the point from which the new Union will start.

The new order also tries to bring out the values, freedoms and rationale of the European Union, including its dual legitimacy. The detailed workings of the Union have also been somewhat simplified, though many would say not enough. So, the Constitutional Treaty is a first attempt at creating a coherent, comprehensible and consistent set of rules and procedures, which may allow the enlarged Union to work effectively. It has also given the Union further elements of flexibility, which can be used to increase or decrease integration. Hence it has the potential to be more effective.

Existing policy competences, rather than being extended, have been tweaked to fit the new structure, with external and domestic security policy brought more into the mainstream. Equally, a few important changes to the institutional structure have been made, changes with which governments can live. And the people may find that it is helpful to have faces to attach to the European Union. Nonetheless, it has also gone some way to reinforcing the position of member states. All this could have been better done as the text was not subject to the final polish that it really needed – as the Poles and the Italians have found. But it is an improvement on the status quo.

For most people, however, its significance can only be measured politically and not technically. And here opinions vary greatly even among those in favour of more integration. For some, it signifies a failure to build a strong and just European Union. They see the Constitutional Treaty as a capitulation to the member states, to neo-liberal economics and even to Donald Rumsfeld, the controversial US Secretary of Defence, by denying Europe and the Union a sufficiently strong central authority to ensure social and economic justice. Moreover, it tips the balance towards member states and opt-outs, opening the way to a more differentiated and less cohesive Union.

For others, it is the coherent, compact and comprehensible document which will catalyse public opinion and organize politics in Europe. It means greater clarity, efficiency and solidarity. It is also significant for its enhanced democracy and legitimacy, thanks to the new powers given to the EP and the incorporation of the Charter of Fundamental Rights. So it is a historic caesura, carrying integration to a higher and more constitutional level.

Paradoxically, this view is partly shared by eurosceptics. Thanks to the new status of the document and the way it grants powers to the institutions, they see it as the coping stone of an anti-democratic superstate. The document completes the transformation of the 'Common Market' into a country hostile to member state sovereignty. To an extent, they see it as symbolically significant, because it uses the term constitution, which for many is, inaccurately, restricted to states. They do not believe it to be the victory for the United Kingdom that Blair claims. Moreover, they see it as entrenching an exhausted protectionist approach to the economy.

The truth – if truth there be – lies somewhere in the middle. There is actually a lot of light and shade in the Constitutional Treaty and its mixed bag of compromises. In partially rationalizing and developing what was already there, its authors sought to respond to conflicting criticisms and needs. Hence it is not coherent. And, like the Union itself it is a hybrid of intergovernmentalism and supranationalism. So its significance is that it goes as far as it can in several directions. Gisela Stuart now admits that it was as good a deal as was then possible.

Equally, it is not as awful and as threatening as has been suggested, especially in policy matters over which it has limited control, being a political framework not a party manifesto. Nonetheless, it is quite clearly political and it is silly to deny this. It enhances the political dimension of the Union at the expense of the economic. But to imagine that there can be, or has been, something 'economic' without political connotations is a muddleheaded illusion. Moreover, in some areas it increases EU powers, in others it limits them.

For us, what stands out is, on the one hand, the consolidation of both the Union and the Community and of the existing treaties. The former are now united while the latter are now concentrated into one higher status document which tries to distil, clarify and simplify the underlying principles of the European Union. On the other hand, small but significant changes are made to procedures in decision making, voting and the involvement of national parliaments. There are also new stresses on values, transparency, rights, flexibility and diversity. Changes in policy and institutions are less remarkable, though both the European Council and the EP gain.

Because of the limitations of the Constitutional Treaty and the conflicting views about them, hopes that it would provide a structure which would last for a generation or more and be a model for the rest of the world are unlikely to be realized. It may last longer than many predict, but it is clear that it will be revised in the not too distant future. But for now the Constitutional Treaty is all that is on the table beyond the status quo, and so it needs to be properly understood before it is ratified.

Our strategy

In looking further at the Constitutional Treaty we will try and bear these things in mind, not insisting on any one extreme view but bringing out the document's differing tones and contradictions. This may not make things simpler but it is the only honest way to go. Given the prevailing ignorance about the European Union it is a necessary one. Unless there is full coverage, any decision which people make will be poorly based.

So, first we look at the context: how the Constitutional Treaty actually emerged and what the politics of the process have been. Then, because of the difficulty of the text, we go on to suggest how it needs to be approached. This raises questions of interpretation, status, role, language and presuppositions. Having done this we print Part I without comment. We then set out what we think are Part I's main themes, looking first at the nature of the 'new' European Union and then at its values and rights; its powers and policies; its laws, instruments and acts; its institutions; its democratic dimensions; its finances; and its external roles. We then try and pull these together by asking what the Constitutional Treaty says about the place of the member states in the new order. By looking at origins, meanings and implications we hope to provide the kind of annotated text for which some have called. Later there is also a brief treatment of the rest of the Constitutional Treaty.

Finally, we turn to the decisions which voters in the United Kingdom and elsewhere will have to make, both nominally and implicitly. This needs an understanding of the ratification process and the implications of possible outcomes. We hope that all this will allow people to make up their minds in an informed and considered way, aware of the complexities of the document and the limitations of the political polemics surrounding it. And, if this is not enough to achieve that aim, there are hints on further readings and explanations of technical terms.

2 The context

One aspect of the UK public's lack of awareness of things 'European' is the assumption that the Constitutional Treaty is a wholly new creation. It certainly emerged from a different negotiating forum, a quasi representative European Convention, whose work was largely accepted by the subsequent intergovernmental conference (IGC). However, it is also the latest outcome of a seemingly non-stop process of reform in the European Union and of its treaties. This means that most of its contents are reworkings of what already exists dispersed across over 20 treaties. Recognizing this is vital to a proper understanding of the Constitutional Treaty.

Treaties, problems and possible solutions

Until now the European Union has rested on a series of treaties which have emerged over the years, beginning, as Box 2.1 shows, in 1951. This was followed by the key 1957 Treaties of Rome and the merging of the various institutions into one. Then followed more than 20 years in which there was very little alteration. Since the late 1980s, however, there has been an accelerating process of change with more treaties, thanks in part to enlargements, and radical revisions to the treaty base. In 1986 the Single European Act made a crucial breakthrough by extending qualified majority voting, among other things. Then in 1993, thanks to the Treaty on European Union (the infamous 'Maastricht Treaty') the Union was established, with the existing European Communities being reformed and becoming part of this broader arrangement.

Since then two major changes have been undertaken, introduced by the Treaty of Amsterdam (1997) and the Treaty of Nice (2001). They have been accompanied by more minor reforms brought about by the accession of three new members in 1995 and a further ten in 2004. So the context of the emergence, and to a degree the content, of the Constitutional Treaty is thus a process of treaty reform – or constitutionalization as some prefer to call it.

Box 2.1 From a proliferation of treaties to a Constitutional Treaty

1951	Treaty establishing the European Coal and Steel Community signed
1952	European Coal and Steel Community (ECSC) established
1957	Treaty establishing the European Economic Community signed Convention on Certain Institutions Treaty establishing the European Atomic Energy Community signed
1958	European Economic Community (EEC) established European Atomic Energy Community (EAEC) established
1965	Treaty merging the institutions signed
1967	ECSC, EEC and EAEC collectively referred to as European Communities (EC)
1973	First Treaty of Accession, allowing Denmark, Ireland and the United Kingdom to join the EC, enters into force
1981	Second Accession Treaty, allowing Greece to join the European Communities, enters into Force
1986	Third Accession Treaty, allowing Portugal and Spain to join the EC, enters into force Single European Act signed
1987	Single European Act enters into force
1992	Treaty on European Union signed
1993	Treaty on European Union enters into force, thus establishing the European Union and changing the name of the EEC to the European Community (EC)
1995	Fourth Accession Treaty, allowing Austria, Finland and Sweden to join the EU, enters into force
1997	Treaty of Amsterdam signed
1999	Treaty of Amsterdam enters into force
2001	Treaty of Nice signed
2002	Treaty establishing the European Coal and Steel Community expires
2003	Treaty of Nice enters into force European Convention adopts Draft Treaty establishing a Constitution for Europe
2004	Fifth Accession Treaty, allowing Cyprus, the Czech Republic, Estonia, Hungary, Latvia, Lithuania, Malta, Poland, Slovakia and Slovenia to join the EU, enters into force Treaty establishing a Constitution for Europe signed
2005	Sixth Accession Treaty, allowing Bulgaria and Romania to join the EU, is signed

Rather than appearing out of the blue it has its origins in developments and debates that have been going on since before the European Union as such was created. In fact, proposals for establishing a European Constitution were first aired in the 1950s and were circulated again in the 1980s as part of proposed reforms of the European Communities.

But to view the Constitutional Treaty simply as the latest stage in a process which, as we have said, is ongoing, does not provide a full explanation of why it emerged when it did – when the Treaty of Nice had supposedly dealt with the 'leftovers' from the previous round of reform and thus prepared the Union for its 2004 enlargement. It also overlooks the many and varied factors which influenced the negotiations that eventually resulted in its adoption in June 2004. Personalities, politics and new procedures played their role and cannot be overlooked.

One result of the treaty reform process is that the key rules regulating the European Union are located in a number of places, notably in the two main treaties on which the Union is based – the Treaty establishing a European Community (1957) and the Treaty on European Union (1992) – but also in the various recent treaties that have amended them. This means that the rules are not easy to find. So, one of the main reasons for the Constitutional Treaty was to simplify the mess of existing treaties and consolidate them in a more coherent and comprehensible form. To this extent the UK government's initial defensive presentation of the Constitutional Treaty as a 'tidying-up' exercise was correct.

The need for such a simplification has long been recognized, but only after the difficulties surrounding ratification of the Treaty on European Union (TEU) in 1992–1993 was it given much attention. But the failure of the Amsterdam and Nice negotiations to bring about a major overhaul meant that there was still a job to be done. Moreover, Nice was universally regarded as the worst drafted treaty so far, its complicated voting procedures being especially derided. Unsurprisingly, it was rejected by many, from enthusiasts for integration at one extreme to eurosceptic Tories at the other.

However, the fact that simplification and constitutionalization then rose up the European Union's agenda had much to do with the calls made in 2000 for the adoption of an EU constitution, or at least an agreement on a long-term model for the Union. Such suggestions came from the German Foreign Minister, Joschka Fischer, and the French President, Jacques Chirac. Tony Blair added to the momentum with a call for a political 'Statement of Principles' on the division of competences between Union and member states. At the same time, the Commission was promoting a debate on 'governance', stressing the need to bring the European Union closer to its citizens. All this had implications for treaty reform, as did the drafting of a Charter of Fundamental Rights by a specially convened Convention during the course of 1999–2000. At the same time, there was a growing belief that further reforms were needed to ensure that the European Union could continue to function after eastwards enlargement. And there were pressures from the German *Länder* for clarification of Brussels' powers and from others who wanted to achieve the long dreamed of constitutionalization of the treaties.

The 'Future of Europe' debate

The emerging 'to do' list was reflected in a 'Declaration on the future of the Union', adopted alongside the Nice Treaty. This endorsed the idea of further discussions on the distribution of powers between the European Union and its member states; the status of the newly 'proclaimed' Charter of Fundamental Rights; a simplification of the treaties 'with a view to making them clearer and better understood'; and an enhancement of the role of national parliaments in 'the European architecture'. These discussions would also focus on improving and monitoring the democratic legitimacy and transparency of the Union 'in order to bring them closer to the citizens of the Member States'. And the 'deeper and wider debate' would involve not just the member states, as previously, but also 'all interested parties', including representatives of national parliaments and civil society as well as the Commission and the EP. Those states set to join the European Union – the so-called 'candidate' states – would also be involved.

The debate, which was formally launched along with a website (europa.eu.int/futurum) on 7 March 2001, failed to attract much attention. Discussion tended to focus on how reform should be taken forward and what other items should be placed on the agenda. Consequently, when the European Council met in December 2001 and reviewed the situation, the 'Laeken Declaration on the future of the European Union' which it adopted contained a far wider range of issues for further discussion. It listed over 50 questions that needed to be asked if the European Union were to meet the three basic challenges it faced: 'how to bring citizens, and primarily the young, closer to the European design and the European institutions, how to organize politics and the European political area in an enlarged Union and how to develop the Union into a stabilizing factor and model in the new, multipolar world'. The questions were arranged under four headings, each of which expanded the scope of the debate beyond that signalled at Nice.

The first talked about 'a better division and definition of competence' in the European Union and referred not only to clarifying the respective competences of the Union and its member states but to the issue of how competences might be reorganized in the light of citizens' expectations, questioning whether the Union's powers should be extended or whether administration and implementation of policy should be left more emphatically to the member states. A second heading focused on the more technical issue of how the European Union's instruments – its laws – might be simplified, while the third reflected on issues concerning democracy, transparency and efficiency. Among the key concerns were how to increase the democratic legitimacy of the institutions and how to increase the involvement of the national parliaments in the European Union's decision-making processes. A review of the roles and functioning of each of the institutions was also encouraged. The final heading raised the question of what form the treaty base should take in order to promote transparency. Should there be reorganization of the existing treaties to include the Charter of Fundamental Rights which, in the longer term, might lead to the adoption of a 'constitutional text' or a 'constitution'?

Responsibility for looking at all this was entrusted to a new body, the 'Convention on the Future of Europe', comprising representatives of a range of EU institutions and bodies and of national governments and parliaments. This reflected both a commitment to promote open debate and the positive experience of the Convention that had recently drafted the Charter of Fundamental Rights. It was unclear, however, whether the new Convention would be able to agree on how to respond to the challenges facing the Union or get its ideas taken seriously by the IGC which, the Laeken Declaration made clear, would, in line with the TEU, take the final decisions. Nevertheless, the new body's involvement in the process of reforming the treaties was a radical departure for the European Union. It represented a concerted attempt to respond to complaints that the Union was too introverted and secretive. This was reinforced by making all its documents available for consultation on-line (see european-convention.eu.int).

The European Convention and the draft Constitutional Treaty

The European Convention duly convened in Brussels on 28 February 2002 with the former French President and MEP, Valéry Giscard d'Estaing, as Chairman. He was joined by two Vice-Chairmen, Giuliano Amato and Jean-Luc Dehaene (the former Italian and Belgian Prime Ministers) and a total of 102 other full members drawn from the governments and parliaments of the member states, including the candidates, the EP and the Commission. In addition, as Box 2.2 shows, the Convention comprised 102 alternates and 13 observers. Serviced by a Secretariat and with a steering group – the Praesidium, comprising Giscard, Amato, Dehaene and initially nine but later ten other members – the Convention represented a unique opportunity to gather views on the future of Europe and to influence and potentially set the agenda of the IGC in 2004. It could also, as Giscard reminded everybody at the opening ceremony, open the way for a 'Constitution for Europe' providing there was consensus on a single proposal.

This does not mean to say that the Convention operated smoothly or attracted much attention. It got off to a slow and poorly publicized start and experienced difficulty agreeing its working methods and agenda, due to the concerns of candidate countries, eurosceptics, regions, small states and wider

Box 2.2 The European Convention: organization

Composition

1 Chairman
2 Vice-Chairman
15 Representatives of member state governments (+15 alternates)
13 Representatives of candidate state governments (+13 alternates)
30 Representatives of member state parliaments (+30 alternates)
26 Representatives of candidate state parliaments (+26 alternates)
16 Representatives of the European Parliament (+16 alternates)
2 Representatives of the European Commission (+2 alternates)
plus
13 Observers (6 each from the Committee of the Region and the Economic and Social Committee plus the European Ombudsman)

Structure

Presidency: Chairman and two Vice-Chairman
Praesidium: Presidency (3) plus 10 others
Convention: Praesidium (13) plus other full members (92) plus alternates (102) plus observers (13) = 220
Secretariat: Secretary-General (1) plus deputy (1) plus 17 others

Working groups

I Subsidiarity (Inigo Méndez de Vigo): reported 23 September 2002
II Charter of Fundamental Rights (Antonio Vitorino): reported 22 October 2002
III Legal personality (Giuliano Amato): reported 1 October 2002
IV National parliaments (Gisela Stuart): reported 22 October 2002
V Competences (Henning Christopherson): reported 4 November 2002
VI Economic governance (Klaus Hänsch): reported 21 October 2002
VII External action (Jean-Luc Dehaene): reported 16 December 2002
VIII Defence (Michel Barnier): reported 16 December 2002
IX Simplification (Giuliano Amato): reported 29 November 2002
X Freedom, security and justice (John Bruton): reported 2 December 2002
XI Social Europe (George Katiforis): reported 4 February 2003

social interests. By midsummer, however, it had completed a 'listening phase' in which its members – the 'conventionnels' as they became known – had the opportunity to give their views on what they expected from the European Union, debate the Union's 'missions' and competences, and discuss in greater detail issues concerning justice and security. A Civil Society Hearing and a Youth Convention was also held as part of a generally unsuccessful effort to generate wider interest. Neither event provided representative input into debates, any more than did the eight civil society contact groups which were later established.

Greater success came with the setting up of 11 working groups charged with examining particular aspects of the Future of Europe debate. These were chaired by members of the Praesidium, although the self-selecting membership of several meant that their composition was not always representative of either the Convention or the Union. A first batch – covering subsidiarity, the Charter of Fundamental Rights, legal personality for the Union, the role of national parliaments, competences and economic governance – was launched in May 2002 and, two months later, was followed by four more on external action, defence, simplification and freedom, security and justice (see Box 2.2 and Box 2.3). An eleventh on 'social Europe' was belatedly established in November, by which time half of the existing working groups had reported. The others reported before the end of the year.

Box 2.3 The European Convention and the 2003–2004 Intergovernmental Conference

2001	
15 December	Laeken Declaration
2002	
27 February	Inaugural meeting of the European Convention's Praesidium
28 February	Inaugural plenary session of the European Convention
21–22 March	First full working plenary session: start of 'listening phase'
8 May	Praesidium announces establishment of working groups I–VI
25 June	Civil Society Hearing
9–12 July	Youth Convention meets
11–12 July	7th plenary session concludes 'listening phase'
18 July	Praesidium announces establishment of working groups VII–X
28 October	Praesidium unveils first 'skeleton' constitution
21 November	Praesidium announces establishment of working group XI
4 December	Commission President unveils draft constitution ('Penelope')
2003	
15 January	France and Germany publish proposals on institutional reform
6 February	Praesidium unveils first set of draft articles
6–7 February	15th plenary session debates Praesidium's initial set of draft articles
28 February	Praesidium unveils second set of draft articles
26 May	Pracsidium unveils revised text of Part I
27 May	Praesidium unveils revised text of Parts II–IV

Continued overleaf

Box 2.3 Continued

5–6 June	23rd plenary session debates revised draft of Parts I and IV
11–13 June	24th plenary session debates and agrees by 'broad consensus' revised Parts I and II of the *Draft Treaty establishing a Constitution for Europe*
20 June	Parts I and II of the *Draft Treaty establishing a Constitution for Europe* presented to the Thessalonica European Council, which agrees that the draft provides 'a good basis' for negotiations in an IGC
4 July	25th plenary session debates revised draft of Part II–IV
9–10 July	Closing plenary session debates and agrees by 'broad consensus' revised Parts III and IV of the *Draft Treaty establishing a Constitution for Europe*
18 July	Complete *Draft Treaty establishing a Constitution for Europe* presented to the President of the European Council (Rome)
2003	
29 September	Intergovernmental Conference (IGC) opens
12–13 December	European Council fails to reach agreement on a *Treaty establishing a Constitution for Europe* and IGC negotiations are effectively suspended
2004	
24 March	European Council decides to resume IGC negotiations
17 May	IGC negotiations resume
18 June	European Council agrees *Treaty establishing a Constitution for Europe*
29 October	*Treaty establishing a Constitution for Europe* signed in Rome

By this time, too, Giscard had published in outline a 'preliminary draft Constitutional Treaty' based on a reorganization of the existing treaties and their presentation in three Parts. This 'skeleton' determined subsequent discussions and defined the form of the text that the Convention ultimately adopted, albeit with an extra Part being created for the inclusion of the Charter of Fundamental Rights. This was more than could be said for many alternative drafts which were circulated, including those from Commission President Prodi, the UK Foreign and Commonwealth Office and Andrew Duff MEP, all of which were essentially ignored or misunderstood.

The existence of so many outlines, partial drafts and complete constitutional texts encouraged a growing consensus that there should be a single constitutional document and not simply a set of options for treaty reform. Giscard had expressed his preference for this, and many of the conventionnels supported a 'constitution'. Others found the term, with its notions of statehood, more difficult to swallow, yet were agreed on a single document.

Even the UK government came round to the idea of a legally binding document and not just a 'statement of principles', with Blair noting in November 2002 that 'a new Constitution for Europe' was needed.

Its shape and content remained to be decided. Soon, however, the Convention Secretariat began to add flesh to the bones of Giscard's 'skeleton'. A first set of draft articles was published in early February 2003, with more appearing over the next few months, before complete and often revised versions were published in May and June. Although many of the draft articles incorporated proposals from the working groups, others were clearly inspired by Giscard himself or by the Praesidium. Some proved highly controversial. The first 16 articles, for example, attracted nearly 1,200 amendments from the conventionnels, a large number focusing on the nature and values of the European Union. Also contentious were those articles on reform of the Union's institutions which appeared in April. Their emphasis on an enhanced role for the Union's more intergovernmental bodies encouraged claims that Giscard was seeking to establish a *directoire* of large states to run the European Union, thus alienating smaller member states, the Commission and the EP. Eventually, revised articles were produced. With the heads of government refusing to allow more time, the final draft was rushed through in mid-June.

The final package contained enough to please most conventionnels. It seemed to justify their belief that the convention method was more open and more effective than that of the IGCs. Giscard was therefore able to present a *draft Treaty establishing a Constitution for Europe* – or at least Parts I and II – to the European Council at Thessalonica on 20 June 2003. Parts III and IV, on which there was broad consensus, were then 'tidied up' and forwarded to the then President of the European Council, Italian Prime Minister Silvio Berlusconi, a month later.

The fact that the Convention had actually managed to produce a draft Constitutional Treaty was a surprise to many and confounded expectations that the diversity of interests present would prevent a broad consensus emerging. Admittedly, there were dissenting voices, and some of these, including UK MP David Heathcoat-Amory, made their opposition clear in a minority report favouring 'an association of free and self-governing European states and an open economic area'. This could not, however, detract from the Convention's achievement – where IGCs had failed – in producing an agreed document, the architecture of which was to last. Nevertheless, the impact that the draft would have was still in the air, the European Council saying only that it would be 'a good basis for starting' in the IGC. It brought this forward to October 2003 leaving little time for reflection on the text, which was especially worrying since public opinion resolutely refused to take much real notice of the Convention's work.

The IGC and the Constitutional Treaty

The IGC opened, slightly earlier than anticipated, on 29 September 2003 with an unprecedented number of states participating. Not only were the 15 member states represented, but so were the ten candidate states that would be joining the European Union in 2004. In addition, the remaining candidate states – Bulgaria, Romania and Turkey – attended as observers. From the outset, the aim of the Italian Presidency was clear: to conclude the IGC at the Brussels European Council on 12–13 December. Four meetings and one 'conclave' of Ministers of Foreign Affairs were held, and it was clear that the member states were willing to accept a vast majority of the Convention's draft, including its structure. In fact, in the end about 13,500 of the draft's 14,800 words survived into the final text.

There were nevertheless institutional issues on which the text, as it stood, was unacceptable. These included the size and composition of the Commission, the role and functions of the proposed Union Minister for Foreign Affairs, the nature and rotation of the Council Presidency and the respective powers of the EP and the Council in deciding the budget. Also outstanding were the extension of majority voting, the revision process for the Constitutional Treaty, the adaptation of the Danish opt-out in justice and home affairs and a mutual assistance clause. Most importantly, there was considerable opposition from Spain and Poland to the proposed double majority voting system in the Council, since they had won a particularly favourable allocation of votes in the Treaty of Nice and were understandably loath to cede this advantage.

Despite the contentiousness of several issues and the European Council's failure in October to make significant headway in resolving them, the Italians still believed agreement on the Constitutional Treaty could be reached at the December European Council. They were proved wrong. The unwillingness of Spain and Portugal to compromise on the issue of votes created an impasse which was exacerbated by poor Italian preparation and a general willingness among other member states to defer conclusion of the IGC. Few insiders were surprised, but media coverage was obsessed with failure and crisis. In fact, the events managed to focus minds on the outstanding issues and gave the incoming Irish Presidency time to reflect on ways forward. Moreover, there was no real desire to abandon the idea of a Constitutional Treaty.

Sensing that a 'cooling off' period was required before negotiations could resume, the Irish government refrained from making concluding the IGC one of the goals of its Presidency. Nonetheless, a change of government in Spain in March 2004 and the adoption by the Polish government of a more accommodating position on the double-majority issue meant that the Irish

Taoiseach, Bertie Ahern, was able in March 2004 to report to the European Council that the prospects for concluding the IGC were now such that the Presidency would resume negotiations. This it did in May and, following three rounds of negotiations at Foreign Minister level, the Constitutional Treaty was agreed at a stormy European Council in Brussels in June.

The key to agreement was Spanish and Polish acceptance of a revised system of double-majority voting. Other member states also had to make concessions, while some were given guarantees to assuage their concerns. For the former, there would, for example, be no reference to Christianity in the preamble, and the size of the Commission would eventually be reduced to less than one member per member state. For the latter, notably the United Kingdom, unanimity was retained for tax harmonization and further guarantees of the restricted application of the Charter of Fundamental Rights were approved.

As with all previous treaties, reaching agreement on the text was not the end of the process. The Constitutional Treaty still had to be 'tidied up' to ensure consistency in the language and phraseology used and accurate cross-referencing of articles. In addition, authentic versions had to be produced in each of the 21 official languages of the now enlarged European Union. This took much of the summer and was accompanied by a number of additional declarations being adopted. A complete version of the Constitutional Treaty along with its protocols and annexes and associated declarations was gradually pulled together and published on 6 August. Late corrections and adjustments were then made before a final version was signed at a ceremony in Rome – in the same building as representatives of the original six member states signed the Treaty of Rome – on 29 October 2004. It later emerged that linguistic adjustments would have to be made to the Polish and Italian versions.

What has changed with the Constitutional Treaty?

For those who followed the work of Convention and IGC, it is clear that much of the Constitutional Treaty signed by the Prime Ministers and Foreign Ministers of the 25 member states has its origins in the existing treaties. Because many people are unaware of this, many of the fiercest attacks have been on things which have been enshrined in the treaties, or in established practice, for years if not decades. Hence the Constitutional Treaty is often blamed for the decisions of previous generations, when all it did was adapt them. Therefore, having a copy of the existing treaties to hand when reading the Constitutional Treaty is little short of a necessity for an accurate appreciation. A proper judgement depends on knowing what is already there, what has changed and what is quite new.

So how does the Constitutional Treaty compare to what is already there? Obviously it is not possible to indicate here exactly what has happened to all the 381 articles of the two main existing treaties: the *Treaty on European Union* and the longer *Treaty establishing the European Community*. However, most of their provisions appear somewhere in the Constitutional Treaty, albeit not always formatted or phrased in the same way. Indeed, when it comes to Part I, it is possible to indicate roughly the origins of each provision. However, as Table 2.1 shows, about a third of the articles are new, but even these generally echo clauses in the TEU and TEC. Given that so many articles are subdivided into separate paragraphs, it is quite often the case that part of an article is new whereas other paragraphs repeat existing clauses. The new articles can also bring in both long-established principles resulting from judgements of the Court of Justice and day-to-day practices that have not been given treaty status in the past.

Table 2.1 The existing treaties and the Constitutional Treaty: a comparison with Part I

Constitutional Treaty	*Existing treaties*
I-1	From Articles 1 and 49 TEU
I-2	Extension of Article 6(1) TEU
I-3	From Preambles, Article 2 TEU and 2 and 3 TEC etc.
I-4	Variation on Articles 3 and 12 TEU
I-5	Article 6 TEU and Article 10 TEC
I-6	New but based on ECJ jurisprudence
I-7	Transfer of Article 281 TEC
I-8	Codifies exiting usages
I-9	New plus Article 6(2) TEU
I-10	Rewriting of Articles 17–21 TEC
I-11	New plus Article 5 TEC etc.
I-12	New plus Articles 4 and 98–9 TEC etc.
I-13	New but summarizes Preamble
I-14	New
I-15	From Articles 98–9 and 126–8 TEC
I-16	Articles 2 and 11 TEU
I-17	New
I-18	Builds on Article 308 TEC
I-19	Articles 3 and 5 TEU and 7 TEC
I-20	From Articles 189–92 and 249 TEC
I-21	Builds on Article 4 TEU
I-22	New
I-23	Revision of Articles 202–5 and 249 TEC
I-24	New
I-25	New
I-26	Articles 201 and 211–14 TEC

Table 2.1 Continued

Constitutional Treaty	*Existing treaties*
I-27	Articles 214 and 217
I-28	New
I-29	Articles 220–45 TEC
I-30	Articles 105–110 TEC
I-31	Articles 246–8 TEC
I-32	Articles 7, 257–8 and 260–4 TEC
I-33	New and Article 249 TEC
I-34	Article 249 TEC
I-35	Article 249 TEC
I-36	Article 211 TEC
I-37	Article 10 TEC
I-38	Articles 5 and 253 TEC
I-39	Article 254 TEC
I-40	Articles 11, 13, 16, 18 and 21–4 TEU etc.
I-41	Articles 17 and 23 TEU etc.
I-42	Articles 29 and 34 TEU
I-43	New
I-44	Article 43 TEU
I-45	New
I-46	Articles 1 TEU, 189 and 191 TEC
I-47	New and Article 194 TEC
I-48	New
I-49	Article 195 TEC
I-50	Articles 1 TEU and 200 and 255 TEC
I-51	New and Article 286 TEC
I-52	New and Declaration 11 of the Treaty of Amsterdam
I-53	Articles 268-80 TEC
I-54	Articles 6 TEU and 269 TEC
I-55	New together with Article 271 TEC
I-56	Article 272 TEC
I-57	New and Article 310 TEC
I-58	Article 49 TEU
I-59	Articles 7 TEU and 309 TEC
I-60	New

Part II is not new in itself, the Charter of Fundamental Rights having been 'proclaimed' in 2000, though it is new as a legally binding document. The only change made when it was incorporated was to add, at the insistence of the UK government, clauses at the end to make it absolutely clear that it does not create new rights and cannot be used to authorize a general right of oversight of national, in particular social, legislation. Part III is even more closely linked to the existing treaties, with virtually all of its clauses coming from the TEU and TEC, albeit in slightly modernized forms. Part IV also draws heavily on existing parallel articles. The two Annexes attached to the Constitutional Treaty, as well as most of the 36 protocols are identical to, at least in terms of content, or draw on the texts of annexes and protocols adopted as part of earlier treaties. The same is true for most of the political declarations. So there is enormous continuity between the Constitutional Treaty and its predecessors.

There are, however, new elements, and in Part I these include Article I-8 which recognizes the use of existing symbols; Article I-7 on fundamental rights; Article I-9 on fundamental principles; Articles I-12–17 on categories of competences; and Article I-17 on involving national parliaments in the monitoring of subsidiarity. When it comes to the institutions, Article I-21 brings in the European Council President; Article I-25 gives qualified majority voting a completely new form; Article I-26(5) phases in changes to the structure of the Commission; and Article I-28 establishes the Union Minister for Foreign Affairs.

In terms of procedures, Articles I-33 and I-37 introduce a new classification of legislative acts while I-40 and I-41 are new in their reference to the role of the Union Minister for Foreign Affairs, while I-43 introduces a solidarity clause. Articles I-45, I-46, I-47, I-51 and I-52 on the European Union's democratic credentials are also new though their content reflects existing realities. There are also new budgetary procedures in Articles I-55 and I-56, while Article I-57 gives a new twist to the idea of association with the European Union for non-members. And the provision for withdrawal in Article I-60 is wholly new.

Understanding the Constitutional Treaty thus requires us to see the limits to its innovativeness. Indeed, the degree of continuity found means that, ironically, if the Constitutional Treaty were to be rejected in favour of the existing treaties, many of the things disliked by critics would remain unchanged. However, such reactions to the Constitutional Treaty show that it needs to be approached carefully and not on the basis of half-truths and misapprehensions. And we now turn to how this can be done.

3 Thinking about the Constitutional Treaty

Knowing roughly what is in the Constitutional Treaty, how it emerged from the European Convention, the IGC and the existing texts, is useful. But this takes us only so far along the road to a full understanding. So how do we go further down the road? It might look as if all we have to do now is pick up the Constitutional Treaty and read on without further thought, but, in fact, it may not be wise to do so given its controversial nature.

This is because the fuss made about the Constitutional Treaty means that many people will have very clear ideas about it, even if they have not actually read the text. Such preconceptions can affect the way they think about it. This is particularly the case in the United Kingdom, which lacks a codified constitution of its own. Equally, most people are likely to have a view on whether it is a treaty or a constitution, and, if the latter, what this means. This is despite the conflicting views on the matter. In other words, we rarely read things wholly innocently and, given what has passed for debate in the United Kingdom, we need to be aware of this. Finally, the way the Constitutional Treaty is drafted needs thinking about. It is a long and difficult document written not to amuse people on trains but to be legally binding and to ensure continuity with the past. We need to bear these things in mind before actually reading the text.

Preconceptions

It may sound odd to say that a major problem about understanding the Constitutional Treaty lies in what we bring to it ourselves, given what we have said of how little the public, notably in the United Kingdom, seems to know about either the European Union or the Constitutional Treaty. Indeed, most people do not seem to want to read the latter, which is perhaps why publishers and newspapers, not to mention governments, have not done more to publish it. Yet lack of knowledge does not produce neutrality. Rather the reverse is true because absence of detailed knowledge leaves people exposed to the images portrayed in the flawed debate.

To begin with, British discussion of the Constitutional Treaty has been very spasmodic and rather general, focusing – even in the House of Common's second reading – on the overall achievements of the European Union and the value of membership. It has been hampered by pro-Europeans' dissatisfaction with the government's inactivity and unwillingness to embrace the euro cause, so myths and stereotypes predominate both generally and in the already hostile press. As this suggests, the Constitutional Treaty has been subsumed into other European issues. In the United Kingdom this includes both membership and the long-running fears of the alleged Brussels 'superstate' with its unelected Commission and invasive Court. This 'sovereignist' fear is also visible in France alongside opposition to Turkish entry, something also visible in the Netherlands. Complaints about agricultural spending, corruption and over-regulation, which also shape British reactions, are less common abroad. Equally, there is little concern in the United Kingdom about the 'Bolkestein' directive on cross-border service provision, which so exercises the French.

In other words, the Constitutional Treaty has often been caught up in broader, and contradictory, arguments about economic policy. Some socialists are opposed because it symbolizes free-market directives and policies, domestic and European, of which they disapprove. They lament the Constitutional Treaty's lack of social and environmental awareness and its failure to create the strong 'political' Europe needed for this. They see it as the defeat of the 'federalist' project by Anglo-Saxon concepts. Conversely, many British critics attack the document less for itself than because they see it reflecting a costly, uncompetitive and low-growth economy. Such ideas also influence the way many look at the Constitutional Treaty even though, as we have already said, this is a framework document and not a set of policy prescriptions. In both cases, attitudes to the governments seen as responsible for such policies colour people's attitudes. Despite the fact that such criticisms cancel each other out, it is always easy to put over a negative case and constant repetition in the popular press inevitably has an impact, making it harder to look at things objectively.

The fact that, across Europe, the contrary case has been put in contradictory and lukewarm ways exacerbates the problem. Many downplay it as a minor change, a 'mere tidying up', or as Bertie Ahern put it, a rationalization out of which 'we'll get a few generations'. Others see it as the dawn of a bright new era or as 'their victory' over the others. Neither the stress on the limited changes it makes nor the claim of prevailing over 'Brussels' helps to counter hostile preconceptions. All this means that the debate is underdeveloped and conducted in local blinkers. Hence the antis have often made more impact on the poorly informed. So many who think about the document, usually without reading it, are likely to approach it from a prejudiced point of view.

British perspectives

Another aspect of the problems created by what we ourselves bring to the Constitutional Treaty is that the British have special difficulties in dealing with such legal texts. This is partly thanks to the unusual nature of the UK constitution. While it is wrong to say that the United Kingdom does not have a 'written' constitution, since its constituent statutes, judgements and conventions are all available in print, there is no agreement as to which acts are 'constitutional'. On the one hand, this is because they are not codified into one agreed document which summarizes them. On the other hand, it is because, whereas in many countries 'the rules of the game' have a special status and require heightened levels of parliamentary or popular support for their adoption and amendment, in the United Kingdom there is nothing really to distinguish a constitutional law from a non-constitutional act. All laws are regarded as being of the same status, although this is beginning to change.

Finally, UK constitutional rules are unentrenched. That is to say they can easily be changed by Parliament or, in the case of conventions, by mere shifts in opinion. Conversely, in most other countries, constitutional changes can only be made with support from the vast majority of the constituent states (as in the United States of America) or by a majority of these and the people (as in Switzerland) or by enhanced parliamentary majorities.

The absence of a codified and popularly endorsed constitutional document certainly provides flexibility, allowing Parliament to respond quickly to events. Yet this flexibility underlies the unease about the pooling of sovereignty within the European Union because there are no domestic rules which either facilitate or place limits on this in the way there are in countries with an overriding and codified constitution. For the absence of a single, superior constitutional document can also mean there are no real restraints on government action. Similarly, it makes for relative unfamiliarity with legal texts and norms. Because we do not have to think about such texts, we can focus on things not necessarily found in constitutional documents, such as personalities and policies.

Thus commentators like Siedentop have remarked that the British lack a constitutional culture, despite what has been called a certain constitutional self-righteousness. Without a codified document, constitutional questions attract little interest, even among political scientists, and are left to lawyers and anoraks. Despite many books on UK constitutional law, the general public does not think in 'constitutionalist' terms of hierarchies of principles, rules and structures. It finds it hard to comprehend the structures of UK governance and is even less comprehending about the governance of other countries. Political education is therefore difficult and is a marginal concern.

This has encouraged both a lack of interest in the emergence of the Constitutional Treaty and an inability to focus on the key texts. In May 2003 the *Daily Mail* launched its first onslaught on the Constitutional Treaty, well before it had been completed. Subsequently, the Foreign Secretary rebuked a leader in *The Times* for basing its arguments on a failed proposal to the Convention. A little later, the same paper also derided the Commission for showing the Convention draft on the Europa website rather than the up-to-date one, even though the Constitutional Treaty was still being negotiated in the IGC, which had, in any case, put all drafts and proposed changes on-line.

Reading the text also poses problems because the British are generally unfamiliar with the grammar and terminology of constitutional reforms. The scorn among parliamentary sketch writers at the idea that the text of the Constitutional Treaty, once agreed at the European Council in June 2004, needed a process of technical textual revision to ensure that it was consistent both internally and between the many languages in which it has to be translated proves the point. Some letter writers clearly believed that no such 'toiletage' – as the process is unfortunately known in EU circles – was necessary and that it was perfectly possible to have a referendum on the draft within a few days of the agreement. This all means that the British, who have the most need of it, have the least background for understanding the text and need to make the most effort to do so.

A treaty and/or a constitution?

We also need to be aware of what we think the document actually is – a treaty or a constitution – because this will affect the way we approach it. Though some say it is a silly debate, it is actually a highly political matter and not just a sterile technical point. The very name has become politicized. But the arguments miss the point because its status is a confusingly mixed one.

Street language in the United Kingdom follows both supporters and opponents alike, who delight in calling the document 'a constitution'. This is because, as we will see, the word has a particular meaning. For supporters, it has an encouraging and legitimating ring whereas opponents see it as menacing. Thus the 'no' campaign initially objected to the referendum question talking of approving 'the Treaty', denouncing this as ponderous and called for the simpler 'constitution', a term that gives them most advantage because of its overtones. The government prefers to talk of it as a 'treaty' since this is more reassuring to public opinion; and critics who want more integration see it as a treaty masquerading as a constitution and never making the link with popular sovereignty, which they see as essential to a constitution.

Admittedly this is the language of most of the document, but reading it simply as a constitution will not give us a fair understanding. The official designation of what was signed on 29 October 2004 is a '*Treaty* establishing a Constitution for Europe' (*our emphasis*) and, legally, it is a treaty requiring unanimous agreement in order to become operative. And, as Box 3.1 shows, there are many other reasons why it should be so regarded. To begin with, it is one of a long series of deals between sovereign states that confer authority on the European Union to take decisions in specific but limited areas and under specific conditions. Hence, it still starts with what the European Union is to do rather than by creating institutions. Its institutions are, moreover, more limited in their number and scope than are similar national bodies. At the same time, the Constitutional Treaty preserves most of the normal style of a treaty, whether in language or, especially, through the addition of things like declarations and protocols. And only states can revise the treaties.

Equally its structure – with the long Part III on policies and Part IV on application – differs from many, if not all, constitutions. No self-respecting constitution, it has been said, would have 448 articles. Interestingly, some critics deny it constitutional status precisely because it is not a brief statement of principles but, to quote a French Socialist opponent, is more like a commercial treaty or a set of house rules. In other words, the length and style of the overall document can only be explained by the fact that it is a treaty and one which seeks to maintain continuity with preceding treaties. It is very detailed, not to say verbose, because its provisions are codes for working the arrangements agreed by the signatory states.

The member states steer the European Union both through the enhanced role of the European Council and by means of the interpretative Declarations. The Constitutional Treaty also leaves almost all implementation of EU decisions to the member states. Furthermore, the member states retain their sovereignty in other areas and can go back on their undertakings and leave without much fuss, something never really possible before.

So, for many observers, the member states remain the 'Masters of the Treaties', and the Constitutional Treaty both reinforces their influence and consolidates the rules they have agreed in the past. The Constitutional Treaty is not a constitution in the same way as a state has one. Nor does it remedy the democratic deficit of the European Union in the way we might expect a true constitution to do. For some purists, because it neither emerges from the people nor creates anything like a political community (with uniform voting rights for all), it does not deserve the title 'constitution'. The fact that it accepts national constitutions has also been seen as a reason for denying it constitutional status. In other words, whatever its superficial changes, the Constitutional Treaty remains a classic treaty in many ways.

Against this, there are an equal number of arguments. Thus, while the title may start with 'Treaty', it is in fact an act establishing a constitution. And

Box 3.1 Treaty or constitution?

The case for saying it is a treaty

- The title and structure
- Enacted as an agreement between existing states which generally retain their sovereignty
- Continues the acquis (content) of earlier treaties
- The requirement for unanimous ratification
- The way states control amendment, finance and strategy (through the European Council)
- The use of member state Declarations to interpret the text
- The fact that it can be revised by future treaties
- The right of withdrawal
- The principle of 'conferral'
- The order, commencing with (limited) policy objectives not institutions
- Prevalence of detailed codes over free action
- The limits to the frame of governance
- The limits of EU powers of enforcement
- Prolix, technical and complex style
- The use of treaty technology such as Protocols and Declarations

The case for saying it is a constitution

- The consistent use of the term in the text and in the title
- Owes its origins to a representative body, claims that the constitution and not the 'High Contracting Parties' establishes the Union, and is being be ratified by referendum in ten member states
- Its formal repeal of all existing treaties
- The possibility of proceeding if unanimity is not achieved
- The possibility of easier amendment in certain areas
- The appeal to the peoples of Europe and the transfer of democratic aspirations to the EU level including citizenship.
- The commitment to the agreement being concluded for an unlimited period
- The merging of the European Union and the EC into onc powerful body with legal personality and no pillars
- The supremacy of European Union over national law and the weakness of subsidiarity
- The existence of 'passerelles' which allow moves to QMV decisions
- Pre-emption of states' rights via the clarification of competences
- The Presidency of the European Council and the Foreign Minister
- The restructuring of policies to fit in with the innovations of Part I
- The clarity of expression and the specification of aims and symbols
- The constitutional feel of Part I and the Charter of Fundamental Rights as a binding code
- Formalizes ongoing constitutionalization

'constitution' is the term used almost exclusively in the rest of the document when it describes itself. Although we are reminded of the 'Treaty' dimension in Part II, albeit on just three occasions, it is only in Part IV (dealing with implementation and amendment) that the term 'Treaty' is widely used. The reference to it being a constitution also extends to the establishment of the European Union, this no longer being described as the work of 'the High Contracting Parties' but of the constitution. This usage, it is argued, emerged from the European Convention, which saw itself as representative of a 'European people' in whose name it claimed to act.

While this is disputed, the fact remains that the Constitutional Treaty was drawn up in a more open and public manner than previous treaties. And, with ratification being carried out through referenda in some of the member states, this could make the European Union a popular rather than a state-based body. Certainly it addresses citizens in ways treaties do not, and it seeks a double legitimacy. Hence, symbolically, it is a constitution. The addition of apparently stable executive offices and the commitment to creating a social market economy increases the symbolism for some authorities. No other international organization has such a structure. Generally the document has a constitutional feel, notably in Part I.

Similarly, while it may be true that the Constitutional Treaty continues the old treaties in many ways, it also repeals them all bar one and continues the process of constitutionalization. This technically makes it the foundation of a new and different political entity and one which, whatever it may say about being based on the conferral of powers and competences, imposes its own law on member states. By merging the pillars and doing away with the European Community – although not the European Atomic Energy Community (EAEC) — it both removes some national safeguards and claims citizenship and a monopoly of democracy and public space, thanks in part to the incorporation of Charter of Fundamental Rights. At the same time, although it clarifies powers, it allows the Union to pre-empt member state action in areas of shared responsibility. And, although the Constitutional Treaty creates a mechanism for withdrawal, this has to be set against the fact that the document is concluded for an unlimited period – implying permanency.

Furthermore, while member states have a power of amendment and revision, this overlooks the fact that there are so-called *passerelle* clauses which allow them to shift the adoption of certain measures from unanimity to qualified majority voting. There are also simplified procedures for revision which limit the authority of the member states. Equally, though the member states will continue to play a major part, some of the institutional reforms in the Constitutional Treaty create influential posts, such as the EU Minister for Foreign Affairs, thus enhancing the role of the institutions.

A final reason for saying it is a constitution follows from its supporters' claims that it as an historic achievement, the reflection of a 'constitutional moment'. It is historic because it is a step change from the old European Community, in that it lays down principles and rights to be observed and accepts symbols associated with statehood (i.e. a flag, an anthem and a currency). And, even if it does not actually transform the European Union into a real European state (as its opponents claim), it certainly does not close the road to this. It could, for Jürgen Habermas, the German intellectual, be the making of a true European 'demos', possibly at the expense of its constituent nations. So, for some supporters and many of its opponents, whatever the technicalities, the Constitutional Treaty has to be regarded as a true, state-like, constitution.

Not all these points, on either side, are valid. Moreover, many of them cancel each other out. The truth is that the Constitutional Treaty – or the treaty–constitution as the French have it – aspires to be both. The differences are as much quantitative as qualitative. It is a treaty in form and style, as well as being a superior codifying and constitutive act which is largely constitutional in import. Equally it exercises a legal force similar to that of many constitutions. It is a hybrid and this causes problems.

One of these problems is that people imagine that treaties and constitutions are totally different, a contention which both supporters and opponents of the Constitutional Treaty have a vested interest in maintaining. In reality there is some overlap, since historically treaties have been used to create constitutional structures. This was frequently the case in nineteenth-century Germany. And some Americans, at least until the Civil War, saw the US Constitution as simply a diplomatic agreement between sovereign states. Moreover, the constitutions of other international bodies, such as the International Labour Organization, were established by treaties. Such precedents reinforce the case for the Constitutional Treaty being a hybrid. So the only reading which really fits the facts is that it is both constitutional and a treaty and is best regarded as a Constitutional Treaty.

What kind of Constitutional Treaty?

Calling the Constitutional Treaty simply a 'constitution 'reflects assumptions that there is only one kind of constitution. Many people have narrow, and not wholly appropriate, understandings of the term. A constitution is too often seen as a tablet of stone chiselled to found a state. But it can be more indicative and more limiting of power.

The eurosceptic view assumes both that constitutions always trump treaties and that they are absolutely clear and wholly binding documents from which there is no escape. This is not so. Many constitutions recognize that international law is, and should be, superior to national law. Moreover, constitutions are, in the main, limited framework documents, not absolute and complete sets of rules. They require other things to fill them out. So they are only part of the story. Much happens outside them.

The idea that the Constitutional Treaty gives no freedom of action often derives from what it says about the primacy of EU law. As we will see, although this is now formally stated in the Constitutional Treaty, it is not new. Moreover, it neither applies as widely as is sometimes thought nor constitutes an unchecked right to overrule all national decisions. And the history of the Union shows that it is not unknown for member states to defy treaties and court rulings, despite the levying of fines.

There is also a certain lack of logic in the related criticism that the document is unusable because of its lack of clarity, leaving it open to the Court of Justice to interpret it. Eurosceptics see the text as being full of traps laid in, non-existent, footnotes and obscure clauses by Machiavellian integrationists. But few, if any, constitutions are so clear as to be incapable of more than one appreciation or understanding. In the case of the Constitutional Treaty, because the text is a compromise there is inconsistency and hence scope for finding what you want. And the use of courts, rather than politicians, to adjudicate on meaning is true of almost all constitutions.

A second misplaced assumption is that only states can have a constitution – and therefore the Constitutional Treaty must be creating a state. This is clearly wrong. All kinds of public bodies can, and do, have constitutions – from student unions through bodies like the British Conservative Party to international organizations. All need statements of aims, means and rules for a corporate body so there is no logical reason why the term can only be used of a state. So the mere existence of a constitution, especially in treaty form, does not mean that the new European Union is a state. It is also wrong to assume that a constitution necessarily fixes social and economic policy.

Third, supporters and opponents also assume that, where states are concerned, there can only be one kind of constitution, the enabling republican model aimed at creating a popularly founded polity. In other words, constitutions are created by the people and not by diplomats. They are seen as documents which not merely set out principles, institutions and structures of governance, but which also involve a populace constituting themselves as a nation state. But if other bodies can, and do, have constitutions this is not necessarily so.

Indeed, the Constitutional Treaty was in part inspired by a different view of a constitution as a document seeking to limit government so as to protect rights and avoid arbitrary rule. There was thus much talk of spelling out who does what so as to prevent creeping competence. For observers like Chris Patten, having such a constitution would comfort doubters by placing clear barriers against the transfer of authority to 'Brussels'. Jack Straw has argued a similar line and Vernon Bogdanor, the Oxford academic, has even called it a eurosceptics' constitution. Yet, while there is some evidence for this, British opinion has not accepted that the term 'constitution' has now lost its threatening and intrusive nature.

It is also worth noting that the belief that the document is a constitution implies that the existing treaties are not. Yet the Court of Justice has, for some 20 years, seen the TEC as 'the constitutional charter' of the European Community, a position shared by most lawyers. And many authorities refer to the process of treaty reform as one of constitutionalization. The 1997 Amsterdam Treaty thus simplified and consolidated the treaties while both repealing some existing acts and incorporating others, without adding new elements of its own. It also cast changes in terms of principles rather than specifying numbers.

So rejecting the Constitutional Treaty would not necessarily lead to a wholly different or wholly 'non-constitutional' situation. If passed it will, like its predecessors, reflect the balance of power prevailing in the European Union. It will also set out the framework of institutional governance and provide a political code for working it. Equally it will establish a superior reference point against which other rules can be assessed. Indeed it goes further in this direction than the existing treaties, as it does in defending rights and freedoms. It will also reinforce limitations on the powers of the institutions.

Some claim that the Constitutional Treaty provides the European Union with an integrative symbol. This may turn out to be the case, but the level of contestation suggests it could be a symbol of opposition. However, although it creates a polity it does not really constitute a European people. Early responses also suggest that it will not play the educational role that many national constitutions do. And its role in embodying tradition is limited, though the continuation of the acquis – as the corpus of existing legislation is known – suggests it is there. So functionally it is only partly a constitution. This schizophrenia may not be helpful but it is typical of the kind of compromises which a body like the European Union is forced to make.

The way the Constitutional Treaty is written

Many people have said that the Convention and the IGC should have produced a much shorter document which eschewed detail, was accessible to any reasonably intelligent person and not open to divergent interpretations. However, the Constitutional Treaty is certainly not short. And few have found it easy to understand or agree upon. So, when parliamentary committees and newspaper leader writers call on governments to explain properly what the Constitutional Treaty means and does, they are not only trying to score political points; they are reflecting the fact that technically it is not easy to come to terms with the text. It needs to be approached with care and not be read like an airport novel. Understanding why the Constitutional Treaty is as long as it is and why it is written in the way it is is a helpful first step towards a meaningful read.

How fair is the criticism of the length of the Constitutional Treaty? Given that Jack Straw once said he wanted a slim volume which would fit into his pocket, many critics have attacked it as immensely long and verbose. The Constitutional Treaty does simplify language, structure and process, but at 480 pages it is not short in absolute terms. However, it does at least fit into one volume, if not into the ordinary pocket, and it is virtually the only volume we will need to find the European Union's ground rules. And it is shorter than both the total size of the twenty or so preceding treaties and some competitors. The former amounted to 600 articles, well over 1,100 pages and innumerable words.

Single member states can also produce far more than this every year. In the case of the United Kingdom, the Supply Estimates for 2004 run to 640 pages and the Budget runs to 320 pages. The 2003 Criminal Justice Bill ran to 350 pages with innumerable chapters. And every year the statute book gains anything up to 6,000 new pages. There are also some 4,000 secondary statutory instruments every year filling 10,000 pages.

The length of the Constitutional Treaty is due to the very fact that it is not just a constitution. If it were, it could have been a relatively short document. But, because it is also an agreement among states, many of which have been involved in integration for more than 50 years, then everything has to be there, including past decisions. In other words, were the Constitutional Treaty to comprise Part I alone then there would be tremendous uncertainty as to the status of what has previously been agreed under the existing treaties. The acquis has to be worked in through Part III. Because of this the Constitutional Treaty has also been criticized for including too many policy statements which have no place in a real constitution.

A related criticism is that the Constitutional Treaty is badly written. As the *Financial Times* put it 'it is a treaty and therefore must have all the clumsy verbiage of law making attached to the relatively pithy first part'. Others have been less kind. It has been criticized for its legalese, for its repetitiousness, its obliqueness, its tortuousness and its turgidness. This is not merely a matter of failing to achieve a good style. For others it is utterly incomprehensible, not to mention inelegant and ungainly. Hence the *Economist* suggested that the only thing to do with the draft produced by the European Convention was to throw it in the bin. More hostile critics see it as a deliberate ploy and as a triumph for Eurocrats and their jargon. They accuse the authors of trying to make it unintelligible to general readers so that they will not appreciate its import. So, for them, profound changes are hidden away in vague details and in the more obscure reaches of the text, notably in Part III.

The reality is more banal. There are several reasons why the language is difficult. First, because it is an intergovernmental treaty, the language reflects the many compromises reached in the pursuit of agreement between 25 member states. This means including extra items to satisfy aggrieved parties. It also means a deliberate vagueness so that competing interests – which read the text in different ways – can all be satisfied with the outcome. Hence it is often deliberately open to different interpretations. This is done not to confuse the general public but to accommodate the needs of governments pushed by their own publics. Nonetheless, this is not very helpful to the ordinary reader.

Second, the Constitutional Treaty, especially its Part I, is meant to be a distillation of fundamentals because no text is likely to be able to provide for all existing and future contingencies. But basic principles can be somewhat abstract and generalized, especially if readers are unaware of the context. Third, it is not written by a single author but is the product of various groups penning lines at different points in time. While this does not make for absolute clarity it is inherent in the negotiation process.

Fourth, and more importantly, its difficult language derives from the status and purpose of the Constitutional Treaty. In other words, it is written in a legalistic and formal language partly because it derives from existing treaties and especially because, like its predecessors, it is a legally effective document and has to be enforceable in courts. Despite the accusations of being a superstate, the European Union is based on an intergovernmental treaty and is held together less by powerful institutions than by a willingness to accept legal judgements. Without this the Union would fall apart. And approachable language will not provide the kind of precise legal code needed.

Finally, documents produced by conventions and IGCs are usually drawn up in one language and translated into others. This does not make for spontaneity of style. Moreover, terms in one language can have a very different resonance or meaning in others, as is notably the case with federalism. And though the English version of the Constitutional Treaty is the one that will be most widely used, it is not a particularly good text because much of it has been translated from French and was not subjected to as much stylistic revision as we would have wished.

Not surprisingly, some commentators believe that anyone could have done better. This is doubtful. While it is clear that the style could have been made more accessible, and that it is not a text easily comprehensible to schoolchildren (as Giscard d'Estaing wanted), there is something to be said for the language. Notably in Parts I and II it is more concise and less official than elsewhere. Equally, the amount of EU jargon has been reduced. The addition of headings for each article is also useful. This makes it more approachable than most acts of parliament, as comparison with the Referendum Bill reveals. So it is not, as has been claimed 'unreadable'. This is a silly statement and one unfair to ordinary readers. It is not beyond most people's abilities to follow most of Part I, provided they bear its origins and purpose in mind.

All this shows that there is a good deal to think about before reading the text. We need to accept the challenge of a kind of document which is uncommon in the United Kingdom, and one which is both a treaty and a constitution. And it is a Constitutional Treaty which is as concerned to limit as to increase EU power. We also have to accept that while its style is imperfect, it is imperfect for a purpose. Doing this may not feed our prejudices but it will allow a reading closer to the complicated compromises of the document itself.

4 Part I – The official text

Treaty establishing a Constitution for Europe

Preamble

HIS MAJESTY THE KING OF THE BELGIANS, THE PRESIDENT OF THE CZECH REPUBLIC, HER MAJESTY THE QUEEN OF DENMARK, THE PRESIDENT OF THE FEDERAL REPUBLIC OF GERMANY, THE PRESIDENT OF THE REPUBLIC OF ESTONIA, THE PRESIDENT OF THE HELLENIC REPUBLIC, HIS MAJESTY THE KING OF SPAIN, THE PRESIDENT OF THE FRENCH REPUBLIC, THE PRESIDENT OF IRELAND, THE PRESIDENT OF THE ITALIAN REPUBLIC, THE PRESIDENT OF THE REPUBLIC OF CYPRUS, THE PRESIDENT OF THE REPUBLIC OF LATVIA, THE PRESIDENT OF THE REPUBLIC OF LITHUANIA, HIS ROYAL HIGHNESS THE GRAND DUKE OF LUXEMBOURG, THE PRESIDENT OF THE REPUBLIC OF HUNGARY, THE PRESIDENT OF MALTA, HER MAJESTY THE QUEEN OF THE NETHERLANDS, THE FEDERAL PRESIDENT OF THE REPUBLIC OF AUSTRIA, THE PRESIDENT OF THE REPUBLIC OF POLAND, THE PRESIDENT OF THE PORTUGUESE REPUBLIC, THE PRESIDENT OF THE REPUBLIC OF SLOVENIA, THE PRESIDENT OF THE SLOVAK REPUBLIC, THE PRESIDENT OF THE REPUBLIC OF FINLAND, THE GOVERNMENT OF THE KINGDOM OF SWEDEN, HER MAJESTY THE QUEEN OF THE UNITED KINGDOM OF GREAT BRITAIN AND NORTHERN IRELAND,

DRAWING INSPIRATION from the cultural, religious and humanist inheritance of Europe, from which have developed the universal values of the inviolable and inalienable rights of the human person, freedom, democracy, equality and the rule of law,
BELIEVING that Europe, reunited after bitter experiences, intends to continue along the path of civilisation, progress and prosperity, for the good of all its inhabitants, including the weakest and most deprived; that it wishes to remain a continent open to culture, learning and social

progress; and that it wishes to deepen the democratic and transparent nature of its public life, and to strive for peace, justice and solidarity throughout the world,
CONVINCED that, while remaining proud of their own national identities and history, the peoples of Europe are determined to transcend their former divisions and, united ever more closely, to forge a common destiny,
CONVINCED that, thus 'United in diversity', Europe offers them the best chance of pursuing, with due regard for the rights of each individual and in awareness of their responsibilities towards future generations and the Earth, the great venture which makes of it a special area of human hope,
DETERMINED to continue the work accomplished within the framework of the Treaties establishing the European Communities and the Treaty on European Union, by ensuring the continuity of the Community acquis,
GRATEFUL to the members of the European Convention for having prepared the draft of this Constitution on behalf of the citizens and States of Europe,

WHO, having exchanged their full powers, found in good and due form, have agreed as follows:

PART I

Title I Definition and objectives of the Union

Article I-1 Establishment of the Union

1. Reflecting the will of the citizens and States of Europe to build a common future, this Constitution establishes the European Union, on which the Member States confer competences to attain objectives they have in common. The Union shall coordinate the policies by which the Member States aim to achieve these objectives, and shall exercise on a Community basis the competences they confer on it.
2. The Union shall be open to all European States which respect its values and are committed to promoting them together.

Article I-2 The Union's values

The Union is founded on the values of respect for human dignity, freedom, democracy, equality, the rule of law and respect for human rights, including the rights of persons belonging to minorities. These values are common to the Member States in a society in which pluralism, non-discrimination, tolerance, justice, solidarity and equality between women and men prevail.

Article I-3 The Union's objectives

1. The Union's aim is to promote peace, its values and the well-being of its peoples.
2. The Union shall offer its citizens an area of freedom, security and justice without internal frontiers, and an internal market where competition is free and undistorted.
3. The Union shall work for the sustainable development of Europe based on balanced economic growth and price stability, a highly competitive social market economy, aiming at full employment and social progress, and a high level of protection and improvement of the quality of the environment. It shall promote scientific and technological advance.

It shall combat social exclusion and discrimination, and shall promote social justice and protection, equality between women and men, solidarity between generations and protection of the rights of the child.

It shall promote economic, social and territorial cohesion, and solidarity among Member States.

It shall respect its rich cultural and linguistic diversity, and shall ensure that Europe's cultural heritage is safeguarded and enhanced.

4. In its relations with the wider world, the Union shall uphold and promote its values and interests. It shall contribute to peace, security, the sustainable development of the Earth, solidarity and mutual respect among peoples, free and fair trade, eradication of poverty and the protection of human rights, in particular the rights of the child, as well as to the strict observance and the development of international law, including respect for the principles of the United Nations Charter.
5. The Union shall pursue its objectives by appropriate means commensurate with the competences which are conferred upon it in the Constitution.

Article I-4 Fundamental freedoms and non-discrimination

1. The free movement of persons, services, goods and capital, and freedom of establishment shall be guaranteed within and by the Union, in accordance with the Constitution.
2. Within the scope of the Constitution, and without prejudice to any of its specific provisions, any discrimination on grounds of nationality shall be prohibited.

Article I-5 Relations between the Union and the Member States

1. The Union shall respect the equality of Member States before the Constitution as well as their national identities, inherent in their fundamental structures, political and constitutional, inclusive of regional and

local self-government. It shall respect their essential State functions, including ensuring the territorial integrity of the State, maintaining law and order and safeguarding national security.
2. Pursuant to the principle of sincere cooperation, the Union and the Member States shall, in full mutual respect, assist each other in carrying out tasks which flow from the Constitution.

The Member States shall take any appropriate measure, general or particular, to ensure fulfilment of the obligations arising out of the Constitution or resulting from the acts of the institutions of the Union.

The Member States shall facilitate the achievement of the Union's tasks and refrain from any measure which could jeopardise the attainment of the Union's objectives.

Article I-6 Union law

The Constitution and law adopted by the institutions of the Union in exercising competences conferred on it shall have primacy over the law of the Member States.

Article I-7 Legal personality

The Union shall have legal personality.

Article I-8 The symbols of the Union

The flag of the Union shall be a circle of twelve golden stars on a blue background.

The anthem of the Union shall be based on the "Ode to Joy" from the Ninth Symphony by Ludwig van Beethoven.

The motto of the Union shall be: "United in diversity".

The currency of the Union shall be the euro.

Europe day shall be celebrated on 9 May throughout the Union.

Title II Fundamental rights and citizenship of the Union

Article I-9 Fundamental rights

1. The Union shall recognise the rights, freedoms and principles set out in the Charter of Fundamental Rights which constitutes Part II.
2. The Union shall accede to the European Convention for the Protection of Human Rights and Fundamental Freedoms. Such accession shall not affect the Union's competences as defined in the Constitution.
3. Fundamental rights, as guaranteed by the European Convention for the Protection of Human Rights and Fundamental Freedoms and as they

result from the constitutional traditions common to the Member States, shall constitute general principles of the Union's law.

Article I-10 Citizenship of the Union

1. Every national of a Member State shall be a citizen of the Union. Citizenship of the Union shall be additional to national citizenship and shall not replace it.

2. Citizens of the Union shall enjoy the rights and be subject to the duties provided for in the Constitution. They shall have:

(a) the right to move and reside freely within the territory of the Member States;

(b) the right to vote and to stand as candidates in elections to the European Parliament and in municipal elections in their Member State of residence, under the same conditions as nationals of that State;

(c) the right to enjoy, in the territory of a third country in which the Member State of which they are nationals is not represented, the protection of the diplomatic and consular authorities of any Member State on the same conditions as the nationals of that State;

(d) the right to petition the European Parliament, to apply to the European Ombudsman, and to address the institutions and advisory bodies of the Union in any of the Constitution's languages and to obtain a reply in the same language.

These rights shall be exercised in accordance with the conditions and limits defined by the Constitution and by the measures adopted thereunder.

Title III Union competences

Article I-11 Fundamental principles

1. The limits of Union competences are governed by the principle of conferral. The use of Union competences is governed by the principles of subsidiarity and proportionality.

2. Under the principle of conferral, the Union shall act within the limits of the competences conferred upon it by the Member States in the Constitution to attain the objectives set out in the Constitution. Competences not conferred upon the Union in the Constitution remain with the Member States.

3. Under the principle of subsidiarity, in areas which do not fall within its exclusive competence, the Union shall act only if and insofar as the objectives of the proposed action cannot be sufficiently achieved by the

Member States, either at central level or at regional and local level, but can rather, by reason of the scale or effects of the proposed action, be better achieved at Union level.

The institutions of the Union shall apply the principle of subsidiarity as laid down in the Protocol on the application of the principles of subsidiarity and proportionality. National Parliaments shall ensure compliance with that principle in accordance with the procedure set out in that Protocol.

4. Under the principle of proportionality, the content and form of Union action shall not exceed what is necessary to achieve the objectives of the Constitution.

The institutions of the Union shall apply the principle of proportionality as laid down in the Protocol on the application of the principles of subsidiarity and proportionality.

Article I-12 Categories of competence

1. When the Constitution confers on the Union exclusive competence in a specific area, only the Union may legislate and adopt legally binding acts, the Member States being able to do so themselves only if so empowered by the Union or for the implementation of Union acts.

2. When the Constitution confers on the Union a competence shared with the Member States in a specific area, the Union and the Member States may legislate and adopt legally binding acts in that area. The Member States shall exercise their competence to the extent that the Union has not exercised, or has decided to cease exercising, its competence.

3. The Member States shall coordinate their economic and employment policies within arrangements as determined by Part III, which the Union shall have competence to provide.

4. The Union shall have competence to define and implement a common foreign and security policy, including the progressive framing of a common defence policy.

5. In certain areas and under the conditions laid down in the Constitution, the Union shall have competence to carry out actions to support, coordinate or supplement the actions of the Member States, without thereby superseding their competence in these areas.

Legally binding acts of the Union adopted on the basis of the provisions in Part III relating to these areas shall not entail harmonisation of Member States' laws or regulations.

6. The scope of and arrangements for exercising the Union's competences shall be determined by the provisions relating to each area in Part III.

Article I-13 Areas of exclusive competence

1. The Union shall have exclusive competence in the following areas:
(a) customs union;
(b) the establishing of the competition rules necessary for the functioning of the internal market;
(c) monetary policy for the Member States whose currency is the euro;
(d) the conservation of marine biological resources under the common fisheries policy;
(e) common commercial policy.

2. The Union shall also have exclusive competence for the conclusion of an international agreement when its conclusion is provided for in a legislative act of the Union or is necessary to enable the Union to exercise its internal competence, or insofar as its conclusion may affect common rules or alter their scope.

Article I-14 Areas of shared competence

1. The Union shall share competence with the Member States where the Constitution confers on it a competence which does not relate to the areas referred to in Articles I-13 and I-17.

2. Shared competence between the Union and the Member States applies in the following principal areas:
(a) internal market;
(b) social policy, for the aspects defined in Part III;
(c) economic, social and territorial cohesion;
(d) agriculture and fisheries, excluding the conservation of marine biological resources;
(e) environment;
(f) consumer protection;
(g) transport;
(h) trans-European networks;
(i) energy;
(j) area of freedom, security and justice;
(k) common safety concerns in public health matters, for the aspects defined in Part III.

3. In the areas of research, technological development and space, the Union shall have competence to carry out activities, in particular to define and implement programmes; however, the exercise of that competence shall not result in Member States being prevented from exercising theirs.

4. In the areas of development cooperation and humanitarian aid, the Union shall have competence to carry out activities and conduct a common policy; however, the exercise of that competence shall not result in Member States being prevented from exercising theirs.

Article I-15 The coordination of economic and employment policies

1. The Member States shall coordinate their economic policies within the Union. To this end, the Council of Ministers shall adopt measures, in particular broad guidelines for these policies.

Specific provisions shall apply to those Member States whose currency is the euro.

2. The Union shall take measures to ensure coordination of the employment policies of the Member States, in particular by defining guidelines for these policies.

3. The Union may take initiatives to ensure coordination of Member States' social policies.

Article I-16 The common foreign and security policy

1. The Union's competence in matters of common foreign and security policy shall cover all areas of foreign policy and all questions relating to the Union's security, including the progressive framing of a common defence policy that might lead to a common defence.

2. Member States shall actively and unreservedly support the Union's common foreign and security policy in a spirit of loyalty and mutual solidarity and shall comply with the Union's action in this area. They shall refrain from action contrary to the Union's interests or likely to impair its effectiveness.

Article I-17 Areas of supporting, coordinating or complementary action

The Union shall have competence to carry out supporting, coordinating or complementary action. The areas of such action shall, at European level, be:

(a) protection and improvement of human health;
(b) industry;
(c) culture;
(d) tourism;
(e) education, youth, sport and vocational training;
(f) civil protection;
(g) administrative cooperation.

Article I-18 Flexibility clause

1. If action by the Union should prove necessary, within the framework of the policies defined in Part III, to attain one of the objectives set out in the Constitution, and the Constitution has not provided the necessary powers, the Council of Ministers, acting unanimously on a proposal from

the European Commission and after obtaining the consent of the European Parliament, shall adopt the appropriate measures.
2. Using the procedure for monitoring the subsidiarity principle referred to in Article I-11(3), the European Commission shall draw national Parliaments' attention to proposals based on this Article.
3. Measures based on this Article shall not entail harmonisation of Member States' laws or regulations in cases where the Constitution excludes such harmonisation.

Title IV The Union's institutions and bodies

Chapter I The institutional framework

Article I-19 The Union's institutions

1. The Union shall have an institutional framework which shall aim to:
- promote its values,
- advance its objectives,
- serve its interests, those of its citizens and those of the Member States,
- ensure the consistency, effectiveness and continuity of its policies and actions.

This institutional framework comprises:
- The European Parliament,
- The European Council,
- The Council of Ministers (hereinafter referred to as the "Council"),
- The European Commission (hereinafter referred to as the "Commission"),
- The Court of Justice of the European Union.

2. Each institution shall act within the limits of the powers conferred on it in the Constitution, and in conformity with the procedures and conditions set out in it. The institutions shall practise mutual sincere cooperation.

Article I-20 The European Parliament

1. The European Parliament shall, jointly with the Council, exercise legislative and budgetary functions. It shall exercise functions of political control and consultation as laid down in the Constitution. It shall elect the President of the Commission.
2. The European Parliament shall be composed of representatives of the Union's citizens. They shall not exceed seven hundred and fifty in number. Representation of citizens shall be degressively proportional, with a minimum threshold of six members per Member State. No Member State shall be allocated more than ninety-six seats.

The European Council shall adopt by unanimity, on the initiative of the European Parliament and with its consent, a European decision establishing the composition of the European Parliament, respecting the principles referred to in the first subparagraph.
3. The members of the European Parliament shall be elected for a term of five years by direct universal suffrage in a free and secret ballot.
4. The European Parliament shall elect its President and its officers from among its members.

Article I-21 The European Council

1. The European Council shall provide the Union with the necessary impetus for its development and shall define the general political directions and priorities thereof. It shall not exercise legislative functions.
2. The European Council shall consist of the Heads of State or Government of the Member States, together with its President and the President of the Commission. The Union Minister for Foreign Affairs shall take part in its work.
3. The European Council shall meet quarterly, convened by its President. When the agenda so requires, the members of the European Council may decide each to be assisted by a minister and, in the case of the President of the Commission, by a member of the Commission. When the situation so requires, the President shall convene a special meeting of the European Council.
4. Except where the Constitution provides otherwise, decisions of the European Council shall be taken by consensus.

Article I-22 The European Council President

1. The European Council shall elect its President, by a qualified majority, for a term of two and a half years, renewable once. In the event of an impediment or serious misconduct, the European Council can end his or her term of office in accordance with the same procedure.
2. The President of the European Council:
(a) shall chair it and drive forward its work;
(b) shall ensure the preparation and continuity of the work of the European Council in cooperation with the President of the Commission, and on the basis of the work of the General Affairs Council;
(c) shall endeavour to facilitate cohesion and consensus within the European Council;
(d) shall present a report to the European Parliament after each of the meetings of the European Council.

The President of the European Council shall, at his or her level and in that capacity, ensure the external representation of the Union on issues

concerning its common foreign and security policy, without prejudice to the powers of the Union Minister for Foreign Affairs.
3. The President of the European Council shall not hold a national office.

Article I-23 The Council of Ministers

1. The Council shall, jointly with the European Parliament, exercise legislative and budgetary functions. It shall carry out policy-making and coordinating functions as laid down in the Constitution.
2. The Council shall consist of a representative of each Member State at ministerial level, who may commit the government of the Member State in question and cast its vote.
3. The Council shall act by a qualified majority except where the Constitution provides otherwise.

Article I-24 Configurations of the Council of Ministers

1. The Council shall meet in different configurations.
2. The General Affairs Council shall ensure consistency in the work of the different Council configurations.
It shall prepare and ensure the follow-up to meetings of the European Council, in liaison with the President of the European Council and the Commission.
3. The Foreign Affairs Council shall elaborate the Union's external action on the basis of strategic guidelines laid down by the European Council and ensure that the Union's action is consistent.
4. The European Council shall adopt by a qualified majority a European decision establishing the list of other Council configurations.
5. A Committee of Permanent Representatives of the Governments of the Member States shall be responsible for preparing the work of the Council.
6. The Council shall meet in public when it deliberates and votes on a draft legislative act. To this end, each Council meeting shall be divided into two parts, dealing respectively with deliberations on Union legislative acts and non-legislative activities.
7. The Presidency of Council configurations, other than that of Foreign Affairs, shall be held by Member State representatives in the Council on the basis of equal rotation, in accordance with the conditions established by a European decision of the European Council. The European Council shall act by a qualified majority.

Article I-25 Definition of qualified majority within the European Council and the Council

1. A qualified majority shall be defined as at least 55% of the members of the Council, comprising at least fifteen of them and representing Member States comprising at least 65% of the population of the Union.

A blocking minority must include at least four Council members, failing which the qualified majority shall be deemed attained.

2. By way of derogation from paragraph 1, when the Council does not act on a proposal from the Commission or from the Union Minister for Foreign Affairs, the qualified majority shall be defined as at least 72% of the members of the Council, representing Member States comprising at least 65% of the population of the Union.

3. Paragraphs 1 and 2 shall apply to the European Council when it is acting by a qualified majority.

4. Within the European Council, its President and the President of the Commission shall not take part in the vote.

Article I-26 The European Commission

1. The Commission shall promote the general interest of the Union and take appropriate initiatives to that end. It shall ensure the application of the Constitution, and measures adopted by the institutions pursuant to the Constitution. It shall oversee the application of Union law under the control of the Court of Justice of the European Union. It shall execute the budget and manage programmes. It shall exercise coordinating, executive and management functions, as laid down in the Constitution. With the exception of the common foreign and security policy, and other cases provided for in the Constitution, it shall ensure the Union's external representation. It shall initiate the Union's annual and multiannual programming with a view to achieving inter-institutional agreements.

2. Union legislative acts may be adopted only on the basis of a Commission proposal, except where the Constitution provides otherwise. Other acts shall be adopted on the basis of a Commission proposal where the Constitution so provides.

3. The Commission's term of office shall be five years.

4. The members of the Commission shall be chosen on the ground of their general competence and European commitment from persons whose independence is beyond doubt.

5. The first Commission appointed under the provisions of the Constitution shall consist of one national of each Member State, including its President and the Union Minister for Foreign Affairs who shall be one of its Vice-Presidents.

6. As from the end of the term of office of the Commission referred to in

paragraph 5, the Commission shall consist of a number of members, including its President and the Union Minister for Foreign Affairs, corresponding to two thirds of the number of Member States, unless the European Council, acting unanimously, decides to alter this number.

The members of the Commission shall be selected from among the nationals of the Member States on the basis of a system of equal rotation between the Member States. This system shall be established by a European decision adopted unanimously by the European Council and on the basis of the following principles:

(a) Member States shall be treated on a strictly equal footing as regards determination of the sequence of, and the time spent by, their nationals as members of the Commission; consequently, the difference between the total number of terms of office held by nationals of any given pair of Member States may never be more than one;

(b) subject to point (a), each successive Commission shall be so composed as to reflect satisfactorily the demographic and geographical range of all the Member States.

7. In carrying out its responsibilities, the Commission shall be completely independent. Without prejudice to Article I-28(2), the members of the Commission shall neither seek nor take instructions from any government or other institution, body, office or entity. They shall refrain from any action incompatible with their duties or the performance of their tasks.

8. The Commission, as a body, shall be responsible to the European Parliament. In accordance with Article III-340, the European Parliament may vote on a censure motion on the Commission. If such a motion is carried, the members of the Commission shall resign as a body and the Union Minister for Foreign Affairs shall resign from the duties that he or she carries out in the Commission.

Article I-27 The President of the European Commission

1. Taking into account the elections to the European Parliament and after having held the appropriate consultations, the European Council, acting by a qualified majority, shall propose to the European Parliament a candidate for President of the Commission. This candidate shall be elected by the European Parliament by a majority of its component members. If he or she does not obtain the required majority, the European Council, acting by a qualified majority, shall within one month propose a new candidate who shall be elected by the European Parliament following the same procedure.

2. The Council, by common accord with the President-elect, shall adopt the list of the other persons whom it proposes for appointment as

members of the Commission. They shall be selected, on the basis of the suggestions made by Member States, in accordance with the criteria set out in Article I-26(4) and (6), second subparagraph.

The President, the Union Minister for Foreign Affairs and the other members of the Commission shall be subject as a body to a vote of consent by the European Parliament. On the basis of this consent the Commission shall be appointed by the European Council, acting by a qualified majority.

3. The President of the Commission shall:

(a) lay down guidelines within which the Commission is to work;

(b) decide on the internal organisation of the Commission, ensuring that it acts consistently, efficiently and as a collegiate body;

(c) appoint Vice-Presidents, other than the Union Minister for Foreign Affairs, from among the members of the Commission.

A member of the Commission shall resign if the President so requests. The Union Minister for Foreign Affairs shall resign, in accordance with the procedure set out in Article I-28(1), if the President so requests.

Article I-28 The Union Minister for Foreign Affairs

1. The European Council, acting by a qualified majority, with the agreement of the President of the Commission, shall appoint the Union Minister for Foreign Affairs. The European Council may end his or her term of office by the same procedure.

2. The Union Minister for Foreign Affairs shall conduct the Union's common foreign and security policy. He or she shall contribute by his or her proposals to the development of that policy, which he or she shall carry out as mandated by the Council. The same shall apply to the common security and defence policy.

3. The Union Minister for Foreign Affairs shall preside over the Foreign Affairs Council.

4. The Union Minister for Foreign Affairs shall be one of the Vice-Presidents of the Commission. He or she shall ensure the consistency of the Union's external action. He or she shall be responsible within the Commission for responsibilities incumbent on it in external relations and for coordinating other aspects of the Union's external action. In exercising these responsibilities within the Commission, and only for these responsibilities, the Union Minister for Foreign Affairs shall be bound by Commission procedures to the extent that this is consistent with paragraphs 2 and 3.

Article I-29 The Court of Justice of the European Union

1. The Court of Justice of the European Union shall include the Court of

Justice, the General Court and specialised courts. It shall ensure that in the interpretation and application of the Constitution the law is observed.

Member States shall provide remedies sufficient to ensure effective legal protection in the fields covered by Union law.

2. The Court of Justice shall consist of one judge from each Member State. It shall be assisted by Advocates-General.

The General Court shall include at least one judge per Member State.

The judges and the Advocates-General of the Court of Justice and the judges of the General Court shall be chosen from persons whose independence is beyond doubt and who satisfy the conditions set out in Articles III-355 and III-356. They shall be appointed by common accord of the governments of the Member States for six years. Retiring judges and Advocates-General may be reappointed.

3. The Court of Justice of the European Union shall in accordance with Part III:

(a) rule on actions brought by a Member State, an institution or a natural or legal person;

(b) give preliminary rulings, at the request of courts or tribunals of the Member States, on the interpretation of Union law or the validity of acts adopted by the institutions;

(c) rule in other cases provided for in the Constitution.

Chapter II The other Union institutions and advisory bodies

Article I-30 The European Central Bank

1. The European Central Bank, together with the national central banks, shall constitute the European System of Central Banks. The European Central Bank, together with the national central banks of the Member States whose currency is the euro, which constitute the Eurosystem, shall conduct the monetary policy of the Union.

2. The European System of Central Banks shall be governed by the decision-making bodies of the European Central Bank. The primary objective of the European System of Central Banks shall be to maintain price stability. Without prejudice to that objective, it shall support the general economic policies in the Union in order to contribute to the achievement of the latter's objectives. It shall conduct other Central Bank tasks in accordance with Part III and the Statute of the European System of Central Banks and of the European Central Bank.

3. The European Central Bank is an institution. It shall have legal personality. It alone may authorise the issue of the euro. It shall be independent in the exercise of its powers and in the management of its

finances. Union institutions, bodies, offices and agencies and the governments of the Member States shall respect that independence.
4. The European Central Bank shall adopt such measures as are necessary to carry out its tasks in accordance with Articles III-185 to III-191 and Article III-196, and with the conditions laid down in the Statute of the European System of Central Banks and of the European Central Bank. In accordance with these same Articles, those Member States whose currency is not the euro, and their central banks, shall retain their powers in monetary matters.
5. Within the areas falling within its responsibilities, the European Central Bank shall be consulted on all proposed Union acts, and all proposals for regulation at national level, and may give an opinion.
6. The decision-making organs of the European Central Bank, their composition and operating methods are set out in Articles III-382 and III-383, as well as in the Statute of the European System of Central Banks and of the European Central Bank.

Article I-31 The Court of Auditors
1. The Court of Auditors is an institution. It shall carry out the Union's audit.
2. It shall examine the accounts of all Union revenue and expenditure, and shall ensure good financial management.
3. It shall consist of one national of each Member State. Its members shall be completely independent in the performance of their duties, in the Union's general interest.

Article I-32 The Union's advisory bodies
1. The European Parliament, the Council and the Commission shall be assisted by a Committee of the Regions and an Economic and Social Committee, exercising advisory functions.
2. The Committee of the Regions shall consist of representatives of regional and local bodies who either hold a regional or local authority electoral mandate or are politically accountable to an elected assembly.
3. The Economic and Social Committee shall consist of representatives of organisations of employers, of the employed, and of other parties representative of civil society, notably in socio-economic, civic, professional and cultural areas.
4. The members of the Committee of the Regions and the Economic and Social Committee shall not be bound by any mandatory instructions. They shall be completely independent in the performance of their duties, in the Union's general interest.

5. Rules governing the composition of these Committees, the designation of their members, their powers and their operations are set out in Articles III-386 to III-392.

The rules referred to in paragraphs 2 and 3 governing the nature of their composition shall be reviewed at regular intervals by the Council to take account of economic, social and demographic developments within the Union. The Council, on a proposal from the Commission, shall adopt European decisions to that end.

Title V Exercise of Union competence

Chapter I Common provisions

Article I-33 The legal acts of the Union

1. To exercise the Union's competences the institutions shall use as legal instruments, in accordance with Part III, European laws, European framework laws, European regulations, European decisions, recommendations and opinions.

A European law shall be a legislative act of general application. It shall be binding in its entirety and directly applicable in all Member States.

A European framework law shall be a legislative act binding, as to the result to be achieved, upon each Member State to which it is addressed, but shall leave to the national authorities the choice of form and methods.

A European regulation shall be a non-legislative act of general application for the implementation of legislative acts and of certain provisions of the Constitution. It may either be binding in its entirety and directly applicable in all Member States, or be binding, as to the result to be achieved, upon each Member State to which it is addressed, but shall leave to the national authorities the choice of form and methods.

A European decision shall be a non-legislative act, binding in its entirety. A decision which specifies those to whom it is addressed shall be binding only on them.

Recommendations and opinions shall have no binding force.

2. When considering draft legislative acts, the European Parliament and the Council shall refrain from adopting acts not provided for by the relevant legislative procedure in the area in question.

Article I-34 Legislative acts

1. European laws and framework laws shall be adopted, on the basis of proposals from the Commission, jointly by the European Parliament and the Council under the ordinary legislative procedure as set out in Article

III-396. If the two institutions cannot reach agreement on an act, it shall not be adopted.
2. In the specific cases provided for in the Constitution, European laws and framework laws shall be adopted by the European Parliament with the participation of the Council, or by the latter with the participation of the European Parliament, in accordance with special legislative procedures.
3. In the specific cases provided for in the Constitution, European laws and framework laws may be adopted at the initiative of a group of Member States or of the European Parliament, on a recommendation from the European Central Bank or at the request of the Court of Justice or the European Investment Bank.

Article I-35 Non-legislative acts
1. The European Council shall adopt European decisions in the cases provided for in the Constitution.
2. The Council and the Commission, in particular in the cases referred to in Articles I–36 and I-37, and the European Central Bank in the specific cases provided for in the Constitution, shall adopt European regulations and decisions.
3. The Council shall adopt recommendations. It shall act on a proposal from the Commission in all cases where the Constitution provides that it shall adopt acts on a proposal from the Commission. It shall act unanimously in those areas in which unanimity is required for the adoption of a Union act. The Commission, and the European Central Bank in the specific cases provided for in the Constitution, shall adopt recommendations.

Article I-36 Delegated European regulations
1. European laws and framework laws may delegate to the Commission the power to adopt delegated European regulations to supplement or amend certain non-essential elements of the law or framework law.

The objectives, content, scope and duration of the delegation of power shall be explicitly defined in the European laws and framework laws. The essential elements of an area shall be reserved for the European law or framework law and accordingly shall not be the subject of a delegation of power.
2. European laws and framework laws shall explicitly lay down the conditions to which the delegation is subject; these conditions may be as follows:
(a) the European Parliament or the Council may decide to revoke the delegation;
(b) the delegated European regulation may enter into force only if no

objection has been expressed by the European Parliament or the Council within a period set by the European law or framework law.

For the purposes of (a) and (b), the European Parliament shall act by a majority of its component members, and the Council by a qualified majority.

Article I-37 Implementing acts

1. Member States shall adopt all measures of national law necessary to implement legally binding Union acts.
2. Where uniform conditions for implementing legally binding Union acts are needed, those acts shall confer implementing powers on the Commission, or, in duly justified specific cases and in the cases provided for in Article I-40, on the Council.
3. For the purposes of paragraph 2, European laws shall lay down in advance the rules and general principles concerning mechanisms for control by Member States of the Commission's exercise of implementing powers.
4. Union implementing acts shall take the form of European implementing regulations or European implementing decisions.

Article I-38 Principles common to the Union's legal acts

1. Where the Constitution does not specify the type of act to be adopted, the institutions shall select it on a case-by-case basis, in compliance with the applicable procedures and with the principle of proportionality referred to in Article I-11.
2. Legal acts shall state the reasons on which they are based and shall refer to any proposals, initiatives, recommendations, requests or opinions required by the Constitution.

Article I-39 Publication and entry into force

1. European laws and framework laws adopted under the ordinary legislative procedure shall be signed by the President of the European Parliament and by the President of the Council.

In other cases they shall be signed by the President of the institution which adopted them.

European laws and framework laws shall be published in the *Official Journal of the European Union* and shall enter into force on the date specified in them or, in the absence thereof, on the twentieth day following their publication.

2. European regulations, and European decisions which do not specify to whom they are addressed, shall be signed by the President of the institution which adopted them.

European regulations, and European decisions when the latter do not specify to whom they are addressed, shall be published in the *Official Journal of the European Union* and shall enter into force on the date specified in them or, in the absence thereof, on the twentieth day following that of their publication.
3. European decisions other than those referred to in paragraph 2 shall be notified to those to whom they are addressed and shall take effect upon such notification.

Chapter II Specific provisions

Article I-40 Specific provisions relating to the common foreign and security policy

1. The European Union shall conduct a common foreign and security policy, based on the development of mutual political solidarity among Member States, the identification of questions of general interest and the achievement of an ever-increasing degree of convergence of Member States' actions.
2. The European Council shall identify the Union's strategic interests and determine the objectives of its common foreign and security policy. The Council shall frame this policy within the framework of the strategic guidelines established by the European Council and in accordance with Part III.
3. The European Council and the Council shall adopt the necessary European decisions.
4. The common foreign and security policy shall be put into effect by the Union Minister for Foreign Affairs and by the Member States, using national and Union resources.
5. Member States shall consult one another within the European Council and the Council on any foreign and security policy issue which is of general interest in order to determine a common approach. Before undertaking any action on the international scene or any commitment which could affect the Union's interests, each Member State shall consult the others within the European Council or the Council. Member States shall ensure, through the convergence of their actions, that the Union is able to assert its interests and values on the international scene. Member States shall show mutual solidarity.
6. European decisions relating to the common foreign and security policy shall be adopted by the European Council and the Council unanimously, except in the cases referred to in Part III. The European Council and the Council shall act on an initiative from a Member State, on a proposal from

the Union Minister for Foreign Affairs or on a proposal from that Minister with the Commission's support. European laws and framework laws shall be excluded.
7. The European Council may, unanimously, adopt a European decision authorising the Council to act by a qualified majority in cases other than those referred to in Part III.
8. The European Parliament shall be regularly consulted on the main aspects and basic choices of the common foreign and security policy. It shall be kept informed of how it evolves.

Article I-41 Specific provisions relating to the common security and defence policy

1. The common security and defence policy shall be an integral part of the common foreign and security policy. It shall provide the Union with an operational capacity drawing on civil and military assets. The Union may use them on missions outside the Union for peace-keeping, conflict prevention and strengthening international security in accordance with the principles of the United Nations Charter. The performance of these tasks shall be undertaken using capabilities provided by the Member States.
2. The common security and defence policy shall include the progressive framing of a common Union defence policy. This will lead to a common defence, when the European Council, acting unanimously, so decides. It shall in that case recommend to the Member States the adoption of such a decision in accordance with their respective constitutional requirements.

The policy of the Union in accordance with this Article shall not prejudice the specific character of the security and defence policy of certain Member States, it shall respect the obligations of certain Member States, which see their common defence realised in the North Atlantic Treaty Organisation, under the North Atlantic Treaty, and be compatible with the common security and defence policy established within that framework.
3. Member States shall make civilian and military capabilities available to the Union for the implementation of the common security and defence policy, to contribute to the objectives defined by the Council. Those Member States which together establish multinational forces may also make them available to the common security and defence policy.

Member States shall undertake progressively to improve their military capabilities. An Agency in the field of defence capabilities development, research, acquisition and armaments (European Defence Agency) shall be established to identify operational requirements, to promote measures to satisfy those requirements, to contribute to identifying and, where appropriate, implementing any measure needed to strengthen the

industrial and technological base of the defence sector, to participate in defining a European capabilities and armaments policy, and to assist the Council in evaluating the improvement of military capabilities.
4. European decisions relating to the common security and defence policy, including those initiating a mission as referred to in this Article, shall be adopted by the Council acting unanimously on a proposal from the Union Minister for Foreign Affairs or an initiative from a Member State. The Union Minister for Foreign Affairs may propose the use of both national resources and Union instruments, together with the Commission where appropriate.
5. The Council may entrust the execution of a task, within the Union framework, to a group of Member States in order to protect the Union's values and serve its interests. The execution of such a task shall be governed by Article III-310.
6. Those Member States whose military capabilities fulfil higher criteria and which have made more binding commitments to one another in this area with a view to the most demanding missions shall establish permanent structured cooperation within the Union framework. Such cooperation shall be governed by Article III-312. It shall not affect the provisions of Article III-309.
7. If a Member State is the victim of armed aggression on its territory, the other Member States shall have towards it an obligation of aid and assistance by all the means in their power, in accordance with Article 51 of the United Nations Charter. This shall not prejudice the specific character of the security and defence policy of certain Member States.

Commitments and cooperation in this area shall be consistent with commitments under the North Atlantic Treaty Organisation, which, for those States which are members of it, remains the foundation of their collective defence and the forum for its implementation.
8. The European Parliament shall be regularly consulted on the main aspects and basic choices of the common security and defence policy. It shall be kept informed of how it evolves.

Article I-42 Specific provisions relating to the area of freedom, security and justice

1. The Union shall constitute an area of freedom, security and justice:
(a) by adopting European laws and framework laws intended, where necessary, to approximate laws and regulations of the Member States in the areas referred to in Part III;
(b) by promoting mutual confidence between the competent authorities of the Member States, in particular on the basis of mutual recognition of judicial and extrajudicial decisions;

(c) by operational cooperation between the competent authorities of the Member States, including the police, customs and other services specialising in the prevention and detection of criminal offence

2. National Parliaments may, within the framework of the area of freedom, security and justice, participate in the evaluation mechanisms provided for in Article III-260. They shall be involved in the political monitoring of Europol and the evaluation of Eurojust's activities in accordance with Articles III-276 and III-273.

3. Member States shall have a right of initiative in the field of police and judicial cooperation in criminal matters, in accordance with Article III-264.

Article I-43 Solidarity clause

1. The Union and its Member States shall act jointly in a spirit of solidarity if a Member State is the object of a terrorist attack or the victim of a natural or man-made disaster. The Union shall mobilise all the instruments at its disposal, including the military resources made available by the Member States, to:

(a) – prevent the terrorist threat in the territory of the Member States;
- – protect democratic institutions and the civilian population from any terrorist attack;
- – assist a Member State in its territory, at the request of its political authorities, in the event of a terrorist attack;

(b) assist a Member State in its territory, at the request of its political authorities, in the event of a natural or man-made disaster.

2. The detailed arrangements for implementing this Article are set out in Article III-329.

Chapter III Enhanced cooperation

Article I-44 Enhanced cooperation

1. Member States which wish to establish enhanced cooperation between themselves within the framework of the Union's non-exclusive competences may make use of its institutions and exercise those competences by applying the relevant provisions of the Constitution, subject to the limits and in accordance with the procedures laid down in this Article and in Articles III-416 to III-423.

Enhanced cooperation shall aim to further the objectives of the Union, protect its interests and reinforce its integration process. Such cooperation shall be open at any time to all Member States, in accordance with Article III-418.

2. The European decision authorising enhanced cooperation shall be adopted by the Council as a last resort, when it has established that the objectives of such cooperation cannot be attained within a reasonable period by the Union as a whole, and provided that at least one third of the Member States participate in it. The Council shall act in accordance with the procedure laid down in Article III-419.

3. All members of the Council may participate in its deliberations, but only members of the Council representing the Member States participating in enhanced cooperation shall take part in the vote.

Unanimity shall be constituted by the votes of the representatives of the participating Member States only.

A qualified majority shall be defined as at least 55% of the members of the Council representing the participating Member States, comprising at least 65% of the population of these States.

A blocking minority must include at least the minimum number of Council members representing more than 35% of the population of the participating Member States, plus one member, failing which the qualified majority shall be deemed attained.

By way of derogation from the third and fourth subparagraphs, where the Council does not act on a proposal from the Commission or from the Union Minister for Foreign Affairs, the required qualified majority shall be defined as at least 72% of the members of the Council representing the participating Member States, comprising at least 65% of the population of these States.

4. Acts adopted in the framework of enhanced cooperation shall bind only participating Member States. They shall not be regarded as part of the acquis which has to be accepted by candidate States for accession to the Union.

Title VI The democratic life of the Union

Article I-45 The principle of democratic equality

In all its activities, the Union shall observe the principle of the equality of its citizens, who shall receive equal attention from its institutions, bodies, offices and agencies.

Article I-46 The principle of representative democracy

1. The functioning of the Union shall be founded on representative democracy.

2. Citizens are directly represented at Union level in the European Parliament.

Member States are represented in the European Council by their Heads of State or Government and in the Council by their governments, themselves democratically accountable either to their national Parliaments, or to their citizens.

3. Every citizen shall have the right to participate in the democratic life of the Union. Decisions shall be taken as openly and as closely as possible to the citizen.

4. Political parties at European level contribute to forming European political awareness and to expressing the will of citizens of the Union.

Article I-47 The principle of participatory democracy

1. The institutions shall, by appropriate means, give citizens and representative associations the opportunity to make known and publicly exchange their views in all areas of Union action.

2. The institutions shall maintain an open, transparent and regular dialogue with representative associations and civil society.

3. The Commission shall carry out broad consultations with parties concerned in order to ensure that the Union's actions are coherent and transparent.

4. Not less than one million citizens who are nationals of a significant number of Member States may take the initiative of inviting the Commission, within the framework of its powers, to submit any appropriate proposal on matters where citizens consider that a legal act of the Union is required for the purpose of implementing the Constitution. European laws shall determine the provisions for the procedures and conditions required for such a citizens' initiative, including the minimum number of Member States from which such citizens must come.

Article I-48 The social partners and autonomous social dialogue

The Union recognises and promotes the role of the social partners at its level, taking into account the diversity of national systems. It shall facilitate dialogue between the social partners, respecting their autonomy.

The Tripartite Social Summit for Growth and Employment shall contribute to social dialogue.

Article I-49 The European Ombudsman

A European Ombudsman elected by the European Parliament shall receive, examine and report on complaints about maladministration in the activities of the Union institutions, bodies, offices or agencies, under the conditions laid down in the Constitution. The European Ombudsman shall be completely independent in the performance of his or her duties.

Article I-50 Transparency of the proceedings of Union institutions, bodies, offices and agencies

1. In order to promote good governance and ensure the participation of civil society, the Union institutions, bodies, offices and agencies shall conduct their work as openly as possible.
2. The European Parliament shall meet in public, as shall the Council when considering and voting on a draft legislative act.
3. Any citizen of the Union, and any natural or legal person residing or having its registered office in a Member State shall have, under the conditions laid down in Part III, a right of access to documents of the Union institutions, bodies, offices and agencies, whatever their medium.

European laws shall lay down the general principles and limits which, on grounds of public or private interest, govern the right of access to such documents.

4. Each institution, body, office or agency shall determine in its own rules of procedure specific provisions regarding access to its documents, in accordance with the European laws referred to in paragraph 3.

Article I-51 Protection of personal data

1. Everyone has the right to the protection of personal data concerning him or her.
2. European laws or framework laws shall lay down the rules relating to the protection of individuals with regard to the processing of personal data by Union institutions, bodies, offices and agencies, and by the Member States when carrying out activities which fall within the scope of Union law, and the rules relating to the free movement of such data. Compliance with these rules shall be subject to the control of independent authorities.

Article I-52 Status of churches and non-confessional organisations

1. The Union respects and does not prejudice the status under national law of churches and religious associations or communities in the Member States.
2. The Union equally respects the status under national law of philosophical and non-confessional organisations.
3. Recognising their identity and their specific contribution, the Union shall maintain an open, transparent and regular dialogue with these churches and organisations.

Title VII The Union's finances

Article I-53 Budgetary and financial principles

1. All items of Union revenue and expenditure shall be included in estimates drawn up for each financial year and shall be shown in the Union's budget, in accordance with Part III.
2. The revenue and expenditure shown in the budget shall be in balance.
3. The expenditure shown in the budget shall be authorised for the annual budgetary period in accordance with the European law referred to in Article III-412.
4. The implementation of expenditure shown in the budget shall require the prior adoption of a legally binding Union act providing a legal basis for its action and for the implementation of the corresponding expenditure in accordance with the European law referred to in Article III-412, except in cases for which that law provides.
5. With a view to maintaining budgetary discipline, the Union shall not adopt any act which is likely to have appreciable implications for the budget without providing an assurance that the expenditure arising from such an act is capable of being financed within the limit of the Union's own resources and in compliance with the multiannual financial framework referred to in Article I-55.
6. The budget shall be implemented in accordance with the principle of sound financial management. Member States shall cooperate with the Union to ensure that the appropriations entered in the budget are used in accordance with this principle.
7. The Union and the Member States, in accordance with Article III–415, shall counter fraud and any other illegal activities affecting the financial interests of the Union.

Article I-54 The Union's own resources

1. The Union shall provide itself with the means necessary to attain its objectives and carry through its policies.
2. Without prejudice to other revenue, the Union's budget shall be financed wholly from its own resources.
3. A European law of the Council shall lay down the provisions relating to the system of own resources of the Union. In this context it may establish new categories of own resources or abolish an existing category. The Council shall act unanimously after consulting the European Parliament. That law shall not enter into force until it is approved by the Member States in accordance with their respective constitutional requirements.
4. A European law of the Council shall lay down implementing measures of the Union's own resources system insofar as this is provided for in the

European law adopted on the basis of paragraph 3. The Council shall act after obtaining the consent of the European Parliament.

Article I-55 The multiannual financial framework

1. The multiannual financial framework shall ensure that Union expenditure develops in an orderly manner and within the limits of its own resources. It shall determine the amounts of the annual ceilings of appropriations for commitments by category of expenditure in accordance with Article III-402.
2. A European law of the Council shall lay down the multiannual financial framework. The Council shall act unanimously after obtaining the consent of the European Parliament, which shall be given by a majority of its component members.
3. The annual budget of the Union shall comply with the multiannual financial framework.
4. The European Council may, unanimously, adopt a European decision authorising the Council to act by a qualified majority when adopting the European law of the Council referred to in paragraph 2.

Article I-56 The Union's budget

A European law shall establish the Union's annual budget in accordance with Article III-404.

Title VIII The Union and its neighbours

Article I-57 The Union and its neighbours

1. The Union shall develop a special relationship with neighbouring countries, aiming to establish an area of prosperity and good neighbourliness, founded on the values of the Union and characterised by close and peaceful relations based on cooperation.
2. For the purposes of paragraph 1, the Union may conclude specific agreements with the countries concerned. These agreements may contain reciprocal rights and obligations as well as the possibility of undertaking activities jointly. Their implementation shall be the subject of periodic consultation.

Title IX Union membership

Article I-58 Conditions of eligibility and procedure for accession to the Union

1. The Union shall be open to all European States which respect the

values referred to in Article I–2, and are committed to promoting them together.

2. Any European State which wishes to become a member of the Union shall address its application to the Council. The European Parliament and national Parliaments shall be notified of this application. The Council shall act unanimously after consulting the Commission and after obtaining the consent of the European Parliament, which shall act by a majority of its component members. The conditions and arrangements for admission shall be the subject of an agreement between the Member States and the candidate State. That agreement shall be subject to ratification by each contracting State, in accordance with its respective constitutional requirements.

Article I-59 Suspension of certain rights resulting from Union membership

1. On the reasoned initiative of one third of the Member States or the reasoned initiative of the European Parliament or on a proposal from the Commission, the Council may adopt a European decision determining that there is a clear risk of a serious breach by a Member State of the values referred to in Article I-2. The Council shall act by a majority of four fifths of its members after obtaining the consent of the European Parliament.

Before making such a determination, the Council shall hear the Member State in question and, acting in accordance with the same procedure, may address recommendations to that State.

The Council shall regularly verify that the grounds on which such a determination was made continue to apply.

2. The European Council, on the initiative of one third of the Member States or on a proposal from the Commission, may adopt a European decision determining the existence of a serious and persistent breach by a Member State of the values mentioned in Article I-2, after inviting the Member State in question to submit its observations. The European Council shall act unanimously after obtaining the consent of the European Parliament.

3. Where a determination under paragraph 2 has been made, the Council, acting by a qualified majority, may adopt a European decision suspending certain of the rights deriving from the application of the Constitution to the Member State in question, including the voting rights of the member of the Council representing that State. The Council shall take into account the possible consequences of such a suspension for the rights and obligations of natural and legal persons.

In any case, that State shall continue to be bound by its obligations under the Constitution.

4. The Council, acting by a qualified majority, may adopt a European decision varying or revoking measures adopted under paragraph 3 in response to changes in the situation which led to their being imposed.

5. For the purposes of this Article, the member of the European Council or of the Council representing the Member State in question shall not take part in the vote and the Member State in question shall not be counted in the calculation of the one third or four fifths of Member States referred to in paragraphs 1 and 2. Abstentions by members present in person or represented shall not prevent the adoption of European decisions referred to in paragraph 2.

For the adoption of the European decisions referred to in paragraphs 3 and 4, a qualified majority shall be defined as at least 72% of the members of the Council, representing the participating Member States, comprising at least 65% of the population of these States.

Where, following a decision to suspend voting rights adopted pursuant to paragraph 3, the Council acts by a qualified majority on the basis of a provision of the Constitution, that qualified majority shall be defined as in the second subparagraph, or, where the Council acts on a proposal from the Commission or from the Union Minister for Foreign Affairs, as at least 55% of the members of the Council representing the participating Member States, comprising at least 65% of the population of these States. In the latter case, a blocking minority must include at least the minimum number of Council members representing more than 35% of the population of the participating Member States, plus one member, failing which the qualified majority shall be deemed attained.

6. For the purposes of this Article, the European Parliament shall act by a two-thirds majority of the votes cast, representing the majority of its component members.

Article I-60 Voluntary withdrawal from the Union

1. Any Member State may decide to withdraw from the Union in accordance with its own constitutional requirements.

2. A Member State which decides to withdraw shall notify the European Council of its intention. In the light of the guidelines provided by the European Council, the Union shall negotiate and conclude an agreement with that State, setting out the arrangements for its withdrawal, taking account of the framework for its future relationship with the Union. That agreement shall be negotiated in accordance with Article III-325(3). It shall be concluded by the Council, acting by a qualified majority, after obtaining the consent of the European Parliament.

3. The Constitution shall cease to apply to the State in question from the date of entry into force of the withdrawal agreement or, failing that, two years after the notification referred to in paragraph 2, unless the European Council, in agreement with the Member State concerned, unanimously decides to extend this period.

4. For the purposes of paragraphs 2 and 3, the member of the European Council or of the Council representing the withdrawing Member State shall not participate in the discussions of the European Council or Council or in European decisions concerning it.

A qualified majority shall be defined as at least 72% of the members of the Council, representing the participating Member States, comprising at least 65% of the population of these States.

5. If a State which has withdrawn from the Union asks to rejoin, its request shall be subject to the procedure referred to in Article I-58.

5 Part I – A thematic analysis of the Constitutional Treaty's fundamentals

One way of looking at Part I, and indeed the Constitutional Treaty as a whole, is to work through its nine Titles (see Box 5.1) article by article. However, as we have said, we think it more helpful to pick out its key aspects and themes. By considering them and their implications, we hope we can address some of the concerns people have about it. Obviously opinions will vary as to what is most significant but our choices derive from our reading of the text and the debate. And, by examining them, we hope that the Constitutional Treaty will become more comprehensible.

What then are the key aspects and themes? For starters there is the contested and unique nature of the European Union itself. Does the Constitutional Treaty create a 'new' European Union which seems either very threatening, hence the talk of a 'superstate', or simply a more streamlined organism which replaces the limited and divided structures of the past? Equally, the often overlooked references to values and rights, which are a

Box 5.1 Part I: an outline

Title I	Definition and objectives of the Union	I-1 to I-8
Title II	Fundamental rights and citizenship of the Union	I-9 to I-10
Title III	Union competences	I-11 to I-18
Title IV	The Union's institutions and bodies	I-19 to I-32
Chapter 1	The institutional framework	I-19 to I-29
Chapter 2	The other Union institutions and advisory bodies	I-30 to I-32
Title V	Exercise of Union competence	I-33 to I-44
Chapter 1	Common provisions	I-33 to I-39
Chapter 2	Specific provisions	I-40 to I-43
Chapter 3	Enhanced cooperation	I-44
Title VI	The democratic life of the Union	I-45 to I-52
Title VII	The Union's finances	I-53 to I-56
Title VIII	The Union and its neighbours	I-57
Title IX	Union membership	I-58 to I-60

running theme throughout the document, have to be taken seriously, since these too can be seen either as allowing the Union to interfere more or as giving it a more ethical and democratic nature. Attention must also be paid to the Union's competences – or powers – and the way these support policies since one claim is that the Constitutional Treaty transfers more powers and responsibilities to 'Brussels'.

This links to three more major aspects of the changes that the Constitutional Treaty introduces: those made to the Union's instruments; the refinements to its financing; and the way in which the Union's institutions are developed. Much has been made of the primacy of EU law, though this is not new, and less of the way the Constitutional Treaty simplifies and re-brands the types of decisions that the European Union takes. And the institutions are both reformed and supplemented by the creation of controversial new posts. The Constitutional Treaty also goes out of its way to assert the Union's democratic credentials, even if many critics deny it all democratic legitimacy. This deserves examination. The new text lays out bases for the financing of the Union and these too can cause concern.

This is even more the case with the provisions for the Union's external action, which may be seen either as denying member states their traditional autonomy and rights or as moving towards giving the European Union a more effective role in the world. All this helps us to assess the final, and perhaps overriding, theme: the way the Constitutional Treaty handles relations between the Union and the member states. Is it the case that the latter lose their individuality and influence? Or are they the real gainers from the Constitutional Treaty? By treating it as both treaty and constitution, an examination of these key points shows that it is a document which reflects its origins, seeks to limit powers and steers an uncertain line between competing forces.

The nature of the 'new' EU

One of the key changes suggested by the Constitutional Treaty is the creation of a new body in the place of the old confusion of Union and Community. This, with its pillars and other communities, was complicated and hard to explain. It represented historical doubts among governments about extending integration but the subtle distinctions they created to defend their positions were ignored by the general public who called everything 'the Union'. The Convention recognized this and created one all embracing Union. Giscard d'Estaing would like to have called this 'United Europe' but was overruled. So the name 'Union' was chosen. As well as being in line with street usage it also reflected the extent to which the 'new' Union borrowed from the old. Yet, ironically, the Convention draft failed to mention this, leaving it to the IGC to point it out, somewhat obliquely, in the Preamble.

Nonetheless, the change has proved very alarming to many eurosceptics. For some the new Union is a very different body from its predecessor: separate from, and superior to, the member states; unitary rather than federal and hence bureaucratic, socialistic and overweening. So it vastly expands EU powers and subordinates national sovereignty and decision making. For supporters of integration this is far from the case. To many it is simply a new verbal construction imposed on a largely unchanged reality. Although it dissolves the old Union in the new, it does not do this properly, leaving many of the weaknesses of the old order with its opt-outs and obstacles to democratic EU-level decision making. In other words the new Union is a contested project, which requires examination.

So, what does the Constitutional Treaty actually say about the Union? The answer is not as much as we might expect. As Box 5.2 shows, it drops a number of hints about its foundations, its objectives, its legal status, its institutional side and some other characteristics. But it never fully and finally defines the Union. Nor does it pull all its threads together. Hence, to get a better idea of what the Union is, we also need to compare it with its predecessor. What we find is that, though it promises to become a more fixed and solid body, it remains a somewhat ambiguous hybrid. Had the drafters really wanted to create a superstate, it is doubtful if they would either have started from where they did or have written things in the way they have.

Foundations

The Constitutional Treaty does not face head on the question of what the Union is. Article I-1 talks of its establishment and implies that it is an empty vessel filled up by powers given it by the member states. Next, Article I-2 lists its five foundations. One is cultural-cum-historical, as the Preamble makes much of the Continent having both a special civilizing role and a tendency to conflict, something which the states desire to leave behind. Given this the Union is open to all European states who share such ambitions.

A second and related foundation is constituted by the values of the member states and their societies: human rights, freedom, democracy, equality and the rule of law. Previously these were principles rather than values and were fewer in number. The odd reference to 'a society' may be meant to suggest that these values belong to EU citizens and not just to government structures. Third, the Constitutional Treaty also makes it clear that the European Union is seen as resting on the will of its citizens and its member states, giving it a double legitimacy.

Fourth, and more significantly, the actual powers of the Union are not self-generated. They are conferred on it by the member states and not

Box 5.2 The new Union and the old

	New Union	*Old Union*
Relationship	Single body	Legally superior to the Community but dependent on it to act
Foundations	Europe	Community and intergovernmentalism
	Values	Policies and closeness to citizens
	Double legitimacy	Organizing relations of states and peoples
	Conferral	Created by states as a new stage in the process of ever-closer union
	Constitutional Treaty	An indeterminate number of treaties of different types
Objectives	Peace	Economic and social progress
	Values	Asserting EU identity on world stage
	Well-being of its peoples both economic and legal	Protection of its citizens
	Freedom, security and justice	Freedom, security and justice
	Sustainable development, cohesion and solidarity	Maintaining and building on the EC acquis
Legal standing	Legal personality	Restricted ability to sign international agreements, while EC had full legal personality
	Explicit legal primacy	Implicit primacy of EC law
	Respect for member states and the rule of law	Largely exempt from ECJ jurisdiction
Structures and *working*	Unitary and inclusive structure	Tied to 'single' institutional framework which excluded the European Council
	More uniform and simplified decision making	Two complex and formal working procedures
Other Characteristics	Voluntary	No formal possibility of exit
	Fixed and organized	Evolutionary and unfinished
	More coherent	Ambiguous

directly by the citizens of Europe. In other words it owes its authority to specific legal acts, not to a generalized popular endorsement. Moreover, the Union is seen as a means of coordinating and implementing the specific objectives on which the member states have decided. Thus the text shows that, while the Union may be a specific political entity, it is both functional and limited. It is created to fulfil given tasks and not just to exist in the way that a nation state does. Finally, the new text is itself a basic foundation since it brings together all the rules surrounding the European Union which have previously been scattered across many treaties. And, as well as being an empowering document, it has also to be seen as text which constrains the Union.

Objectives

So what aims is the new European Union supposed to pursue on behalf of its member states and citizens? According to Article I-3 (1) the overriding aim is to promote what the Union is most concerned with: peace, values and the well-being of its peoples. All three echo the Preamble. Paragraph (3) spells out the specific dimensions of that well-being, including a competitive social market economy and various social hopes. And Paragraph (4) sets down the precise international objectives it is required to meet, presumably in its pursuit of peace.

This is straightforward enough, if somewhat general, but the article complicates things by then adding what seems to be an obligation rather than an aim, this is to provide an internal market and an area of freedom, security and justice. Both suggest that the European Union is responding to its reliance on its citizens and to their needs. Equally, the text adds cohesion, solidarity and cultural diversity within the Union. The fact that these things are required by the member states, and are subject to them, re-appears in the requirement of paragraph (5) that the Union pursue these objectives within the powers conferred on it. It has to 'work', 'safeguard' and 'combat' in seeking these large aims.

Legal status

Having set out, however sketchily, the bases and objectives of the European Union the Constitutional Treaty then goes on to deal with its actual standing. Article I-5 makes it clear that the Union cannot dispose of the member states as it chooses. It must respect and cooperate with them just as they are expected to help and not hinder the Union. Thus the Constitutional Treaty envisages mutual partnership, not dictatorship.

Nor does the fact that Article I-6 states that EU law is also said to enjoy primacy, or supremacy, over national law mean that in the future member states are to be denied all rights of self-determination as some fear. In fact, as we have seen, legal primacy already exists. The Constitutional Treaty gives it a more formal, clear and authoritative foundation. Previously it was hidden in case law and never fully endorsed by member states and their constitutional courts. It is now stated very – perhaps too – baldly as a general principle, even though it is specifically limited to areas where the member states have conferred power. It applies mainly to the institutions, only involving member states when they are applying EU law. So it is doubtful that this should be read as allowing the Union to overrule national constitutions. Indeed, recent rulings by the Spanish Constitutional Court suggest that, on key issues, states remain free to take actions in contradiction of EU rules. In any case, to confer powers and then to have the right to disregard them would be a bit odd to say the least. A Declaration makes it clear that this is intended as codification of existing Court of Justice jurisprudence. However, the way it is formulated could be taken to imply that it spreads beyond Community matters into the diplomatic and judicial domains. So an element of ambiguity remains.

The phrase, in Article I-7, that the European Union shall have 'legal personality' has also caused much alarm. This status, which establishes the Union as a body able to negotiate international agreements, was, in the past, enjoyed by the Community since the Union as such had only vestigial negotiating rights. The Constitutional Treaty merely transfers it to the new Union. It does not mean new powers, merely a simpler and, potentially, more effective way of working. Without it the Union would not be recognized by international law and its decisions would have no effect.

The fact that the European Union is endowed with symbols and citizenship is also, as we will see, a reflection of existing reality. It is not a new claim for superiority. This point is reinforced by the stress in Article I-9 on the European Union's acceptance of fundamental rights, whether internally or externally generated. All in all, the Union is very much subject to the rule of law even if decisions collectively made by the member states can take precedence over conflicting domestic rules. This is rather different from the past when some EU activities were not subject to ECJ jurisdiction.

Structure and working methods

In institutional terms the new Union maintains the legacy of the European Community. It has an institutional framework which, according to Article I-19, is to be devoted to achieving the European Union's objectives, ensuring consistency and generally serving the interests of the Union, the member states and the citizens. It no longer has to use the term 'single institutional framework' since, self-evidently, there will be only one framework under the Constitutional Treaty. Moreover, the European Council is integrated into the framework, which is a considerable simplification. Previously this was not technically an 'institution', being restricted to the Union. Now it sits alongside the EP, ECJ and Commission with its own semi-permanent President and, according to Articles III-341 and 367, its own rules of procedure. Equally, it can now be sued by member states and other institutions for failure to act. It also gains new quasi legislative and appellate roles. So it is now institutionalized as the key institution of the new Union, responsible for providing impetus, direction and priorities. The existence of the President is essential to the fulfilment of its roles, roles which enhance the influence of the member states in the Union rather than excluding them.

The EU Minister for Foreign Affairs, the other official innovation, also takes direction from guidelines laid down by the European Council. Below the latter come the Commission and the new dual legislature of the EP and the Council. The European Union's financial basis remains unchanged and is still ultimately dependent on monies coming from the member states. The Union does not, in other words, collect its own taxes. This is another example of the checks and balances built into the institutional structure.

In the past the Union and Community had a series of working procedures. These have now been simplified and limited thanks to the new definitions of decision making, legal acts and powers. The clear division between the Community method and the intergovernmentalism of the old pillars has been whittled down although, as we will see, there are separate procedures for diplomatic and judicial affairs 'hidden underground'. The Union can also work by coordinating member state activities as well as simply legislating on its own. Equally, as well as paying more attention to subsidiarity it has both to be transparent and to accept flexible working by member states. These changes should make the European Union more coherent and efficient.

Other characteristics

This is not all that the Constitutional Treaty suggests about the nature of the European Union. Articles I-58 and 59 make it clear that it is committed to democracy and human rights. This is part of a new stress on its values. The Union is also essentially rule based and is expected to obey its own rules. Hence the remits of both the ECJ and the Ombudsman now extend throughout the Union.

Article I-60 establishes it as an essentially voluntary association. For all that the European Union is said to be committed to a common destiny, and rests on a treaty with no expiry date, member states can leave when they choose even if the other member states do not want this. And it is they which provide its security. Despite the myths, there is no EU army.

A comparison with the old

How does this compare with the previous incarnation of the European Union? Previously the Union was seen as 'a' union, and as a construction of the treaties, rather than 'the Union' of the Constitutional Treaty, and with vaguer duties apparently centred on organizing inter-state cooperation. Now it is the entire enterprise and is more political and less ambiguous than before.

Previously, while it enjoyed superior status, the European Union had no legal personality and depended on the European Community to act. Equally, it was much more complex and dispersed with its three pillars, diverse working methods and frequently changing Presidency. And the position of the European Council was uncertain. So the old Union remained more a matter of evolutionary process rather than a finished article.

The 'new' Union re-assessed

The changes made by the Constitutional Treaty have clearly simplified the Union. It is now more organized and designed to last. But it is still not as carefully defined as we might wish. Nor is it as open and straightforward as it might be. It still involves a unique mix of state and collective powers and operation, although the balance may have been shifted towards the former. In fact, doubts among the member states continue to ensure that the mutual trust to create a Federation remains lacking.

The stress on conferred powers, which is imposed on the institutions as well as on the Union as a whole, and the other limitations on the Union's competences rather suggest this. So does the fact that it is still portrayed in the Constitutional Treaty as essentially a functional organization, designed to meet the specific policy aims of the member states. Nonetheless, much of this has to be teased out from the text. And the fact that this is so means that the nature of the Union is still open to several interpretations.

Values and freedoms

If one of the main aims of the new European Union is to promote its values, these have been less debated than other aspects of the Constitutional Treaty and thus there are probably fewer preconceived ideas in this area. Yet they deserve attention. For their inclusion is not an odd rhetorical flourish but represents a deliberate and important theme in the Constitutional Treaty:

the promotion of values, rights and freedoms. This is true not merely in domestic but also in foreign affairs. For many Continental commentators, one of the document's major strengths is that it shows that the European Union is more than just a single market. It is to be a more democratic structure, subject to universal values and partly remedying the existing deficit in rights. The fact that, as we will see later, the Charter of Fundamental Rights and Freedoms will be given binding status underlines this theme and also gives the document a more constitutional feel. This is reinforced by the way that such principles, which had previously been divided up somewhat contradictorily between the Union and the Community, are here more clearly codified and stated.

All this has sometimes been queried in the United Kingdom – although perhaps less so than other aspects of the Constitutional Treaty, such as its powers and policies and their effects on sovereignty. This is partly because the British see themselves as pragmatic and are less used to thinking in terms of rights. However, eurosceptics would argue that rights can only be provided by states and are not needed in what should be only a treaty for a free-trade area. They would also say that rights can be used to subvert both UK law and social–economic management.

In fact, the European Union is, and always has been, more than a free-trade area, and therefore there is a strong argument for it being required to respect individuals' rights and values, especially if it is as large and threatening as is often assumed. If the Union has no respect for rights and values, it cannot but be oppressive. This surely is to be avoided. Moreover, because the Constitutional Treaty is partly constitutional, the stress on rights and freedoms needs to be seen as a restraining matter and not as something menacing.

So we need to ask precisely what the Constitutional Treaty says about rights and freedoms. Here we need to consider not just Part I but also Part II, which contains the Charter of Fundamental Rights. Equally we need to ask exactly why there is this stress on rights and principles. And do the provisions of the Constitutional Treaty justify the claims made for their centrality? What we find is that, although the idea of a Union based on unimpeachable values and usable rights exists, the way they are expressed in the Constitutional Treaty is not always consistent; nor is it free from problems.

Values in Part I

Although Part I of the Constitutional Treaty more or less begins with an article (Article I-2) entitled 'The Union's values', references to values also occur in other places, often with slightly different emphases. Thus the Preamble argues that Europe is the birthplace of universal values: human rights, freedom, democracy, equality and the rule of law. It also hints that such rights are to be balanced with responsibilities to future generations and the environment. Then, in Article I-1, acceptance of its values is made a condition of entry to the Union. Signing up to the European Convention of Human Rights (ECHR) means that the barrier for entry has been raised a little higher. Similarly, foreign and neighbourhood policies are to be based on EU values.

Within the European Union the member states are also required not to jeopardize EU objectives, one of which, as Article I-3 makes clear, is promoting EU values. Later on, in Article I-59, the Constitutional Treaty makes non-adherence to these values a cause for a suspension of voting rights, thereby reinforcing the Union's commitment to its values in the eyes of some commentators. Equally, the institutions are required to promote EU values. Flexibility and enhanced cooperation, as in Articles I-18 and 44, can also be used to achieve such objectives.

The values themselves, as spelled out in Article I-2, are largely the same as in the Preamble and the existing treaties, although they are described as principles in the latter. However, respect for human dignity, whether of individuals in general or of those belonging to minority groups, is now added to the list. The article also talks of another range of values which mark European societies: pluralism, non-discrimination, solidarity, tolerance and justice. The IGC then wrote in gender equality, while the Irish made combating social exclusion an objective.

Things are then slightly confused by Article I-4 which is headed 'Fundamental freedoms and non-discrimination'. This guarantees the freedom of establishment and the free movement of people, services, goods and capital, the established bases of the internal market. However, because it covers economic freedoms, it is not in Title II, which covers fundamental freedoms and citizenship. Here, Article I-9, which is headed 'Fundamental rights', states that the European Union will recognize the rights, freedoms and principles set out in Part II. It also accepts the fundamental rights laid down by both the ECHR (to which the Union will adhere) and the member states. Signing up to the ECHR carries implications of statehood for some eurosceptics and also threatens to increase the powers of the Court of Justice. A Declaration provides for cooperation between this and the European Court of Human Rights.

The rest of the Title is given over to citizenship, which, as before, is described as additional to national citizenship and subject both to constitutional law and to unspecified duties. There are three categories of rights in citizenship: free movement, diplomatic protection and voting. More details of these are found in Part II, which also provides a slightly different gloss on the Union's values. Title VI of Part I exemplifies democratic principles and values, and there are also guarantees on data protection in Article I-51. So, although usages are variable and there is some repetition, Part I is clearly much concerned with values.

Values in Part II

Because the Convention only agreed at the last moment to include the Charter of Fundamental Rights in its draft and preferred not to disturb its carefully crafted compromises, there are some overlaps, and the odd contradiction, between Part I and Part II. As Box 5.3 shows, while the latter reinforces the identification of the values established in Part I, it also raises solidarity to the rank of a major value. Equally, the former sees rights and the rule of law as principles, whereas it treats democracy and other things as values. However, because it makes it clear that the European Union is based on values and has the duty of preserving and developing them, it takes us further towards understanding them and their relation to freedoms and rights. In fact, the Charter sets out rights and freedoms in terms of the Union's basic values. Thus, under dignity, it lists rights to life and bans on slavery and torture.

Given the stress on solidarity, and the rights which go with it, some commentators believe there is a new social dimension to the Union's rights and values. However, many of these rights can only be invoked if they are present in national legislation. Citizenship likewise includes a small number of limited political rights, along with consular protection where needed. All this spells out the values embraced by the Union and some of their – often controversial – practical implications. It also makes clear that there are many limitations.

Motives

So what explains this cautious promotion of values and rights? To begin with there has been a historical dynamic. As the European Community expanded beyond its initial economic activities, questions were asked – notably in Germany – as to the rectitude of belonging to a body which seemed to ignore human rights. In response, the ECJ began to refer to them in some of its judgements. This was followed up by a series of treaty amendments so that rights became justiciable once the Treaty of Amsterdam came into effect. Because it was then technically difficult for the European Union to sign up to the ECHR, maintained by the Council of Europe in Strasbourg, it was decided in 1999 to create a Convention to produce a statement of what rights already existed under EU legislation. The resultant Charter was then 'proclaimed' in December 2000.

Box 5.3 Values, rights and freedoms

Democracy and citizens' rights	Preamble, I-2, I-10, Part II
Equality	Preamble, I-2, Part II
Freedom	Preamble, I-2, Part II
Free movement	I-4
Human dignity	I-2, Part II
Human rights	I-2
Justice	I-2, Part II
Non-discrimination	I-2, I-4
Pluralism	I-2
Rule of law	I-2, Part II
Solidarity	I-2, Part II
Tolerance	I-2

At the same time, the alarm about the growing gap between the European Union and its populations, mentioned at Laeken, made the new European Convention responsible for trying to bridge this. And, because the Declaration argued that there was support for the Union's goals as well as resistance to the way they were implemented, the stress on rights and values was enhanced in an attempt to place the individual at the heart of EU activity through citizenship and the creation of an area of freedom, security and justice. Finally, many people were aware that the European Union was never going to have a homogenous population, so any linking identity could only come, as it does in Switzerland, from shared political values. If people accepted the way things were done and saw this as both just and exemplifying the things in which they believed, then they would support the enterprise even though they did not share blood, culture or language. And, because the assumption is that nation states will continue to exist, the stress on values and rights is partly also a defence of member states' essential identities.

So the European Convention promoted values from being mere principles to being fundamental bases. Their importance in continental Europe was highlighted by the IGC arguments over whether there should be a reference to God and Christianity in the Preamble. This was reinforced by the revelation of the difference in values between most Europeans and the supporters of both George W. Bush and Catholic Commissioner elect Rocco Buttiglione, whom the EP rejected in 2004.

Evaluating the values

This calls into question the Constitutional Treaty's claim that the values of the European Union are universal. Admittedly, they seem to be available to all inhabitants of the Union, not just to EU citizens, and to apply beyond the Union. Yet, such is the diversity of beliefs throughout the world that the values we have identified are very much the product of European history. And they can be contested. A recent report commissioned by Romano Prodi, former Commission President, made it clear that there is no fixed list, and indeed there are considerable differences between western and eastern Europeans given the latter's post-1945 history. Moreover, the strength of secularism and the desire not to offend Muslim and other religious minorities prevented both the Convention and the IGC from finding a consensus on admitting the role of Christianity in shaping the Continent. However, a dialogue with churches and other similar bodies was incorporated in Article I-52.

Given this, the claim that the stress on values and rights gives the Union a new legitimacy and helps to redress the gap with citizens, is not wholly convincing. It does show that the Union is not just a market and is trying to cope with its democratic deficit. However, there is obviously some dispute about such values. Because they are unspecific they appeal to differing conceptions of liberty and rights. Equally they are said to oscillate between laying down norms and accepting national differences. Furthermore, some say they are too liberal and individualistic, paying too little attention to shared social rights. Others, notably in the UK, see them as too close to a costly and oppressive 'European social model'. So there is far from full agreement on values and how they are to be understood. Democracy is a case in point.

Moreover, there are only limited sanctions to support them. Not all values have a special article in Part III to ensure that, like gender equality and non-discrimination, they are properly pursued across the Union. If many member states were to move away from them, it is not clear that the Union would be able to cope. So, in political terms, this does not really add up to a manifesto or a 'veritable social contract' which will unify the peoples of the European Union.

There are further problems. For some there is too much of a Christmas tree effect about the over-enthusiastic approach to identifying values. Indeed, some say there is a superfluity of values. The way that lists of values vary in both definition and location is not very helpful, any more than are the overlaps. Moreover, the values stated have been criticized as being diffuse and lacking in effect. Thus not all of them are justiciable. Subsidiarity also fails to get a real look in.

Finally, the Constitutional Treaty does not clearly differentiate between values – normally seen as abstract principles – and practical enforceable rights as means of protecting interests. Nor is it clear which rights are fundamental and which are not. Many people would not accept that some of them, notably the social rights, are incontestable. Freedoms also seem to overlap with rights. Some tighter editing would have been helpful here as elsewhere. As it is, the appeal to rights is worthy but unconvincing. Nonetheless, the underlying commitment to values and rights in the existing treaties and in the Charter of Fundamental Rights means that, even were the Constitutional Treaty to be rejected, they would still endure.

Powers and policies

We know from our discussion of the nature of the European Union and from Article I-1(1) that powers – or competences – have been conferred on it by the member states and are exercised in the pursuit of common objectives. We also know from the Constitutional Treaty's opening article that the role of the European Union is a mixed one. On the one hand it coordinates agreed policies and, on the other, it exercises those powers conferred on it. But which policy areas does it coordinate and where is it competent to act? Moreover, what sort of powers does it have and for how long has it had them?

Opponents of the Constitutional Treaty often maintain that the European Union has all-encompassing powers and that the Constitutional Treaty significantly increases these. This preconception is misleading. The Union's powers, while extensive, are limited, and the Constitutional Treaty, rather than significantly increasing them, helps clarify exactly what the Union can do and where. There are some new policy competences and the so-called 'flexibility' clause that allows the European Union to act in areas not explicitly mentioned is retained. Yet the Constitutional Treaty cannot be compared to earlier treaties, such as the Treaty on European Union, which introduced a wide range of new and significant policy areas, notably economic and monetary union. The former also simplifies provisions on enhanced cooperation to allow for a more multi-speed Europe.

Appreciating what the European Union can do is made decidedly easier by the Constitutional Treaty. Part I outlines in its third Title the categories and areas of competence, but before then, in Article I-11, it outlines the three *principles* that govern the limits and exercise of its powers. The first is *conferral*, the principle that the Union can only act in line with the competences that the member states have given it. In other words, the Union has no powers by right and cannot arrogate any to itself. Moreover, the Constitutional Treaty makes it clear that primacy exists only because of conferral, so that this is something the member states endorse. In other words, the European Union does not have what authorities call 'competence-competence'. All powers come from the member states, and any competence not conferred on the Union remains with the member states. This has always been the case;

although it can only be inferred from the wording of existing treaties, none of which mention 'conferral' as a principle. That the Constitutional Treaty gives it such prominence is designed to clarify the status quo and assuage the concerns of those critics and opponents who see in the European Union some power-grabbing centralizing entity that is bent on wresting powers away from defenceless member states. The reality is quite different, although those keen to see powers 'returned' to the member states will be disappointed that no mechanism for this has been included.

The second principle provides a second-best solution but is better known. This is *subsidiarity*, which applies in all instances except those where the European Union enjoys exclusive competence. The principle is that the Union will act only if the member states themselves cannot achieve the desired objective of a proposed action and if the desired objective can be better achieved at EU level. In other words, the European Union should only act where and when appropriate. To this end, a protocol dating back to the Treaty of Amsterdam details the mechanisms, now involving national parliaments to a greater degree, to be used to monitor compliance by the Union's institutions. The default is therefore for action to be taken by the member states although, as the Constitutional Treaty now notes, this may be at a regional or local level. This has always been the preferred wording of more federal states, such as Germany and Belgium. In the past, UK governments have sought to retain the emphasis on the national level, a stance now at odds with devolution.

The third principle is *proportionality*, and this also acts as a constraint on unfettered EU action. It holds that the European Union should do no more than is necessary to achieve the objectives of the Constitutional Treaty. With this in mind, the associated protocol requires all legislative drafts – but not other actions – to contain a detailed statement justifying them and setting out their financial and legislative implications. Established practice, based on the case law of the Court of Justice, means that the less onerous measure should be adopted.

Once the principles have been explained, Article I-12 sets out the different *categories of competence* that the Union possesses. In doing so, it brings greater clarity to what has to date been a particularly confusing issue: what exactly can the European Union do? It identifies three basic types of competences: exclusive, shared and what we might term 'complementary' (see Box 5.4). Then it lists a number of policy areas where the Union's competence defies simple categorization – although it is implicitly 'shared' – before going on in Articles I-13 to 17 to explore these further and categorize all the other policy areas. More than 30 policy areas are identified, further provisions for which are contained in Part III (see Table 5.1). These, as Article I-12 reminds us, set out the scope of each competence and the arrangements governing their

Box 5.4 Powers and competences: exclusive, shared and supporting

Exclusive competence	*Shared competence*	*Supporting, coordinating or complementary action*
Customs union	Internal market	Protection and improvement of human health
Competition rules necessary for the functioning of the internal market	Social policy (as defined in Part III)	Industry
Monetary policy in the eurozone	Economic, social and territorial cohesion	Culture
Conservation of marine biological resources under the common fisheries policy	Agriculture and fisheries	Tourism
Common commercial policy	Environment	Education, youth, sport and vocational training
Conclusion of certain international agreements	Consumer protection	Civil protection
	Transport	Administrative cooperation
	Trans-European networks	
	Energy	
	Area of freedom, security and justice	
	Common safety concerns in public health matters (as defined in Part III)	
	Research and technological development	
	Space	
	Development cooperation	
	Humanitarian aid	
	Economic policy Employment Common foreign and security policy	

exercise, although there are specific provisions governing some policies in Part I. The problem is that the words used to describe the various classes are such as to raise hackles, which is a good example of the way that simplification is not always as much of a blessing as critics of the Constitutional Treaty's language assume.

When the Constitutional Treaty talks of *exclusive competences* it is referring to areas in which the European Union alone may legislate and adopt acts that bind the member states. There are obvious areas where this is the case: the customs union, competition policy as it affects the internal market, monetary policy for the eurozone and the common commercial policy. Yet in these, as in the other areas listed in Article I-13 – the conservation of marine biological resources under the common fisheries policy and certain international agreements – the fact that it enjoys exclusive competence does not

Table 5.1 Part III on powers and competences

Exclusive competence	
Customs union	III-151
Competition	III-161 to III-166
Monetary policy	III-185 to III-191
Conservation of marine biological resources	III-225 to III-232
Common commercial policy	III-314 to III-315
Conclusion of certain international agreements	III-323 to III-326
Shared competence	
Internal market	III-130 to III-150
	III-152 to III-160
	III-167 to III-176
Social policy	III-209 to III-219
Economic, social and territorial cohesion	III-220 to III-224
Agriculture and fisheries	III-225 to III-232
Environment	III-233 to III-234
Consumer protection	III-235
Transport	III-236 to III-245
Trans-European networks	III-246 to III-247
Energy	III-256
Area of freedom, security and justice	III-257 to III-277
Common safety concerns in public health matters	III-278
Research and technological development	III-248 to III-255
Space	III-248 to III-255
Development cooperation	III-316 to III-320
Humanitarian aid	III-321
Supporting, coordinating or complementary action	
Protection and improvement of human health	III-278
Industry	III-279
Culture	III-280
Tourism	III-281
Education, youth, sport and vocational training	III-282 to III-283
Civil protection	III-284
Administrative cooperation	III-285
Others	
Economic policy	III-178 to III-184
Employment	III-203 to III-208
Common foreign and security policy	III-294 to III-313
	III-322

mean that all legislation comes from the Union. The member states adopt legislation implementing EU decisions – when, as we will see, these take the form of framework laws – and may also be empowered to adopt other acts. The empowerment comes from the Union, underlining the fact that, in these policy areas, it is the case that powers have been ceded to the Union. As we will see in the discussion of institutions below, this does not mean that the member states have lost all policy responsibility, for they play a considerable role in the adoption of legislation at the EU level.

They obviously retain a much greater role in areas of *shared competence*. These are primarily those areas listed in Article I-14 (e.g. the internal market, the environment, the area of freedom, security and justice), although they also include the coordination of economic and employment policies (Article I-15) and the common foreign and security policy (CFSP) (Article I-16). With a shared competence, both the European Union and the member states can legislate, although member states must defer to the Union. So a member state may act only 'to the extent that the Union has not exercised, or has decided to cease exercising, its competence' (Article I-12(2)). As critics point out, this raises questions about the suitability of the term 'shared competence'. Clearly, once an issue is covered by EU legislation, a member state may not legislate in a manner that conflicts with this. Equally, just because the European Union is active in a particular area, this does not mean that member states forego the opportunity to act and lose all rights and influence. Moreover, in certain shared competences – research, technological development, space, development cooperation and humanitarian aid – the Constitutional Treaty makes it clear that the Union cannot prevent member states from exercising their competences.

There are also limits on what the European Union can do in some specific policy areas. In economic and employment policies, the Union's remit is restricted to promoting coordination. And, even if the provisions in Part I on the CFSP envisage – as has been the case since Maastricht – the framing of a common defence policy that might in time lead to a common defence, the goal is not the replacement of national foreign policies. Member states will retain these and will be able to use them. This is indeed implicit in the fact that CFSP issues are a shared competence. A similar position exists with justice and home affairs. The emphasis is very much on mutual recognition, minimum rules and approximation as opposed to the harmonization or abolition of national legislation and practices, as some critics maintain.

Although the Constitutional Treaty increases the range of areas in which the European Union shares competences with the member states, there are clear limits to what it can do. Judicial cooperation in civil matters, for example, is restricted to matters that have cross-border implications. Moreover, Article III-257 is clear that the Union must respect the different legal systems and traditions of the member states in promoting the area of freedom, security and justice. Its role is not to undermine or replace them. Also, the Constitutional Treaty may talk of a new 'common policy' on asylum, immigration and external border control, but many of the provisions already exist. In the case of the United Kingdom, the default position is that measures adopted either here or on immigration or judicial cooperation in civil matters do not apply unless the UK government itself decides to opt in.

As for the complementary competences – or more accurately '*areas of supporting, coordinating or complementary action*' – these are listed in Article I-17. In these the role of the European Union is generally limited to promoting cooperation between member states and it has little scope or opportunity for legislative action. Indeed, the harmonization of national legislation or rules is expressly ruled out both in Article I-12(5) and in relevant parts of Part III. The Constitutional Treaty also excludes harmonization of national legislation in a range of other areas where the European Union is competent to act, including employment policy, combating racial and religious discrimination, the integration of immigrants, and industry. This is notwithstanding the fact that supporters of more intense EU engagement areas wish this were not so. Here it is worth recalling that the treaty-based nature of the European Union means that it can change the rules to allow for harmonization only if the member states unanimously agree to do so.

This is also reflected in the '*flexibility clause*' found in Article I-18. Inspired by the so-called 'catch-all' Article 308 TEC, it allows the Council to agree unanimously to pursue 'action' without there being an express competence to do so in the Constitutional Treaty. Some argue that this gives the European Union carte blanche to pursue whatever measures it pleases, particularly since its application is no longer restricted to the operation of the 'common market' but extends to all EU activities. Yet there are clear limits, not least the need for there to be both an unfulfilled objective in the Constitutional Treaty and unanimity within the Council. Moreover, any such action must be within the framework of the policies set out in Part III, be based on a European Commission proposal, have the backing of the EP and be drawn to the attention of national parliaments. And, so as to assuage concerns of its opponents, no measure can entail the harmonization of national legislation.

These constraints remind us how far the Constitutional Treaty is from being a constitution creating one centralized and uninhibited state. Indeed, it bears all the marks of a treaty between somewhat suspicious member states. Nonetheless, the provision does and will have its uses, allowing the European Union to pursue measures where the existing competences, legally speaking, do not allow. It has often been used in the past and many of the 'new competences' that the Union has gained over time followed on from previous use of the 'catch-all' or 'flexibility' clause.

This brings us to the questions of the *origin of the competences* and which competences are actually new. For the most part, the competences listed in the Constitutional Treaty come from the existing treaties. This is certainly true of the exclusive competences, to which the Constitutional Treaty does not add, which generally date back to when the European Economic Community was established in 1958 (see Table 5.2). It is equally true that the clear majority of shared competences are already in the existing treaties. Agriculture, fisheries and transport were in the original Treaty of Rome, whereas the likes of the environment and economic and social cohesion were added by the Single European Act in 1987. Others were inserted later by either the Treaty on European Union (e.g. trans-European networks) or the Treaty of Amsterdam (e.g. the area of freedom, security and justice). Only space, energy, humanitarian aid and territorial cohesion are mentioned for the first time in any detail in the Constitutional Treaty.

This is not to say that the various competences have remained unaffected by past treaties. Most have seen their substance changed. And the Constitutional Treaty does bring additional changes to some, as highlighted in our overview of Part III, although these are not particularly extensive or overly significant. Indeed, the purpose of these additions and extensions is often to confirm existing practice, although it is clear that some embody new aspirations. Hence, the European Union has been involved in space-related projects, notably the Galileo satellite, for some time, particularly as part of its research and development policy. Humanitarian aid has also been part of its external activities for over a decade and is implicit in the humanitarian assistance role that the European Union pursues through the CFSP. What the Constitutional Treaty does is provide a clearer legal basis.

The same is true for those areas of supporting, coordinating or complementary action that cannot be found in the existing treaties. Tourism and civil protection were first mentioned in a declaration adopted at Maastricht as areas in which policies would be pursued, and they have been. And concerns over the need to ensure civil protection were very much behind the inclusion of the solidarity clause found in Article I-43. As for sport, a dedicated declaration was adopted at the time of the Treaty of Amsterdam, and activities along the lines of those envisaged in Articles III-282 are already under way. This leaves administrative cooperation, which has been inspired by the Union's efforts since the mid-1990s to assist applicant and candidate countries with the development of the administrative capacities necessary to assume the obligations of membership.

So, although the longer list of areas of competence contained in the Constitutional Treaty implies an expansion of EU competences, this does not automatically follow. What the Constitutional Treaty does is to clarify the status quo. In doing so, it does formally extend the competence of the European Union, and we should not forget that there are existing policy areas where the Constitutional Treaty also increases the Union's powers. These are limited, however, as we will see later.

Hence, as we have said, it would be inappropriate to conclude that the

Table 5.2 Policy areas: new and old

Policy area	*TEC 1958*	*SEA 1987*	*TEU 1993*	*TA 1999*	*TN 2003*	*CT*
Administrative cooperation						✓
Agriculture and fisheries	✓					A
Area of freedom, security and justice			✓	A	A	A
Citizenship			✓	A	A	A
Civil protection						✓
Common commercial policy	✓		A	A	A	A
Common fisheries policy	✓					A
Common foreign and security policy*			✓	A	A	A
Competition	✓		A			A
Consumer protection			✓	A		
Culture			✓	A		A
Customs union	✓					
Development cooperation			✓	A		A
Economic and social cohesion		✓	A	A	A	A
Economic policy	✓	A	A		A	A
Education			✓			A
Employment				✓		
Energy						✓
Environment		✓		A	A	
Humanitarian aid						✓
Industry			✓		A	A
Internal market	✓	A	A	A		A
International agreements	✓	A	A	A	A	A
Monetary policy		✓	A		A	A
Public health (as defined in Part III)			✓	A		A
Research and technological development		✓		A		A
Social policy (as defined in Part III)	✓	A	A	A	A	A
Space						✓
Sport						✓
Taxation	✓		A			A
Territorial cohesion						✓
Tourism						✓
Trans-European networks			✓	A		
Transport	✓		A	A		A
Vocational training	✓		A	A	A	A
Youth			✓			A

Key
✓ first appeared as a competence
A competence amended

Note
* Provisions for the predecessor of the common foreign and security policy, European political cooperation, first appeared in the treaties with the 1987 Single European Act.

Constitutional Treaty embodies a significant extension of EU competences. Equally, if we consider the range of competences which the European Union can exercise, it is difficult to see what convincing evidence there is to substantiate the conflicting claims of the Constitutional Treaty's critics that it is either too socialistic in its orientations or enshrines neo-liberal economic principles to the exclusion of any notion of social welfare. What the European Union is empowered to do generally reflects past compromises and agreements to modify these in the light of experience. A greater understanding of what the Union actually does and is doing therefore explains much of what is in the Constitutional Treaty, and how it both builds on the existing treaties and lays down new restraints.

Familiarity with the existing European Union also helps us understand *how policies will be pursued and implemented* under the Constitutional Treaty. Generally, as we showed earlier, there is a standard approach which involves all member states assuming the same obligations; decisions being made jointly by the Council and the EP on the basis of a Commission proposal; and the Court of Justice having jurisdiction over these. Yet, as has been the case to date, special procedures apply in certain instances.

First, there are CFSP and justice and home affairs matters. These are currently found in the Union's two intergovernmental pillars, which the Constitutional Treaty formally removes. Yet their ghosts remain in the form of dedicated articles in Part I. These set out the broad framework for EU activity and note specific institutional arrangements and procedures. With regard to the CFSP, the prominent role of the European Council becomes evident, as does the marginal role of the EP (Articles I-40 and 41). Where the area of freedom, security and justice is concerned, the Constitutional Treaty notes the key components of the policy, a particular role for national parliaments and the right of initiative for member states in the field of police and judicial cooperation (Article I-42). Added to this, the existing exclusion of the CFSP from the jurisdiction of the Court of Justice is maintained thanks to Article III-376. Exclusions relating to aspects of justice and home affairs are also retained.

Second, a number of *opt-out* and *opt-in* arrangements exist that allow certain member states to exempt themselves from some activities. The most well known is the UK opt-out from economic and monetary union. Yet other cases exist, such as those on UK and Irish non-participation in the Schengen area, UK, Irish and Danish detachment from the area of freedom, security and justice, and Danish exemptions from aspects of the CFSP. These were negotiated either as part of the Treaty on European Union or of that of Amsterdam and remain effective.

Third, Article I-44 contains provisions on *enhanced cooperation*, the – as yet unused – mechanism that allows groups of member states to proceed with closer cooperation without obliging others to follow suit. The provisions have been revised to change the minimum number of participating member states to one-third of the total membership, and their coverage has been extended so that only those areas in which the European Union enjoys exclusive competence are excluded. Whether this will result in enhanced cooperation being pursued remains to be seen, but with 'permanent structured cooperation' in defence matters also being envisaged, a core or avant-garde of member states could possibly emerge. If it did, it would provide further proof that the European Union is far less rigid and monolithic than many perceive it to be.

Finally, there is the matter of resources. As we will see, the Union's financial resources are far less than those of the member states. This places considerable limits on what the European Union can actually do. Hence, not all competences are pursued. Equally, despite the popular perception that the Union comprises a huge bureaucracy, its institutional and human resources are, by comparison with those of the member states, decidedly small. Indeed, the European Union relies heavily on the latter to implement policy. This, and the willingness of the member states to fulfil their legal obligations, also constrains what the Union can and does do. As the Stability and Growth Pact saga shows, member states may agree rules but this does not ensure they will abide by them.

A discussion of powers and policies helps reinforce the idea, highlighted earlier, that the European Union is essentially a functional entity designed to fulfil the specific policy aims of the member states. This is evident from the preceding analysis, notably where the principle of conferral is concerned. It is also reflected in the evolution of the Union's policy competences. And it is clear that, in limiting what the European Union can actually do, the member states have usually sought to keep as much power for themselves as possible.

Some admittedly wish to do more, and this may be possible through enhanced cooperation. Yet its treaty-based nature means that empowering the Union to do more requires unanimity among all the member states. Some fear that the European Union has the power to assume more competences, and to harmonize member state rules, almost at will. This, like the assumption that primacy is new and all embracing, is wrong.

However, the fact that the European Union has significant powers cannot, and should not, be denied. This is evident not only from the lists of competences contained in Part I but also, as we shall see, from the numerous laws and other acts that the institutions have adopted over time. It might also be asked how far the Constitutional Treaty will prevent further creeping competence. Nonetheless, EU policies are now subject to more constitutional restraints than previously, and many of these are essentially regulatory and do not involve transfers of resources.

Laws, instruments and acts

Although it has attracted less attention than primacy and policies, one of the major aspects of the Constitutional Treaty is the way it has consolidated the legal forms in which policies and powers take shape. In doing this it was responding to one of the main concerns of Laeken, the need to simplify the European Union so that it became more comprehensible and transparent. An important element of this was the simplifying of what are called 'instruments' or legal 'acts', the technical and procedural forms which EU decisions take (presently regulations, directives, decisions, opinions and recommendations). Over time these had multiplied and become more complex, to the point that nobody was quite certain how many forms and procedures there actually were, some estimates running to 40. And many were described in terms which did not accord with British usages. Moreover, 'directives', which were meant to be statements of principles which member states could implement in ways that suited their own situations, had become disproportionately detailed.

So the Constitutional Treaty seeks to rationalize and regularize such acts, rebranding them so that now they have slightly more comprehensible titles than before. Second, it provides clearer, if more detailed, definitions of the six permitted instruments, presenting them in three classes, as Box 5.5 shows. Third, it revises the rules as to how EU legal acts should be based, implemented and published. This is in line with the Constitutional Treaty's stress on the EU's democratic values; so, although Chapter I of Title V is somewhat technical, it also touches on the powers of member states and institutions. Hence the way the European Union legislates when exercising its legal primacy is much codified, constitutionalized and, to an extent, constrained.

Rationalization

The European Convention made a real effort to consolidate the European Union's instruments so that the IGC accepted its work with only stylistic alterations. Having defined the Union's competences, the Constitutional Treaty goes on to regularize the number of legal acts by creating a new category for previously unclassified Commission acts. At the same time, it renames them in what was thought to be a more comprehensible manner, although the way so many are described as 'European' – presumably to make it clear that they are not national acts – is a bit over the top. Moreover, 'EU' would be more accurate than European. And, for some, the decision to talk of 'laws' is threatening, symbolizing a proliferation of legislation by a state, not by an international organization. This overlooks the fact that

Box 5.5 Instruments

Old instruments	*New instruments*	*Nature*
Legislative acts		
Regulation	European law	Of general, direct and binding application in all member states. No domestic legislation needed. As with framework laws must be passed by the statutory legislative procedures.
Directives	European framework law	Binding on all member states as to the actual objective but implemented by member states in ways appropriate in their circumstances. Requires domestic legislation to activate.
Non-legislative acts		
Unclassified Commission rulings under Article 202 TEC	European regulations	General binding secondary acts for implementation. Like laws can be *either* directly applicable *or* adaptable to member state circumstances.
	European decision	Binding act taken by the European Council, the Council, the Commission and the European Central Bank as laid down in the Constitutional Treaty. Can be applicable to all or just addressed to specific recipients. Often used in CFSP.
Recommendation	Recommendation	Non-binding advice issued by the Council, the Commission and the European Central Bank
Opinion	Opinion	Non-binding views issued by the Commission, the Court of Justice, the Court of Auditors, the Economic and Social Committee and the Committee of the Regions.
Delegated regulations		Rules laid down by the Commission in virtue of provisions in laws and framework laws.

international law is not necessarily made by states, but the new usage is clearly more honest and comprehensible than the present term 'Regulation'.

Although the Constitutional Treaty does not specify the forms set aside, it does make it clear what the permitted new forms are. And it also guards against the introduction of new instruments. Article I-33 implies that the form of the Union's legal acts reflects the way its powers are conferred by the member states. Because of this, the European Union does not have freedom of action to decide how, and in what ways, it will act. It has to work within the rules laid down by the Constitution, notably those in Part III. However, there was obviously some doubt as to whether the rules will be obeyed. Consequently, the second paragraph warns the Council and EP not to use unauthorized forms as they had done in the past. Nonetheless, there are alternatives in foreign and judicial policy.

Definitions

Article I-33 sets out and briefly defines the permitted instruments: laws, framework laws, regulations, decisions, recommendations and opinions. These have to be seen as a hierarchy with laws at the top and opinions at the bottom. All this is in line with most national usages.

The Constitutional Treaty then goes on, in Article I-34, to define the first class of instrument, those which involve formal and binding legislation. These owe their predominance partly to their overriding effects and partly to the fact that they have to be passed by a process involving all three main decision-making institutions (the EP, the Commission and the Council). As we will see, this is normally by what used to be called co-decision and is now described as the 'ordinary legislative procedure'. Some commentators see this as consecrating the Commission's right of legislative initiative. However, in some cases the Council and the EP can legislate more independently, through what are called European laws. Equally, in specified cases, member states and other institutions can initiate legislation.

There are two acts in this class, European Laws and Framework Laws, which are simply new names for the existing Regulation and Directive of Article 249 TEC. The former remains generally applicable and comes into effect automatically without further national action. The Framework Law lays down general objectives which are left to the member states involved to achieve in the most suitable way for their own circumstances. No general rules about when the two forms should be used are given, although Laeken urged greater use of the Framework form. However, later, Article I-38(1) says that, where the Constitutional Treaty does not specify, a judgement will have to be made on the case. But the lowest level of act possible should be used.

The Constitutional Treaty then provides, in Article I-35, for the second class of instrument: non-legislative acts, so called because they are taken in simpler ways, usually follow on from primary legislation and are not always binding. Of these, decisions are specific acts, all of which are effective. But they are binding only on those to whom they are addressed, though this can involve the whole European Union. The European Council's right to issue decisions is now recognized, bringing it further into the mainstream.

As before in Articles 110 and 249 TEC, the other main institutions can, alongside decisions, issue regulations, recommendations and opinions. Regulations are the most complicated as they are implementing acts which can be generally applicable or locally adjusted. Giving them a clear title and role is an important simplification. Recommendations are non-binding advice on action. In the case of the Council, its recommendations usually need a Commission proposal. Opinions, which are only mentioned in passing, are essentially position statements, issued by bodies like the Committee of the Regions and the Economic and Social Committee as part of consultation processes. The ECJ also issues opinions. Individual articles of the Constitutional Treaty spell out when all these various acts can be adopted.

Article I-36 echoes existing Articles 192 and 211 TEC but controls and streamlines what had been a controversial third class of instrument: delegated legislation. This involves subordinate acts that are felt necessary to ensure that primary legislation works well. They had previously emerged in a non-transparent way through advisory committees working for the Commission in a process known as 'comitology'. This attracted much criticism from other institutions and from outsiders. The Constitutional Treaty now requires that primary legislation specifies where delegation is allowed, limits where it can be done and requires that any grant should be within specific conditions. The EP and Council now have a right to block or revoke any such delegation.

Procedures

Obviously such acts are not produced in a vacuum. As has already become clear, they emerge from specific decision-making processes such as the ordinary legislative procedure. The key questions about these involve the weightings used to get majorities in the relevant institutions. These have now been simplified and spelled out in Articles I-23 to 25 and III-396. We will come back to them in more detail when looking at the institutional aspect of the Constitutional Treaty.

Defining and passing legal acts is, of course, only part of the process. So the Constitutional Treaty goes on to think about putting them into practice.

This, as Article I-37 makes clear, is an obligation on the member states unless uniformity is essential, in which case the Commission and, where foreign policy is concerned, the Council get involved. However, for European laws, the text must specify conditions to limit the Commission's role.

All acts also have to conform to a set pattern which means that the reasons for an act must be set out, along with preceding legislation and initiatives (Article I-38). As a result EU laws should make it clear why they have been adopted, albeit in a somewhat formalistic way. This was equally true of legislation adopted on the basis of Articles 253 and 308 TEC. They must also be signed by an appropriate authority – as is done by the Crown in the UK – and published in hard copy form in one place, the *Official Journal of the European Union* (Article I-39). They are also freely available in electronic form.

What does all this amount to? The EP claims that the changes promote more efficiency, legitimacy and transparency. Certainly there will be a less complicated and more organized set of instruments than is now the case. The rules on delegated legislation should make it easier for Council and the EP to concentrate on principle, leaving execution to the Commission.

However, the main acts have more than one form, and there are some exceptions to the general rules on forms and procedures in specific areas. Moreover, the EP feels that the European Union does not make enough use of the ordinary legislative mode. So simplification has only gone some way. As to legitimacy, the changes made to comitology and the new controls available to the EP and member states mean that delegated legislation – intended also to take some of the burden off the EP and the Council – is both less of a mystery than previously and also more constitutional in nature. All this is expressed in simpler and clearer language than at present. And for many citizens the language will be more familiar, although perhaps not in the United Kingdom.

Institutions

While the European Union's powers and policies have been bitterly criticized in the United Kingdom, the institutions needed to turn them into reality have been less discussed. There have been ritual attacks on European bureaucrats and courts, and some have attacked the President of the European Council as being an American-style executive President, but it is the overall package which has been at the centre of eurosceptic opposition. To an extent this reflects British lack of comprehension of the responsibilities and powers of the main institutions of the European Union. For many, the myriad bodies that make up the Union's system of governance are beyond comprehension. They are all seen as part of one 'Brussels' monolith.

The situation is compounded by common misunderstandings. It is often assumed that the Commission is some form of unaccountable government that imposes its will on the member states, while the EP is simply a talking shop stuffed with has-been politicians eager to jump on the purported Brussels gravy train. To a degree such incomprehension can be blamed on the existing treaties, which actually shed little light on the institutions in the provisions detailing responsibilities and procedures which are scattered throughout them.

For many others, and notably for supporters of integration, the institutions are the crucial element of the whole operation since they give the European Union its shape and its ability to function. Therefore, it was institutional questions which aroused most controversy in the Convention, especially given the way that proposals were handed down by the Praesidium at the last moment. Institutional questions, including voting procedures, also helped to derail the IGC in December 2003. Since then, they have continued to shape many reactions to the Constitutional Treaty. For this reason they should be taken seriously.

In fact, while it does not really change the overall structure, the Constitutional Treaty does go some way to clarifying how the various institutions are made up and what they do. Also, in an attempt to ensure the continued functioning of the enlarged European Union, it introduces a number of reforms to the existing institutions, through the creation of new posts, changes to composition, or revision of voting procedures. These are designed primarily to ensure efficiency; yet equally some are also introduced in the pursuit of key policy goals, notably regarding the external role of the Union.

Part I, in Articles I-19 to 32, identifies the institutions that make up the Union's *institutional framework* (see Figure 5.1). It also establishes its collective aims, though the idea of a framework rather than an institution having aims is a bit odd. It then outlines how they are composed and operate and what purposes they serve. It also introduces 'other' institutions and 'bodies' of the European Union, which, for differing reasons, stand slightly apart. More detailed provisions concerning the composition and roles of all of these are then provided in Part III (see Table 5.3), where the mechanics of the main decision-making procedure – the ordinary legislative procedure – are laid down in Article III-396. We also need to turn to various provisions scattered throughout Part III to find out which procedures apply in given instances. To make matters more difficult, there are a number of protocols, notably one on transitional provisions for the period to 2009, and declarations affecting the institutions.

Article I-19 lists five institutions that make up the European Union's institutional framework: the EP, the European Council, the Council of Ministers, the European Commission and the Court of Justice. These are widely seen as the key bodies of the Union, and according to the Constitutional

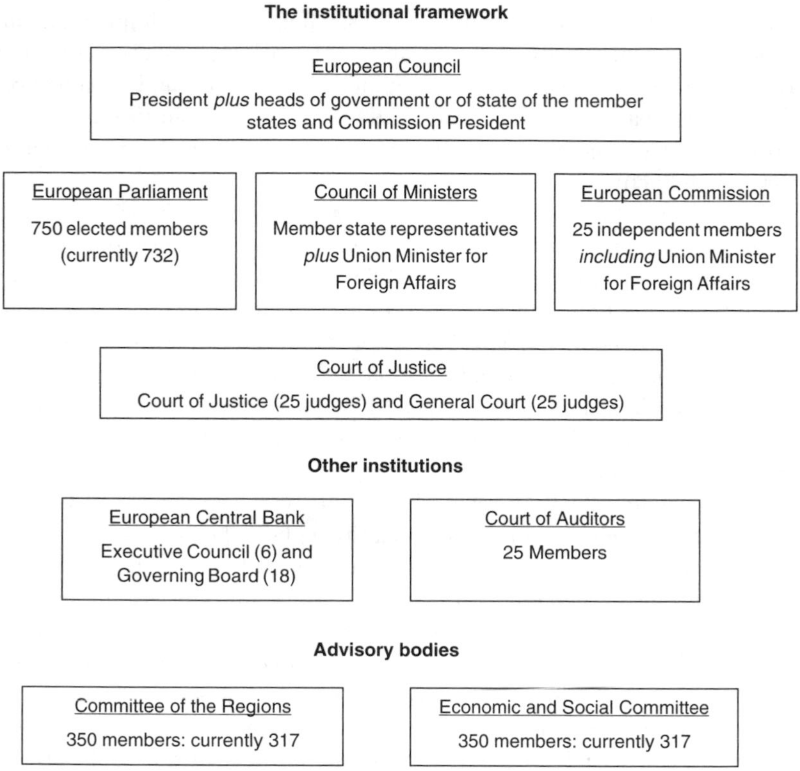

The institutional framework

European Council
President *plus* heads of government or of state of the member states and Commission President

European Parliament
750 elected members (currently 732)

Council of Ministers
Member state representatives *plus* Union Minister for Foreign Affairs

European Commission
25 independent members *including* Union Minister for Foreign Affairs

Court of Justice
Court of Justice (25 judges) and General Court (25 judges)

Other institutions

European Central Bank
Executive Council (6) and Governing Board (18)

Court of Auditors
25 Members

Advisory bodies

Committee of the Regions
350 members: currently 317

Economic and Social Committee
350 members: currently 317

Figure 5.1 The EU's institutional structure.

Treaty they come together to promote the Union's values, advance its objectives, serve its interests and ensure the consistency, effectiveness and continuity of its policies and actions. As part of the general attempt to bring the European Union closer to its citizens and underline the fact that it is there for its members, the institutional framework also aims to serve the interests of both EU citizens and states. It emphasizes conferred powers, and the institutions must operate within the limits of these and in conformity with procedures and conditions contained in the Constitutional Treaty. The institutions are therefore far from being free agents. Moreover, like the member states, they must practise 'mutual sincere cooperation'.

First to be presented is the *European Parliament* because it symbolizes the democratic foundation of the European Union. Although many of its roles are shared with the Council of Ministers, it has to be seen as the main institutional beneficiary from the Constitutional Treaty. It has been

Table 5.3 Institutions and bodies

	Part I	*Part III*
European Parliament	I-20	III-330 to III-340
European Council	I-21 to I-22	III-341
Council of Ministers – the 'Council'	I-23 to I-25, I-28	III-342 to III-346
European Commission – the 'Commission'	I-26 to I-28	III-347 to III-352
Court of Justice	I-29	III-353 to III-381
European Central Bank	I-30	III-382 to III-383
Court of Auditors	I-31	III-384 to III-385
Committee of the Regions	I-32	III-386 to III-388
Economic and Social Committee	I-32	III-389 to III-392
European Investment Bank		III-393 to III-394
Provisions common to EU institutions, bodies, offices and agencies		III-395 to III-401

strengthened thanks to the extension of the ordinary legislative procedure (see Figure 5.2), which makes it a joint legislator with the Council in most of the Union's spheres of activity. This is recognized in the Constitutional Treaty. As Article I-20 shows, it cannot legislate on its own but only in agreement with the representatives of the member states.

The EP also gains new budgetary authority so that it can now approve the whole of the budget and not just specified items. However, this has to be within guidelines laid down by the member states. It does, however, exercise political control independently, notably with regard to the Commission, which it must approve and may dismiss and whose President it will in future 'elect'. Because the Constitutional Treaty says that the selection of the President must reflect the outcome of European elections, some people think this could lead to parties suggesting candidates. The EP is also consulted on, and at times has to consent to, a wide range of issues, including accession, trade and justice and home affairs. So despite the low public profile that it enjoys in the United Kingdom, the EP is an institution to be reckoned with. It wields influence and power, albeit not in the same ways as national parliaments.

In theory at least, the 750 members now allocated by the Constitutional Treaty represent the view of the Union's citizens, although turnout has been falling. Reallocation means that some states, like Germany, will lose seats, while the smallest have been guaranteed a minimum of six seats. With further enlargement to include Bulgaria and Romania, the European Council will, from 2009, have to make a further reallocation of seats, although in the interim the number of MEPs will increase to 785. The decision on how exactly seats will be reallocated has not been made, although the maximum number of seats per member state has been set at 96 (see Table 5.4).

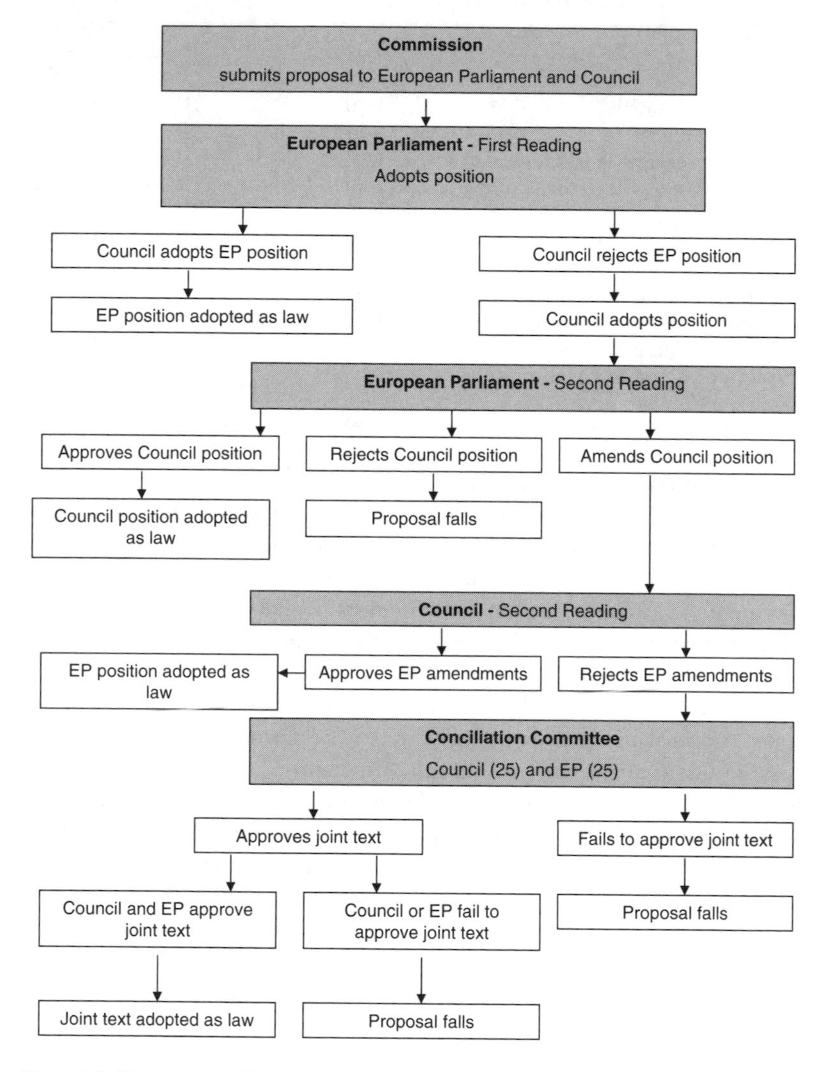

Figure 5.2 Decision making: the ordinary legislative procedure (Article III-396).

Having dealt with the EP, the Constitutional Treaty turns to the *European Council* and the Council of Ministers, two institutions that are often confused. This is partly because of their names and partly because they both represent the member states. In the past the European Council, which is made up of the heads of state or government of each of the member states plus the President of the Commission, was not regarded as part of the institutional

Table 5.4 Seats, votes and populations

	EP seats		*Council votes*		*Population*[1]	
	2004–9	*2009–14*	*(to 31.10.09)*	*(from 1.11.09)*	*Total*	*%*
Germany	99	96	29	1	82,531,700	18.0
United Kingdom	78	tbc	29	1	59,651,500	13.0
France	78	tbc	29	1	61,684,700	13.5
Italy	78	tbc	29	1	57,888,200	12.6
Spain	54	tbc	27	1	42,345,300	9.2
Poland	54	tbc	27	1	38,190,600	8.3
Netherlands	27	tbc	13	1	16,258,000	3.5
Greece	24	tbc	12	1	11,041,100	2.4
Czech Republic	24	tbc	12	1	10,211,500	2.2
Belgium	24	tbc	12	1	10,396,400	2.3
Hungary	24	tbc	12	1	10,116,700	2.2
Portugal	24	tbc	12	1	10,474,700	2.3
Sweden	19	tbc	10	1	8,975,700	2.0
Austria	18	tbc	10	1	8,114,000	1.8
Slovakia	14	tbc	7	1	5,380,100	1.2
Denmark	14	tbc	7	1	5,397,600	1.2
Finland	14	tbc	7	1	5,219,700	1.1
Ireland	13	tbc	7	1	4,027,500	0.9
Lithuania	13	tbc	7	1	3,445,900	0.8
Latvia	9	tbc	4	1	2,319,200	0.5
Slovenia	7	tbc	4	1	1,996,400	0.4
Estonia	6	tbc	4	1	1,350,600	0.3
Cyprus	6	tbc	4	1	730,400	0.2
Luxembourg	6	tbc	4	1	451,600	0.1
Malta	5	6	3	1	399,900	0.1
Total – EU (25)	**732**	**n.a.**	**321**	**25**	**458,599,000**	**100.1**
Romania	35	tbc	14	1	tbc	tbc
Bulgaria	18	tbc	10	1	tbc	tbc
Total – EU (27)	**785**	**750**	**345**	**27**	**tbc**	**tbc**

Note

1 As of 1 November 2004. See *Council Decision of 11 October 2004 amending the Council's Rules of Procedure*, Official Journal L 319, 20 October 2004. Population figures are to be revised annually.

mainstream. The Constitutional Treaty changes this. The European Council, because of the merging of the old Union with the Community, now becomes one of the ordinary institutions of the new European Union, subject to EU law and processes. However, it enjoys only a semi-permanent existence, with its members normally coming together for a day or so four times a year. Its rules of procedure are laid down in Article III-341. These do not include a formal legislative role, although the European Council is empowered to take 'decisions'.

Nonetheless, despite the complaints of some French eurosceptics, it is very much the senior state organization, responsible for setting the agenda, giving the European Union dynamism and defining its international strategies. It also has the power to change many details of institutional arrangements, including voting, as well as hear complaints from the Council in a sort of appellate capacity. So it is now institutionalized as the key institution of the new Union. It is a very political body. Indeed, many see its new role as giving the member states ultimate control of the reformed Union. Also, with the Constitutional Treaty, an attempt is made to reduce its size by limiting the rights of other ministers to attend. However, the Union Minister for Foreign Affairs and the European Council President will participate (Article I-21).

Currently, responsibility for presiding over meetings of the European Council rotates among the member states and coincides with the rotating presidency of the Council. If the Constitutional Treaty goes through, Article I-22 will establish a new post of European Council President. The name, for English speakers, is distinctly unhelpful because 'Chair' would be more accurate and acceptable. It was changed because the distinction does not exist in Latin languages and it was also thought that the holder ought to be on the same level as the heads of the EP and the Commission. In any case, the post is a two-and-a-half-year appointment, the holder being elected by the member states through a qualified majority. The post is not an executive President of Europe, as has been claimed, since the holder will enjoy few powers beyond preparing, chairing and driving forward the work of the European Council. Indeed, the President will have neither a vote nor a dedicated secretariat. The holder will also have to work with the President of the Commission and others, something which may not be easy. There is also a potential for conflict with the Union Minister for Foreign Affairs over who is responsible for external representation. Despite this, the post is likely to give the European Council and the European Union more coherence and continuity.

By contrast the *Council of Ministers* – generally if confusingly referred to as 'the Council'– is apparently a more permanent body, with its own secretariat and buildings in Brussels. Its purpose is to provide a forum in which the member states can come together to exercise legislative (increasingly in tandem with the EP), budgetary, policy-making and coordinating powers (Article I-23). So the Council remains the main decision-making institution in the European Union. Except in rare instances, and where the Council has delegated powers to the Commission, all EU legislation must be approved by member states. When they do so, they now have to do it in public.

However, the IGC rejected the idea of having a Legislative Council which would meet regularly to ratify the decisions of specialist Councils. So, though it is described as one body, the Council is actually a changing meeting of specialist ministers. The most important of these are the General Affairs Council, which prepares the work of the European Council, and the Foreign Affairs Council, which deals with the Union's external policies and activities. There will be other configurations too, presumably along the lines of those already in existence (see Figure 5.3). Apart from the Foreign Affairs Council, all these Councils are to be chaired by teams of three states, the composition of which was agreed in late 2004 (see Table 5.5). Each member state in the team will normally chair each Council configuration for six months.

Also, the Constitutional Treaty, through a dedicated protocol, gives formal endorsement to the Euro Group, the informal meeting of economic and finance minister from the eurozone countries. This will now have a President, elected by majority vote for a two-and-a-half year term, to provide political visibility for the eurozone. Its first President, the Luxembourg Prime Minister Jean Claude Juncker was elected in September 2004. Thus the Council is less united and permanent than might at first appear. Nonetheless, it is the command post of the European Union.

Current		*Under the Constitutional Treaty*	
General affairs and external relations	All Council formations chaired by member state holding the six-monthly Presidency of the Council	General Affairs Council	Chaired by a member state from the Council Presidency team
Economic and financial affairs		Foreign Affairs Council	Chaired by the Union Minister for Foreign Affairs
Justice and home affairs		(tbc)	Chaired by a member state from the Council Presidency team
Employment, social policy, health and consumer affairs		Economic and financial affairs	
Competitiveness		Justice and home affairs	
Transport, telecommunications and energy		Employment, social policy, health and consumer affairs	
Agriculture and fisheries		Competitiveness	
Environment		Transport, telecommunications and energy	
Education, youth and culture		Agriculture and fisheries	
		Environment	
		Education, youth and culture	

Figure 5.3 Council configurations.

Table 5.5 Council: Team Presidencies

Team	*Start date*	*End date*
Germany, Portugal, Slovenia	2007 (January)	2008 (June)
France, Czech Republic, Sweden	2008 (July)	2009 (December)
Spain, Belgium, Hungary	2010 (January)	2011 (June)
Poland, Denmark, Cyprus	2011 (July)	2012 (December)
Ireland, Lithuania, Greece	2013 (January)	2014 (June)
Italy, Latvia, Luxembourg	2014 (July)	2015 (December)
Netherlands, Slovakia, Malta	2016 (January)	2017 (June)
United Kingdom, Estonia, Bulgaria	2017 (July)	2018 (December)
Austria, Romania, Finland	2019 (January)	2020 (June)

Increasingly, Council decisions are being taken using *qualified majority voting* (QMV) and the Constitutional Treaty extends its use so that it becomes the default procedure (see Box 5.6). Unanimity is, however, retained for a significant number of issues. And it remains the case that, in the overwhelming majority of instances, legislation must have either the explicit or implicit approval of a clear majority of the member states. Indeed, the embedded custom of proceeding in the Council on the basis of consensus means that it is rare that a majority in the Council imposes its will on a member state. Compromise and consensus are the norm.

This has not assuaged concerns over the extension of QMV provided for in the Constitutional Treaty, the establishment of QMV as the norm, or the introduction of a new form of QMV, the so-called double majority system (Article I-25), which will apply from 1 November 2009. Until then, the existing QMV system based on weighted votes will continue to be used. Indeed it was the desire to persist with the status quo and resistance to a double majority system that delayed conclusion of the Constitutional Treaty. The double majority system will mean that in order to obtain a qualified majority, 55 per cent of the member states representing 65 per cent of the population of the European Union will have to be in favour (see Table 5.6). When, however, the Council is not acting on a proposal from the Commission or the Union Minister for Foreign Affairs, 72 per cent of the member states (i.e. 18 in the current Union) must be in favour.

While this would suggest that the European Union is moving towards a more comprehensible majority voting system, there are a number of other conditions that must be met before a decision can be adopted. First, at least 15 member states must be in favour. This means that only when the Union admits its 28th member will the 55 per cent criterion come into play. Second, it has already been decided that if a minority of member states representing 75 per cent of either the number of members or the population needed to

Box 5.6 The extension of qualified majority voting

I-22	Election of European Council President
I-24	Presidency of Council configurations
I-28	Appointment of European Union Foreign Minister
I-32	Composition: Committee of the Regions and the Economic and Social Committee
I-37	Comitology
I-47	Citizens' initiatives
I-54	Implementation of own resources decisions
I-60	Negotiation of withdrawal agreement
III-122	Services of general economic interest
III-127	Diplomatic and consular protection measures
III-136	Social security*
III-141	Coordination of provisions for self-employed persons
III-167	Repeal of exemption from state aids policy for areas of Germany affected by division
III-176	Authorization, coordination and supervision of intellectual property rights protection
III-187	Amendments to certain parts of the Statute of the European System of Central Banks
III-191	Use of the euro (only applicable to member states with the euro)
III-194	Measures relating to the broad economic guidelines and excessive deficit procedure (only applicable to member states with the euro)
III-198	Procedure for entry into the euro
III-236	Transport
III-243	Repeal of exemptions from transport policy in areas of Germany affected by division
III-251	European research area
III-254	Space policy
III-256	Energy
III-260	Mechanism for peer review of member states' implementation of policies in the area of freedom, security and justice
III-265	Border checks (UK opt-in)
III-267	Immigration and frontier controls (UK opt-in)
III-270	Judicial cooperation in criminal matters*
III-271	Minimum rules for criminal offences and sanctions*
III-272	Crime prevention
III-273	Eurojust
III-275	Police cooperation
III-276	Europol
III-280	Culture
III-281	Tourism
III-282	Sport
III-284	Civil protection
III-285	Administrative cooperation
III-300	Role of the European Union Foreign Minister in CFSP implementing measures*

Continued overleaf

Box 5.6 Continued

III-312	Membership of structured cooperation in defence
III-313	Urgent financing of CFSP measures
III-315	Aspects of the common commercial policy
III-320	Urgent aid to third countries
III-321	Humanitarian aid operations
III-329	Implementation of solidarity clause.
III-357	Judicial appointments panel.
III-359	Specialized courts
III-364	ECJ jurisdiction on intellectual property rights
III-381	ECJ statute
III-382	Appointment of ECB Executive Board
III-398	Principles of European administration
III-412	Financial regulations

Source: The content of the box is derived from Foreign and Commonwealth Office, *Treaty establishing a Constitution for Europe: Commentary*, London, 26 January 2005, Annex 1.

* Emergency brake available.

Table 5.6 Qualified majority voting: the rules (EU = 25)

	Until 31 October 2009	*From 1 November 2009*
Total number of votes	321	25
Voting on a Commission proposal		
Qualified majority	232	55%
Minimum number of states	13	15
Minimum population	62%	65%
Blocking minority – states	13	11
Blocking minority – population	39%	36%
Deferred decision - states	n.a.	9
Deferred decision – population	n.a.	29%
Voting without a Commission proposal		
Qualified majority	232	72%
Minimum number of states	17	18
Minimum population	62%	65%
Blocking minority – states	9	12
Blocking minority – population	39%	36%
Deferred decision - states	n.a.	6
Deferred decision – population	n.a.	29%

block a qualified majority exists, the Council will discuss the proposal further in the hope of finding within 'a reasonable time . . . a satisfactory solution'. This is all laid out in a Declaration and is set to last until at least 2014. What it means is that in the current Union of 25 member states – where the blocking minority can be either 11 member states or less, provided they represent 36 per cent of the population – a minority of up to eight member states, representing 29 per cent of the population, can also postpone a decision. Emergency brakes will also be operative until 2014.

One very important addition to both the European Council and Council of Ministers is the proposed *Union Minister for Foreign Affairs*. The rationale for the post is to give greater emphasis and unity to the common foreign and security policy (Article I-28) by combining the existing Commissioner for External Affairs with the Council's High Representative for the Common Foreign and Security Policy. Indeed, the European Council has confirmed that the current High Representative, Javier Solana, will be the first Union Minister for Foreign Affairs. This so called 'double hatting' means that the post-holder will not only chair the Foreign Affairs Council, but will also be a Vice-President of the Commission. Hence, while answerable to his appointees – the member states – who not only issue him with mandates but may also sack him, Solana will be bound by Commission procedures when exercising his responsibilities as a Commissioner. Whether this will work remains to be seen.

Such conflicts of interest could make it hard for the EU Minister to fulfil his main tasks of proposing and, especially, conducting the European Union's foreign policy. This does not, in fact, mean a great accretion of power and certainly not the authority to run a 'European army', for he will be appointed solely by the European Council, bearing in mind 'a geographical balance' with the other Presidential posts. Moreover, the EU Minister can only fulfil this task within the guidelines laid down by the European Council.

He will also need support in both devising and implementing policy. Hence work has also already begun on the establishment of a European External Action Service comprising Council and Commission personnel as well as staff seconded from national diplomatic services. This embryo EU diplomatic service will, as envisaged in the Constitutional Treaty, work in cooperation with the diplomatic services of the Member States. In many respects it builds on the existing Policy Planning and Early Warning Unit created by the Treaty of Amsterdam.

For the *Commission*, the transformation of one of its Vice-Presidents into the Union Minister for Foreign Affairs is only one of a number of reforms introduced by the Constitutional Treaty. As Article I-26 notes, the Commission exists 'to promote the general interest of the Union and take appropriate initiatives to that end'. Hence it ensures the application of EU law; manages the Union's finances and programmes; and exercises the 'coordinating, executive and management functions' bestowed on it. For the most part, the Commission's roles and powers remain unchanged and it is not transformed into a 'European government', as some either fear or hope. The CFSP remains in the hands of the Council, and the areas in which the European Union now has a formal competence to act are generally areas where, as we have seen, action has already been taken. The Commission must now take on board the views of the European Council and of national parliaments when proposing legislation, but beyond this there are few new demands made of it. Thus it retains its monopoly of the right to propose legislation, and this is now explicitly stated as a general principle.

However, the composition of the Commission will be radically altered by the Constitutional Treaty. For while, as is currently the case, the Commission is to be composed of members 'chosen on the grounds of their general competence and . . . whose independence is beyond doubt', there is now a controversial requirement that Commissioners should have a 'European commitment'. This may sound unfair but it is essential if the machinery is to work smoothly.

More importantly, although until 2014 the current arrangement of one Commissioner per member state will be maintained, thereafter the size of the Commission will be reduced to two-thirds of the number of member states, provided the European Council does not unanimously decide otherwise. In a Union of 27 members, therefore, there will be 18 Commissioners. These will be selected on the basis of equal rotation among the member states, meaning that each member state will have one of their nationals in two out of every three Commissions. The exact rotation, which must reflect 'satisfactorily the demographic and geographical range' of member states, is to be determined by a unanimous European Council decision. A declaration also requires that 'appropriate organisational arrangements' be adopted to ensure that member states' political, economic and social realities are not overlooked by the Commission.

In addition, there are changes to the way in which the Commission President is chosen (Article I-27). Instead of the member states appointing someone, the Constitutional Treaty allows the EP to share the responsibility. A candidate will be proposed by the European Council, and it will be for the EP to formally elect the person as Commission President. If the requisite absolute majority is not achieved, the European Council will have to propose another candidate. Once the process has been completed, the Council and the president-elect will adopt a list of potential Commissioners on the basis of suggestions made by the member states. The list, complete with the names of the Commission President and the Minister for Foreign Affairs, will then be presented to the EP for a vote of approval. Assuming this is forthcoming, the

European Council will, acting by a qualified majority, formally appoint the Commission. All this should make the process more transparent and political than has previously been the case. It should also raise the profile of the Commission President and of elections to the EP, for the European Council, thanks to a Declaration, is obliged to take into account the outcome of the latter when agreeing on a candidate. In other words, if there is a left of centre majority, the European Council will have to nominate someone of that political complexion, even if the majority of governments represented happen to be on the centre right. The status of the office is also somewhat upgraded by having a full separate article. And this gives the post more authority over the organization of the Commission bureaucracy as well as over its political strategy.

The fifth and last element in the Union's 'institutional framework' is the *Court of Justice* (Article I-29). This comprises the ECJ itself, the Court of First Instance (which the Constitutional Treaty renames the 'General Court') and a series of 'specialised courts'. The first is to include a judge from each member state, assisted, as before, by Advocates-General. In the case of the General Court, there will be at least one judge from each member state since this is the body which will have most business in future. The courts are to rule on actions brought before them and give preliminary rulings on the interpretation of EU law and acts. Beyond this, Article I-29 says little about the Court of Justice except that judges are to be independent and may serve a renewable six-year term of office. Far more detail about the operation of the Court is provided jointly by Part III and a dedicated Statute contained in a Protocol. The specialized courts will include tribunals for staff and copyright matters. Rejecting these provisions means a denial of the rule of law and of the way the UK constitution works.

EU law, and therefore the Courts, have primacy over that of the member states. This gives the ECJ powers similar to those of a supreme court, albeit only in so far as the Constitutional Treaty gives it jurisdiction. There are still clear limits to this, even within the European Union itself, notably in those areas currently dealt with in the Union's two intergovernmental pillars. Even when the Charter of Fundamental Rights is concerned, the Court does not have the free rein to change national laws, as is feared by some. However, the Constitutional Treaty does now require that member states make it easy for citizens to invoke European law.

Even though they are not listed in the main 'framework', the Constitutional Treaty recognizes two other institutions. These are separated out because they are not part of the decision-making nexus and need to have their independence recognized, albeit for different reasons. Including them with the other bodies might, symbolically, call this into question. However, they have the same status and rights as the other institutions.

The first is the *European Central Bank* (ECB), which has responsibility, along with the national central banks of the member states in the eurozone, for the conduct of monetary policy (Article I-30). Based in Frankfurt, the ECB – like most national banks – is wholly independent and exists to maintain price stability for the European Union as a whole and to support its economic policies. Hence it has no political representation. How it does this is set out in Part III and in the Statutes of the ESCB and the ECB.

Article I-30 does remind us, however, that the ECB has sole responsibility for authorizing the issue of the euro, enjoys certain other decision-making powers and must be consulted on all relevant EU and national laws. It also makes it explicit that, as is already the case, member states outside the eurozone retain their powers for monetary matters. The only change to current provisions made by the Constitutional Treaty is to allow its Executive Board to be appointed by a qualified majority.

The second is the *Court of Auditors*. This examines the accounts of the European Union and seeks to ensure sound financial management (Article I-31). Because its role is to scrutinize the rest of the Union it was thought best to make it clear that it was not involved in day-to-day policy making. This is part of the European Union's ongoing, and not always successful, attempts to eliminate fraud and misappropriation.

Finally, the Constitutional Treaty notes the existence of two advisory bodies: the *Committee of the Regions* and the *Economic and Social Committee*. Their role, set out in Article I-32, is to assist the EP, the Council and Commission. The first was established by the Treaty on European Union in 1993 and comprises representatives of regional or local authorities, with each member of the Committee either holding elected office or being politically accountable to an elected assembly. The Economic and Social Committee has been around since the 1950s and brings together representatives of employers, employees and other representatives of civil society. Each committee has a maximum membership of 350 (currently 317) and is consulted on matters of relevance to their members. These are determined by provisions in Part III. They lack the standing of the other institutions, in assisting rather than deciding, and the Convention refused to change this.

So what do all these institutions and bodies amount to? For some, they provide the Union with state-like characteristics. There is an executive of sorts in the Commission, there is a legislature-like entity in the EP and there is obviously a judiciary. But there is also a European Council exercising executive functions and a Council, which generally holds ultimate decision-making authority. In other words there is no straightforward division of powers, and the member states play a key role within and beyond the institutions. The architecture is complex and navigating one's way through the institutional maze of the European Union is no easy task. The

Constitutional Treaty helps us understand why each institution exists by outlining their main roles in Part I and setting down the principles that guide their actions.

It does little, however, to simplify the system. Nor does it always recognize the way that the states, as a corporate body, really function as an institution. Moreover, in creating some new posts, it arguably adds to the complexity. Equally, in establishing these it may raise the profile of the institutions. This could go some way to encouraging understanding and promoting engagement, something which may also follow from the greater emphasis the Constitutional Treaty places on enhancing the Union's democratic credentials.

Democracy

One criticism often directed against the present European Union, albeit for very differing reasons, is its lack of democracy. Opponents decry it as frankly undemocratic, and even supporters lament what is called a 'democratic deficit'. So one of the Laeken challenges was 'how to bring citizens, and primarily the young, closer to the European design and the European institutions'. Various suggestions were made during the European Convention, most focusing on either raising the profile of the Union and its institutions or making it more democratic through increased transparency, accountability and popular engagement. Most of the proposals were taken up by the IGC, so the Constitutional Treaty makes a real effort to develop the Union's democratic credentials. To do this it makes seven changes to existing provisions.

First, the Constitutional Treaty brings a wholly new *stress* on democracy. It is mentioned in the Preamble as both a source of inspiration for the Union and as something to be developed. The opening article states that the European Union exists because of the will of its citizens and this is followed up in Article I-2. The Constitutional Treaty also makes it clear elsewhere that the task of the European Union is to aid the people. Thus the institutions are required to work for the people, and proportionality and rights of appeal are there to help them (Articles I-11 and 19).

To promote the idea of the European Union as a democratic entity further, Part I introduces a specific Title on 'The democratic life of the Union'. This brings together a variety of existing assumptions, practices and treaty provisions as well as a number of innovations. The opening articles of the new Title confirm two basic assumptions concerning the European Union today: that it observes the principle of equality of its citizens (Article I-45) and that it is based on the principle of representative democracy (I-46).

Second, there is a stress on *representative* democracy. This may surprise those critics of the European Union who regard its institutions and practices as remote and bureaucratic. Yet, in terms of the Union's democratic credentials, Article I-46, while it does not provide a clear definition of the 'principle', does provide a reminder of the fact the Council and the European Council, along with the EP, contribute to the European Union as a representative democracy. Those that meet in the first two institutions are representatives of democratically elected governments and, in most instances, hold elected office. It also reminds us of the role that political parties 'at the European level' are meant to play in expressing citizens' views.

Equally, in Article I-48, the Constitutional Treaty provides the European Union with a role in promoting dialogue between the social partners, namely employers and employees, at a European level. The mechanics, which must take into account different national systems and have been in the existing treaties for more than a decade, are set out at greater length in Articles III-211 and 212. Article I-48 also notes that the Tripartite Social Summit for Growth and Employment will provide a forum for such dialogue. The summits, the first of which was held in March 2001, were formalized in 2003 and bring together the 'social partners' with the Commission and the Council.

Third, while the Constitutional Treaty gives priority to representative democracy, it tries to go beyond this to '*participatory*' democracy. Although this is not well differentiated from representative democracy – since it is mainly concerned with avenues for consultation, which presupposes that representatives make decisions – it does go further in one way. Article I-47 requires the European Union to maintain 'an open, transparent and regular dialogue with representative associations and 'civil society', notably, as Article I-52 states, with churches and non-confessional organizations.

Article I-47 also introduces the option of a citizens' initiative, inviting the Commission to submit appropriate proposals. This was inserted into the Convention draft late on – as a result of pressure from enthusiasts for direct democracy and as a sop to those who wanted a general referendum for ratification – in the hope that it would make the document easier to sell, and it builds on the existing mechanism for petitioning the EP (now found in Article III-334). It is more than a mere right of petition and could give citizens a new power. Whether it will be possible to bring together the required signatures of one million citizens remains to be seen, as does the nature of the causes which may be taken up. Prima facie the constitutional changes, which some wish to use it for, seem to be ruled out.

Fourth, the Constitutional Treaty also increases the legislative and control functions of the European Union's only directly elected institution, the *European Parliament*. This is clearly intended as a further move towards democratization. Thus, as Box 5.7 shows, it envisages an increase in the range of policy areas where measures will have to be adopted by the EP and the

Box 5.7 Extensions to the ordinary legislative procedure (co-decision)

I-37	Comitology
I-47	Citizens' initiatives
III-122	Services of general economic interest
III-139	Official and government employment
III-144	Freedom to provide services for established third country nationals
III-147	Freedom to provide services
III-157	Movement of capital to or from third countries
III-160	Freezing of assets
III-174	Distortion of competition
III-176	Intellectual property rights
III-179	Multilateral surveillance procedure
III-187	Amendments to certain parts of the Statute of the ESCB
III-191	Use of the euro
III-223	Structural and cohesion funds
III-231	Agriculture and fisheries
III-236	Transport
III-251	European research area
III-254	Space policy
III-256	Energy
III-265	Border checks
III-267	Immigration and frontier controls
III-270	Judicial cooperation in criminal matters
III-271	Minimum rules for criminal offences and sanctions
III-272	Crime prevention
III-273	Eurojust
III-275	Police cooperation
III-276	Europol
III-281	Tourism
III-282	Sport
III-284	Civil protection
III-285	Administrative cooperation
III-315	Aspects of the common commercial policy
III-319	Economic, financial, and technical cooperation with third countries
III-321	Humanitarian aid operations
III-359	Specialized courts
III-364	ECJ jurisdiction on intellectual property rights
III-381	ECJ statute
III-398	Principles of European administration
III-412	Financial regulations
III-427	Staff regulations of Union officials

Source: The content of the box is derived from Foreign and Commonwealth Office, *Treaty establishing a Constitution for Europe: Commentary*, London, 26 January 2005, Annex 1.

Council using the ordinary legislative procedure (formerly co-decision). As we have seen, the EP ranks ahead of the European Council and has new powers in the election of the President of the Commission, changes which are meant to enhance democracy.

The fifth and much noted development in this respect is the increased involvement of *national parliaments* in monitoring compliance with the subsidiarity principle. This 'yellow card' procedure is described in Article I-11 and two protocols. These require that all consultation documents – policy and legislative proposals issued by the Commission as well as those based on the initiatives of other institutions – are forwarded to national parliaments. Within six weeks they may then, in conjunction with regional parliaments where appropriate, submit reasoned opinions on whether proposed legislation respects subsidiarity. If a third of the national parliaments believe this not to be the case, the Commission, or any other relevant authority, must review the proposal. National parliaments are also involved in consideration of extensions to EU powers and activities under the flexibility procedures of Article I-18.

This certainly increases the input of national parliaments to decision making at the EU level, even if they cannot force the Commission to withdraw – or 'red card' – a proposal. It should also enhance the European Union's democratic credentials, although this will depend very much on the extent to which the consultation process can be made to work. The volume of paper that each national parliament will have to process is considerable and, with the exception of the Danish Folketing, none has traditionally shown the necessary inclination or capacity for scrutinizing the Union's activities fully. This is despite claims that only national parliaments can embody true democracy.

Sixth, the emphasis placed on the *transparency* of the institutions' proceedings – as part of efforts to promote 'good governance' and the participation of civil society (Article I-50) – is also intended to make the European Union more approachable and understandable. The EP, as it has always done, will meet in public. So too now will the Council when considering and voting on legislation. Furthermore, Article I-50 affirms the right of access, of all residents, to documents of the Union's institutions and bodies, although there are restrictions noted here and in Article III-399 which some feel make it no more than a mere gesture. The idea of 'good governance' also presumably includes the principle set out in Article I-46 that decisions shall be taken 'as openly and as closely as possible to the citizen'. This may be achieved through subsidiarity. However, whether people will really be motivated to take more interest in EU affairs than they presently do – and thus come to esteem the Union more – must be a very doubtful proposition.

Finally, *citizens* are the beneficiaries of a new concern. Alongside the restatement of the existing provisions, this now includes safeguards in Article I-51 on the protection of personal data. These follow on from the broad commitment in the existing treaties to respect fundamental rights and extend to all EU bodies the application of provisions introduced by the Treaty of Amsterdam. A declaration notes, however, that there are exceptions where the protection has implications for national security.

Where citizens wish to complain about maladministration, Article I-49 reminds us that they may turn to the independent European Ombudsman elected (rather than, as formerly, appointed) by the EP. Operational since 1995, the Ombudsman received over 8,000 complaints and pursued 1,100 inquiries between 2000 and 2003. Around 30 per cent of complaints were within its mandate, two-thirds of them concerning the Commission. By contrast, the UK office has an annual caseload of approximately 2,300. The Ombudsman wanted to be made an institution, but the authors of the Constitutional Treaty insisted on treating the post as part of democratization.

Most assessments of what the Constitutional Treaty does to address the democratic deficit view its reforms positively. Yet, their contribution to reducing the gap between the European Union and its citizens will depend on their implementation and the extent to which citizens choose to make use of the various options that exist to influence the Union. The early stages of ratification did not bode well. Despite the attempts to make the Constitutional Treaty and the European Union more citizen-oriented, there was little evidence that people were either interested or felt well informed. Nor was there much evidence of a willingness to use the new, or existing, channels for making their views felt. This reflects the general lack of popular interest in governmental processes and a disaffection with politics. So the Union cannot do more than provide new possibilities.

This is not to deny that the European Union could do more to promote popular engagement and affinity. But, it raises the question of whether simply altering structures and procedures is enough. Citizens need to feel that the Union belongs to them and brings them benefits. In the past, the answer was often to spend money on them. Over time, however, this has become an increasingly less viable option, not least because of the changing financial position of the European Union, to which we now turn.

Finance

The financing of the European Union is an aspect of the Constitutional Treaty that is of great concern to the United Kingdom given that debate on the merits or otherwise of the Union was for many years dominated by financial cost–benefit analyses of membership and a parochial obsession with the rebate that was negotiated in 1984. While the issue may not be as prominent as it was during the Thatcher governments, it still casts its shadow. No UK government would ever dare to consider, publicly at least, unilaterally foregoing the rebate. Scrapping the *chèque britannique,* as Jacques Chirac wishes, is simply not up for discussion, even if – in an enlarged European Union where the Common Agricultural Policy accounts for far less of the budget than it ever did, and the British economic situation is much improved – the rebate appears increasingly anachronistic and distinctly non-communautaire. Unsurprisingly, the UK government went into the 2003 IGC determined to defend the status quo; as regards maintaining the veto over any changes to the rebate, the government achieved its objectives.

However, the Constitutional Treaty does alter the way the European Union goes about financing its activities, but it does this in a way which seeks to address some existing problems and concerns. By writing in the member states' ultimate control over the amount spent, increasing EP influence and stressing financial control, Title VII on the Union's finances shows up the limiting nature of the Constitutional Treaty, and even some improvement in style. However, due to Spanish demands, the new procedures will not be operative for some time.

Part I details *basic principles and procedures* but leaves detailed provisions on the EU budget to Articles III-402 to 416. For the most part, its content draws on existing provisions and, where this is not the case, effectively formalizes existing practice. So, according to Article I-53, the budget is to be annual and include estimates of all items of revenue and expenditure. It must balance – unlike national budgets, which may be in deficit– and all expenditure must be authorized not just by the Council, as is currently the case, but also by the EP, thanks to a switch to the ordinary legislative procedure.

In addition, implementation of the expenditure requires legislation and must be pursued in accordance with the principle of sound financial management, with the European Union and the member states being committed to countering fraud and other legal activities. Presently, the Commission alone is responsible. Furthermore, in order to maintain budgetary discipline, no acts that might have 'appreciable implications' for the budget may be adopted unless they can be financed within the limits of what are referred to as the Union's 'own resources' and in line with the 'multiannual financial framework'.

The first of these is the focus of Article I-54, which obliges the European Union – the member states and the institutions – to provide the 'means necessary to attain its objectives and carry through its policies'. The *revenue* comes from three main sources, although these are not identified in the Constitutional Treaty: traditional resources, comprising customs duties and duties on agricultural products; income from member states' VAT receipts; and member state contributions based on gross national income. These can be changed, as the Constitutional Treaty notes, with new and existing categories being created or abolished. Both require the unanimous agreement of the member states and ratification by national parliaments. For the UK government, this provides a double-lock on the maintenance of the budget rebate. No such lock is envisaged for 'implementing measures', however. With the Constitutional Treaty it will be possible for these to be adopted by a qualified majority in the Council, provided the EP gives its consent and the overall agreement on own resources allows the changes.

So how are the funds raised – currently around €120 billion – actually spent? Here, the Constitutional Treaty introduces the key idea of the '*multiannual financial framework*' (Article I-55). This is not new because it has been used since the mid-1980s under the unhelpful title of 'Financial Perspectives'. But by writing it in now, the Constitutional Treaty makes it clear that not merely must the European Union not overspend but that all its spending must be limited to what the member states and the EP have agreed. This is not something we would expect to find in a superstate.

The framework, which covers at least five years, is there to ensure that expenditure develops in 'an orderly manner' and 'within the limits' of the Union's own resources. It sets out annual ceilings for expenditure under categories corresponding to the major areas of EU activity (see Table 5.7) and is agreed by the member states in the Council, although it must receive the approval of an absolute majority of the EP's members. Initially, the Council will act by unanimity, primarily due to Dutch insistence, yet assuming the European Council can at some future point reach unanimous agreement, the Council may be authorized to proceed on the basis of a qualified majority.

Once the framework has been agreed, annual budgets will be decided in line with a separate procedure based on existing practice. As Article I-56 notes, all this is set out in Article III-404, which also simplifies the current procedure in so far as the arcane distinction between 'compulsory' and 'non-compulsory expenditure' is ditched. This means that the EP is granted full co-decision powers over the annual budget. Currently it has only a limited say over 'non-compulsory expenditure'.

The *changes* included in the Constitutional Treaty – and they extend in Part III to include a new duty on member states to accept control and audit obligations in implementing the budget, reflecting the fact that much of the fraud and poor accounting in the European Union is down to the member states – help clarify how the Union is financed and who decides the budget. The combination of an enhanced role for the EP and the absence of any mention of the old distinction between non-compulsory and compulsory

Table 5.7 The EU-25 budget 2004–2006*

	2004 Euro	2005 Euro	%	2006 Euro
Agriculture	49,305	51,439	43.07	52,618
Common agricultural policy	*42,769*	*44,598*	*37.35*	*45,502*
Rural development	*6,536*	*6,841*	*5.73*	*7,116*
Structural actions	41,035	42,441	35.54	44,617
Structural funds	*35,353*	*37,247*	*31.19*	*38,523*
Cohesion fund	*5,682*	*5,194*	*4.35*	*6,094*
Internal policies	8,722	9,012	7.55	9,385
External policies	5,082	5,119	4.29	5,269
Administration	5,983	6,185	5.18	6,528
Reserves	442	446	0.37	458
Pre-accession aid	3,455	3,472	2.91	3,566
Compensation (10 new members)	1,410	1,305	1.09	1,074
Total	**115,434**	**119,419**	**100.00**	**123,515**

Source: European Commission, *Technical Adjustment of the Financial Perspective for 2006 in Line with Movements in GNI and Prices*, COM(2004) 837 final, Brussels, 28 December 2004, Annex 1.

Note
*In thousands, at current prices.

expenditure – which included the CAP and was not subject to EP control – suggests that the Constitutional Treaty could pave the way for further reductions in agricultural spending.

What the changes do not do, however, is determine the actual size of the budget, despite suggestions that the current maximum of 1.27 per cent of EU GDP be included. What the Constitutional Treaty sets out in terms of the European Union's activities heavily influences what the budget must cover, but the amount of expenditure needed is left to negotiation. This explains why, in the midst of the ratification process, there is ongoing debate on the next multiannual financial framework for 2007–2013, all of which will be decided using existing procedures. This helps underline the point made earlier that treaty provisions provide frameworks in which institutions operate, decisions are made and policies implemented. Much of the rest is left to an ongoing process of negotiation. Nonetheless, finance is one area where the Constitutional Treaty clearly improves on present arrangements.

External role

The Constitutional Treaty is very much about what the European Union can and should do for its members. For the most part, the emphasis is on internal EU policy. Yet it also makes it clear that, in line with its basic values (Article I-3), one of the Union's objectives is to contribute to encouraging peace, justice and solidarity throughout the world. So the new European Union has a range of external roles to play, whether through trade, the common foreign and security policy (CFSP) or enlargement. Each of these is referred to in Part I which, in giving greater prominence to external relations and membership, seeks to show how seriously the Union intends to take its external role.

The days when the European Union could be accused of being an economic giant but a political dwarf are essentially gone, at least in a European context where enlargement has been and continues to be used to promote economic and political security. But it is also increasingly true internationally, even if the Union has not established itself as the effective counterbalance to US influence on the world stage that some federalists wish. Critics may persist in accusing the European Union of policy weaknesses and failures at times of international crises – notably over the former Yugoslavia and, more recently, over Iraq – but the evidence is that the gap between what the European Union aspires to do and what it has the capacity to achieve is narrowing. Part I reminds us of this with its attempts to identify common diplomatic interests, new references to a 'common security and defence policy' and a 'special relationship' with its neighbours as well as with institutional innovations such as the creation of a Union Minister for Foreign Affairs.

This is not to say that the Constitutional Treaty heralds any major changes in the substance of the Union's external relations. What it does is restate the roles and aspirations found in the existing treaties, give recognition to ongoing developments, notably regarding security and defence, and provide the European Union with new and improved mechanisms for implementing policy objectives. As such, it either promotes or formalizes a number of processes that have been taking place over the last decade. It does not represent a significant departure from existing practices, and certainly not one which either replaces national foreign policies or which will see member states' foreign ministries and diplomatic services usurped by, or become subordinate to, the Union.

The pillar structure of the European Union may have been abolished, but the Constitutional Treaty maintains the CFSP as a policy run on essentially intergovernmental lines and outside the threefold classification of normal EU competences (Article I-12), even if the existence of a Union Minister for Foreign Affairs is a further sign of institutionalization. Similarly, the goal of a common defence may have been brought marginally closer, but a common EU army is still a distant, and probably unrealistic, prospect. Assertions that the Constitutional Treaty creates an EU force with a Commission-based commander-in-chief designed to rival and ultimately replace NATO are simply false.

What the Constitutional Treaty does in Part I is to sketch out the European Union's external roles in a number of areas and then expand on them in Part III (see Table 5.8), especially in Title V on the Union's 'external action'. One of the first areas to be mentioned is the *common commercial policy*, an area in which the European Union has exclusive competence. This has been used to develop a vast network of bilateral and multilateral trade agreements with non-member states and provides the basis for the Union – through the Commission – to act as a single entity in various international negotiations within the framework of the World Trade Organization. Second, the European Union has a competence to carry out a common policy covering *development cooperation and humanitarian aid*. This is to complement, not replace, the policies of the member states.

Third, the European Union can now conclude *international agreements*, such as association agreements, in those areas where it has the competence to act internally. These can be restricted to single issues (e.g. the euro, for which special procedures apply) or cover a comprehensive range of policy areas, as many of the agreements with states seeking EU membership have done over the last decade or so. Previously, such treaty-making power was invested only in the EC, although the Treaty of Nice went some way to extend it to the European Union as a whole. In granting the Union legal personality, the Constitutional Treaty completes the process and, as we have seen, reduces some of the present legal complexities. Equally, while EU agreements with non-member states or organizations bind the member states, they are far from exhaustive in their coverage and do not prevent member states developing their bilateral relations as long as these do not conflict with those of the European Union.

The fourth area of external action is the *CFSP*, under whose umbrella the common security and defence policy (CSDP) also falls. This whole area is relatively new, dating back to the early 1990s and the actual establishment of

Table 5.8 The EU's external roles

	Part I	*Part III*
Common commercial policy	I-13(1)	III-314 to III-315
Development cooperation and humanitarian aid	I-14(4)	III-316 to III-321
Association and other agreements	I-13(2)	III-323 to III-328
Relations with other organizations	–	III-327
Common foreign and security policy	I-12, I-16, I-28, I-40	III-292 to III-308 and 313
Common security and defence policy	I-41	III-309 to III-313
Neighbourhood policy	I-57	
Enlargement	I-58	

the European Union. The defence dimension is more recent, only really gaining substance following a joint initiative of the UK and French governments at St Malo in 1998 to ensure that the Union has the capacity for autonomous action in international crises. Since then, developments have been rapid. In terms of the CFSP generally, various institutional adjustments were made under the Treaty of Amsterdam and in 2003 a European Security Strategy was adopted. The same year saw the establishment of a European Rapid Reaction Force (ERRF) of 60,000 persons drawn from the member states which would be capable of undertaking the full range of the so-called Petersberg Tasks – peacekeeping, conflict prevention, crisis management and humanitarian assistance – within 60 days. This has been accompanied by the creation of a specialist Military Committee comprising representatives of the member states. Being part of the Council – and not the Commission – it is answerable to the member states.

This emphasis on intergovernmental arrangements for the CFSP and CSDP is maintained under the Constitutional Treaty in Article I-40, even though new posts and structures are established which some view as constraining member state interests. The key new post is the Union Minister for Foreign Affairs. This post, which many see as the Constitutional Treaty's main innovation in external relations, replaces the 'High Representative for the CFSP' and will be responsible for ensuring the consistency of the Union's external relations in general, a task facilitated by the post-holder presiding over meetings of member state foreign ministers in the Council and being a member of the Commission. This is likely to involve a difficult balancing act. And, although the Foreign Affairs Council is now formally detached from the General Affairs Council, the Minister's powers are limited by the need to secure consensus.

The position may also be complicated by the involvement of the new President of the European Council, who is to ensure the Union's external representation on CFSP and related matters. This reflects the fact that the European Council also sees its role enhanced, since it is here that the European Union will develop its overall external strategies. The EP is also made a sounding board for external policies.

Such developments will further the institutionalization and 'Brusselsization' of the CFSP, particularly given the creation of a European External Action Service of seconded national diplomats and the establishment of a European Defence Agency to identify operational requirements and encourage improvements in member states' military capabilities. This is introduced because of the limited success of previous initiatives aimed at developing the actual military capacity of the European Union. It shows that decisions concerning the CFSP generally, as well as those concerning the CSDP and the two new bodies, remain firmly in the hands of the member states acting, for the most part, unanimously and certainly after consultation. Moreover, implementation of any CFSP measures is to be done by the EU Minister for Foreign Affairs *and* the member states. The Constitutional Treaty makes it very clear that without the member states there can be no foreign or security policies. Thus Article I-41(5) envisages groups of states being entrusted with key tasks.

The Constitutional Treaty does, however, require that member states 'actively and unreservedly support' the CFSP 'in a spirit of loyalty and mutual solidarity' and refrain from action contrary to the Union's interests. This wording, contrary to the claims of eurosceptics, is far from new, having been agreed in Maastricht in 1991 in a more binding form. The intention of the European Union to frame a common defence policy 'that might lead to a common defence' is of the same vintage, although the Constitutional Treaty does now assume that the European Council will ultimately, and unanimously, agree to create a common defence, though exactly what is meant by this is somewhat unclear. A common European defence force may therefore emerge in time. Such an eventuality could possibly see the European Union displacing NATO as the organization responsible for defence in Europe. There is no certainty here, since any decision will require unanimous agreement, and the Constitutional Treaty seeks to reassure those fearful of such a scenario by stating that commitments and cooperation under the CSDP shall be consistent with member states' commitments as NATO members.

It also emphasizes that for the 19 member states that are also members of NATO – i.e. including France and Germany – NATO remains the 'foundation of their collective defence and the forum for its implementation'. Similar guarantees are provided to neutral states who dislike most forms of militarization. They are therefore allowed (Article I-41(7)) to stay outside the mutual defence undertakings of the other member states. Yet with the Constitutional Treaty allowing enhanced cooperation in all areas of the CFSP and encouraging 'permanent structured cooperation' on defence matters between interested member states, the status quo is unlikely to survive.

The fifth area in which the Constitutional Treaty provides for Union engagement beyond its borders is in what is now called its own *neighbourhood* (Article I-57). By this is meant mainly countries to the south and east of the enlarged Union. Such explicit reference to the neighbourhood is relatively new – although a similar policy was launched in 2002 – and follows recognition of the fact that the ongoing process of enlargement provides the European Union with new neighbours and that existing arrangements may need revising. It provides the Union with a new mechanism – somewhere short of association – for developing relations. And given that its emergence coincides with the development of a European Neighbourhood Policy, it can be expected that the relationship will not be designed explicitly to lead to EU membership.

This brings us to the final area of EU engagement with the world outside: *enlargement*. Article I-58 sets out the mechanisms by which a state can join, provided it respects the Union's values and is committed to promoting them. Beyond this, it says little, except that enlargement requires unanimous agreement of the member states. Enlargement has nevertheless become a major instrument in the Union's toolbox for managing its external relations with much of the wider Europe. Pre-accession partnerships, financial assistance, regular reports and accession negotiations have provided the European Union with considerable opportunities to promote reform in non-member states. Provided the carrot of membership appears genuine, then this brings influence and contributes to the strengthening of the Union as the core of a regional European integration process. With enlargement set to continue – witness the controversy over accepting Turkey as a future member – this will remain the case. Whether this will enable the European Union to project itself on the world stage, as many in the Convention wished, remains to be seen.

States in the 'new' Union

The last theme to be examined is, for many people, the crucial one and the question which determines their appreciation of the Constitutional Treaty as a whole. What does the document do to the balance between member states and the new Union? Does it demote the former and turn them into helpless provinces of a new centralized superstate, or (less emotively) does it reinforce the power of the institutions at the expense of the states? Or, conversely, does it reinforce the power of the member states, better define the division of competences and bring in national parliaments, thus blocking off further integration? Is it, in other words, the endgame in the creation of a superstate, brought about by strengthening the power of the EU institutions, or even 'the eurosceptics charter', which precisely prevents this by the way it reinforces state power, recognizing that the collectivity of states is the ultimate authority in the Union? Such preconceptions are a major obstacle to understanding what the Constitutional Treaty actually says.

The answer is that neither is true because the Constitutional Treaty does not change the existing balance all that much. There are points at which the European Union and its institutions gain: symbolically, structurally and through changes in decision making. However, many of these apparent gains are either limited or simply carried over from the past. It is equally true that – as many fervent supporters of integration realized to their dismay – the

Constitutional Treaty goes out of its way to respect the rights and influence of the member states (see Table 5.9). Hence, while there are obligations on the member states, there are also symbolic and procedural guarantees for them. So it is possible to see the Constitutional Treaty as shifting the balance somewhat towards the member states. For some, they are the essential EU institution even if the Treaty does not say so. In other words, the Constitutional Treaty does not really succeed in setting out exactly what the division of responsibilities now is. The outcome, as we have already suggested, is yet another fudged compromise. Because the Constitutional Treaty is both a limiting and an empowering document, the European Union is, and will remain, an unusual mixture of the supranational and the intergovernmental.

For some critics, the *member states lose out in a variety of ways*, beginning with the very fact of the new draft setting itself up as a 'constitution' and not the normal state-based treaty. The fact that the Preamble commits the European Union to forging a common destiny (and the commitment to 'ever closer union' is repeated in Part II) leads some to believe that, under the Constitutional Treaty, the Union is still on line for far more integration. Indeed it makes it much more of a state with its own leadership, personality and, especially, symbols. Hence, the Constitutional Treaty opens the way to a loss of control, creeping competence and new obligations, via new transfers of power and new modalities. This threatens the very existence of member states and their autonomy or, less emotively, transfers too much power from states to institutions.

Table 5.9 States in the EU

	Part I	*Part III*
Principle of conferral	I-1(1), I-11(1)	III-115
Relations of member states and the EU	I-5	III-122
Subsidiarity	I-11, I-18(2)	III-111, III-259
Competences	I-12 to I-16	III-122, III-205, III-308, III-315, III-417, III-445
Voting	I-25(1)	III-179, III-184, III-194, III-198, III-312, III-396
Solidarity	I-40(5), I-43(1)	III-294, III-298, III-305, III-329
Autonomous action	I-41(2), I-44	III-131, III-299
Democratic obligations	I-2, I-59	–
Withdrawal	I-60	–
EMU	I-15, I-30(4)	III-197, III-198
National parliaments	I-18, I-43, I-46, I-58	III-259-61, III-273, III-276, IV-443, IV-444
Loyalty to the Union	I-5, I-16	III-294

Not all these claims stand up to close examination. Thus the creation of President of the European Council is something which aids the member states rather than threatens them. By giving the European Council a permanent chair, with relatively limited powers and a brief to achieve consensus and continuity, the member states are more likely to be able to imprint their will on the European Union. Equally, the establishment of the Union Foreign Minister merely replaces two existing offices with one office, which, again, is obliged to share power with the states and to seek consensus. This suggests that the authors of the Constitutional Treaty were well aware that the member states can be divided and recalcitrant. Nor is it certain that there will be a Public Prosecutor. So, while it is true that the creation of such offices will give the European Union a more visible face and, possibly, greater efficiency, it is unlikely to change the status quo. In any case, in making appointments to such offices the Union is required to respect geographical balance among the member states.

Equally, much has also been made of the facts that the new European Union will have legal personality and primacy. However, as we have argued, neither of these is as new or as dramatic as has been claimed. Legal personality merely allows the Union to function internationally and to deny it would render the Union impotent. It does not mean that states lose their own treaty-making power.

Where primacy is concerned, some believe that the principle has been phrased in a relatively moderate way to take account of UK reservations. It does not seem to apply to national constitutions, only to laws. Elsewhere the Constitutional Treaty makes it clear that national constitutions are to be respected. Against this, critics would point out that in Article I-1 states come second to citizens, and it is true that the Constitutional Treaty does mean to set up a dual legitimacy.

Nonetheless, as we have argued, primacy and personality do not constitute an unchecked right to overrule national decisions nor, historically, have they prevented member states from defying treaty and court rulings. Even the introduction of fines has not stopped this, and it is doubtful that the speeding up of the process permitted by Article III-362 will make much difference. Moreover, primacy does not apply as widely as is sometimes thought.

When it comes to symbols, too much should not be made of the use of the term 'constitution' as signifying a qualitative change. As we have already shown, the distinction between a treaty and a constitution can be overdrawn, as can its links to statehood. It does mean that the EU's rules do take on greater authority. But this is because of the member states' own decisions. In Article I-5, which was written in by state representatives during the Convention, it is clear that only states confer powers on the Union, admittedly through the Constitutional Treaty rather than as 'High Contracting Parties' as in the past. States are also recognized both as the source of democratic values and rights and as having their own identities and rights, including control of citizenship. The European Union is also excluded from questions regarding national security.

It does seem that the inclusion of Article 1-8 is meant to suggest that the new Union has an enhanced political standing at the expense of the member states. But it might equally be argued that the insistence on the euro as a symbol makes it harder to avoid. In practice of course, the anthem, the currency, the flag and the day already exist and have done for some years. Rejecting the Constitutional Treaty would not change this though it might prevent the use of the motto: 'United in Diversity'. So the Constitutional Treaty recognizes the status quo, though the changes do emphasize the EU's political nature.

Where the exercise of power is concerned, it is certainly true both that the scope of unanimity is diminished – being replaced by QMV in some 27 areas – and that the European Council can switch more to QMV if it decides unanimously. Unanimity remains in key areas such as taxation, social security and finance. Crucially, the European Union does not have the power to decide on its own competences. Foreign policy also remains subject to special rules. Eurosceptics have also contested the idea that national action appears to be excluded in shared competences if the Union has already acted, although this goes against the rules that member states' policies cannot be harmonized unless this is specifically provided for.

It is also true that the Constitutional Treaty imposes a series of *obligations on member states*, which some have seen as limiting their freedom of action. They are required to be democratic (Article I-2) and can suffer sanctions if they depart from this. They are also seen (Article I-5) as having obligations to the European Union, such as fulfilling legal duties and not hindering the EU's work, which is a fairly obvious necessity for any voluntary organization. The requirement of 'loyal cooperation' has been much criticized, as has the request in Article I-43 to act in solidarity. However, the way the former is formulated is probably less restrictive than that in the existing treaties, while the fact that the European Union has to ask for solidarity shows the reality of the situation: that whatever they may have signed up to, states put their own interests first and have to be persuaded to think of others.

Moreover, contrary to the old Article 6 TEU, the European Union itself now has obligations to its member states (Article I-5(2)). Article I-1 also sees the Union as restricted to coordinating policies which the member states have decided are necessary to achieve their common objectives, and not, as now, coordinating peoples and member states. Admittedly, Article I-15 does subject member states to coordination in the socio-economic field, but this is already the case. Interestingly, Part III provides for voluntary measures to help states improve their administrative capacity to do this. This points well away from a US-style Federal power.

So, the evidence of the Constitutional Treaty is mixed. It is clear that the Constitutional Treaty changes the rules in ways which will lead to more being done through the institutions. It also gives the European Union a more political feel. But this is far from creating a superstate in which member states have all their autonomy taken away from them. If any thing, the real criticism is that the Constitutional Treaty does not handle the problem consistently.

Hence, it is also possible, as we have already seen, to read the Constitutional Treaty differently: as curbing supranational integration and enhancing the *essential role of the member states*. Thus the fact that the new Union gets all its powers – not to mention its finances – from grants from the latter, through the principle of 'conferral' laid down in Article I-1, is highly significant. This has not been said before, any more than has the statement that powers not conferred on the European Union remain with the member states (Article I-11). This is a slightly grudging recognition of the essential sovereignty of member states, although some commentators see the formulation as actually tighter than what exists in Article 5 TEC. This is because conferral is linked to specific powers and not to the Union as such, suggesting that the European Union remains a functional association and not a state. The placing of the institutional chapters of the Constitutional Treaty after the policy articles also points in this direction. States are also recognized as the source of both democratic values and civil rights, as in Article I-9. And citizenship is based on nationality.

Elsewhere the European Union is committed to recognizing the foundations of member states: constitutional structures, identity and regalian powers. Their multiplicity and diversity is also something the Union sees itself as preserving. States can also now act as a group in the specific circumstances laid down in Articles I-41 and 42. The IGC's upping of the percentages of member states needed to pass legislation also helps the latter.

Member states now also count because of their size and not just because of their sovereignty, though not everyone is happy with this. However, they retain their rights to representation in all the institutions. And, despite the references to the people and states as the essential basis of the European Union, only states – all of which are equal, irrespective of size – can actually join it. There is also a clear recognition in Article I-40 that the Union's foreign policy rests on states getting together. They are also recognized as having their own resources and their own rights of proposal in diplomatic affairs and foreign policy orientations, not to mention their own role in overseas aid. Equally, in Article I-43, they are seen as a separate element in solidarity, along with the Union.

One often overlooked strength of the member states is that they are responsible for implementing virtually all EU legislation. However, this is a real power because the European Union as such is, by implication, debarred from implanting laws itself. One early draft explicitly established the member states as the implementing authority of the Union, but the final Constitutional Treaty restricts itself to accepting, in Article I-12, that they do actually implement legislation. It gives them some freedom of action since, where the legislation is a framework law, they can pass regulations on what are otherwise exclusive competences of the Union. Hence, the European Union cannot work without the member states.

Beyond this the Constitutional Treaty also provides the member states with a series of *guarantees* which allow them to defend their position. Some of these derive from what was not included in the Constitutional Treaty, such as ideas of a small executive Commission with an elected President. These would have had a dramatic effect on the nature and balance of the European Union. However, most relate to more positive provisions, whether procedural, structural or those involving subsidiarity. And there is now a right of unimpeded exit.

Procedurally, the member states are protected by things like the principles of conferral and proportionality in Article I-11, which, like the necessity for respect of national identities, places restraints on the way the European Union treats its member states. Articles I-12(5), 17 and 18 also provide that the Union cannot interfere with national sovereignty when exercising supporting competences or flexibility. At the same time, institutions are, by Article I-19, required to work for the interest of member states, among others. All these things can be invoked before the Court of Justice by dissatisfied states. And four member states can block a qualified majority.

When states are in difficulties with the Union they also have a number of rights under the Constitutional Treaty. Thus, if they are unhappy about foreign policy matters, they have to be consulted and can even refer the issue up to the European Council if necessary. They also have to be heard if they are accused of defaulting on their democratic rights obligations. Equally, states not participating in enhanced cooperation also have a voice. And, of course, if they are not involved in something like EMU they cannot be forced to take part, even if they are required to consider the European implications of their policies.

Structurally, the member states' dominance of the reformed European Council, and the continuation of rotating presidencies in most sectoral Councils, is a further guarantee that their wishes cannot be overruled. The upgrading of the 'multiannual financial framework', with its unanimity requirement, places a real constraint on the Union's financial powers. The procedural rules on things like energy resources, development policy and the right to refer certain questions up to the European Council, reflecting the old Luxembourg veto, are also significant. Furthermore, constitutional revision is subject to a state-lock in most cases.

Even more important than this is the new involvement of national parliaments in the political life of the European Union. From being on the fringes, national parliaments have been brought into the constitutional main stream – thanks to a wider and more emphatic role – in line with the recognition that they are one of the bases of representative democracy. Parliaments now have equal rights of information with other interests (such as the EP) so that they can exercise a monitoring role. They also have a right to give a yellow card to the Commission if enough of them think the latter's proposals breach subsidiarity rules. This also applies when the Union's competences may be extended through the flexibility rule or in the area of freedom, security and justice. They also have a power of oversight of Europol and Eurojust, together with a right of notification about new applications for membership (Article I-58). While some eurosceptics deride this as a mere fig leaf, and worry that the right of petition threatens national parliaments, it is taken seriously by others who see it as a threat to the EP and a way of transferring powers back to the member states – assuming it works properly and does not lead to destabilizing oppositionism.

Subsidiarity itself has also been given more emphasis, even though it remains restricted to areas where the European Union lacks exclusive competence, something which is now more narrowly defined. The Charter indicates it is now a sort of right of citizens. All institutions are required to take it into consideration, and legislative acts have to carry a virtual certificate of compliance. Moreover, the Commission has to consult more widely, monitor its legislation for compliance and draw national parliaments' attention to acts where the principle is involved. It will have to think again if a third objects. If this fails, national parliaments can ask their governments to take the case to the ECJ. This is a real channel for influence if national parliaments can get their act together.

Finally, Article I-60 now provides states with an unprecedented right to leave the European Union and thus go back on their original conferral of power. All that is required is that the departing state decides constitutionally in its own terms. It has the facility of negotiating an act of secession but, if this cannot be done, it will find itself outside two years after notifying the European Union of its wish to leave. This is very different from now.

All this adds up to a substantial body of evidence that the Constitutional Treaty does not sweep states away and subvert their sovereignty. Ultimately, they create the European Union and not vice versa. The drafters were all too aware that members remain sovereign states before they are constituents of the Union. Admittedly, this is not the scenario desired by the eurosceptic minority report, which wanted a treaty-based arrangement in which laws were only passed in a limited number of areas and would only be valid if passed by a majority of the national parliaments, who would also elect the Commission. Equally, it is true that the Constitutional Treaty makes the European Union more cohesive and effective, but it remains far from a state, let alone a superstate. The text does not, despite some of the wilder criticisms, endow the Union with its own self-contained army, customs service, local government, police force or tax collectors.

The only sensible way to look at the European Union is as a body based on an inherent tension between individual national action and collective state action through the institutions. This is a partly streamlined version of the existing situation. Because of this tension and of their continuing fears, the member states have continued to impose complicated rules to control what they have collectively agreed. And, though these rules may be disliked and misunderstood by the public, they are often there because of government fears of public displeasure over the extent of integration.

All this is important practically and symbolically and makes the dual legitimacy of the European Union very clear. This is certainly the view of those who lament the maintenance of so many 'vetoes' and 'opt-outs'. Indeed, the Constitutional Treaty writes the key EMU opt-out into the treaty proper in Article I-30(4). They also appear in the Protocols. So, as a matter of principle, the member states are recognized as the ultimate basis of the Union. However, it would be wrong to assume that the member states have now taken over from the institutions, or vice versa. The Constitutional Treaty says nothing like this. It merely tweaks the existing balance so that member states and institutions both have something to gain from it.

In any case, talking of the tension between states and the European Union implies that the member states are a homogenous block. In fact they are very divided, often between smaller and larger states, when it comes to institutional questions. The Constitutional Treaty struggles to treat all states equally, but its new decision-making procedures have probably tipped the balance towards the larger states in some areas. Hence smaller states may well continue to look to the Commission and other institutions as their defender, a fact which makes it harder than ever to see the new balance as anything but complicated and subtle. This shows up not just in Part I but also in the rest of the Constitutional Treaty, to which we now turn.

6 Parts II–IV and beyond

An introduction

Although we have, for reasons of space and simplicity, concentrated on Part I of the Constitutional Treaty, we have to remember that it is only part of a larger document. Indeed, several of the things which worry people are contained in the other three Parts and, perhaps, even in the Protocols and Declarations which follow. These both add to the constitutional nature of the document and emphasize its status as a treaty. Moreover, much of the detail concerning the policy competences and workings of the European Union is contained in these Parts. So, while we cannot print the whole text or go into a great deal of analysis, we think it is important to outline the main points of Parts II–IV and what follows and provide a brief assessment of their significance.

Part II

The first of the Constitutional Treaty's three other Parts is the Charter of Fundamental Rights, now installed as Part II. This is not a new text, but its presence gives the Constitutional Treaty a more constitutional feel. Its detailed provisions also provide some added value to the status quo in that citizen's rights are now set out more clearly in a politically symbolic and legally binding document. However, the extent of its influence can be exaggerated.

As we have seen, the Charter was originally drawn up in 1999–2000 by a dedicated convention. Its purpose was to consolidate in a single document the rights that EU citizens already enjoy as a consequence of the existing treaties, the European Convention on Human Rights and the constitutional traditions common to the member states. This it did, and without too much attention being paid to its work. Indeed, the then UK Minister for Europe, Keith Vaz, dismissed it as irrelevant. Nonetheless, it came into effect after the Nice Council of December 2000.

Partly in order not to waste the work carried out then and partly to avoid raising hackles in the United Kingdom, where some saw it as infringing on national and business freedom of action, no substantive changes to the text were made by either the Convention or the IGC. All that has altered is that the articles have been renumbered and that various provisions on interpretation and application have been revised at the behest of the UK government. That the Charter is the same as that proclaimed in 2000 is reflected in the fact that, unconventionally, its preamble has been retained and has not been incorporated into the one which opens the Constitutional Treaty. This set the Charter apart from the rest of the Constitutional Treaty. However, much to the annoyance of those eurosceptics and others who thought that all traces of the phrase had been wiped from the treaty text, 'ever closer union' among the peoples of Europe appears in the opening line.

What follows is less a charter for further integration, but more an attempt to clarify what the member states and the Union's institutions see as the values on which the European Union is founded and the role that the Union plays in their preservation and development. It is nevertheless made clear that the protection of fundamental rights needs to be strengthened in the light of social change and scientific and technological developments. How this is to be achieved is not made clear, although Article I-9 provides some guidance, noting that rights constitute general principles of EU law.

The rights contained in the Charter are dealt with in six Titles (see Box 6.1). The first concerns 'dignity', and it starts by establishing that human dignity is 'inviolable' and must be 'respected and protected'. The next articles confirm the right to life and to the physical and mental integrity of the person and contain provisions that outlaw torture, the death penalty, the sale of human organs and the cloning of human beings. The fourth and final article prohibits slavery, compulsory labour and trafficking in human beings.

Box 6.1 Part II: an outline

The Charter of Fundamental Rights of the Union

Preamble		
Title I	Dignity	II-61 to II-65
Title II	Freedoms	II-66 to II-79
Title III	Equality	II-80 to II-86
Title IV	Solidarity	II-87 to II-98
Title V	Citizens' rights	II-99 to II-106
Title VI	Justice	II-107 to II-110
Title VII	General provisions governing the interpretation and application of the Charter	II-111 to II-114

Having set out what cannot be done to people, the second Title lists the range of economic, social and political freedoms that the people within the European Union enjoy. It starts with the right to liberty and security, a right which the area of freedom, security and justice is designed to ensure. There then follows the right of privacy and a number of family-related rights, including the right to respect for one's home life and the right to marry and found a family. This last, it is made clear, is guaranteed by national laws. Title II also covers data protection rights, freedom of thought, conscience, religious belief, expression, assembly and association, the 'freedom and pluralism' of the media, and academic freedom. Each of these is simply stated without any definition being provided. The right to education and access to vocational training is spelt out, as are the freedoms to conduct business and choose an occupation and the right to engage in work, although the right to seek employment is restricted to EU citizens. No such restriction is imposed on the right to own and use property, although Denmark, as a later Protocol notes, has restrictions where second residences are concerned. And there is a public interest exemption to the right not to be deprived of one's possessions. The protection of intellectual property is also provided for. The final two articles then turn to asylum and extradition. This first is guaranteed in line with the international law commitments of the member states, while the latter is outlawed in cases where extradited individuals risk death or torture. The collective expulsion of peoples is also prohibited.

Title III deals with equality, whether before the law or between women and men. It also commits the European Union to respect cultural, religious and linguistic diversity. This echoes provisions found in Title II in Part III on non-discrimination and, even more so, in Article II-81, which prohibits discrimination 'based on any ground such as sex, race, colour, ethnic or social origin, genetic features, language, religion or belief, political or any other opinion, membership of a national minority, property, birth, disability, age or sexual orientation'. This is, to some extent, reinforced in Title II of Part III. The rights and protection of children and the rights of the elderly are then set out, before the Title concludes with a statement on the rights of people with disabilities.

The fourth Title deals with solidarity in the sense of the socio-economic rights of workers and individuals. Workers have a right to information and consultation – a right echoing the commitments contained in Article I-48 and elsewhere – while a second article on the right to free placement services reflects commitments found in the Union's Social Charter, which was adopted in 1989. Other articles confirm rights against unfair dismissal and rights to fair and just working conditions, especially where health and safety are concerned. Child labour is prohibited, and legal, economic and social protection is to be afforded to the family as a unit. This entails maternity-related rights and the right to paternity leave. The Title then turns to the entitlement – as opposed to the right – to a range of social security benefits and social services. The right of access to preventative healthcare and medical treatment follows. The last three articles echo Articles III-122, 119 and 120 in setting out, respectively, a right of access to 'services of a general economic interest' and the principles of high levels of environmental and consumer protection.

The content of Title V on EU citizens' rights follows very closely the citizenship rights already outlined in Article I-10. The right to vote and stand in elections to the European Parliament and in municipal elections is confirmed, as are the right of access to documents of EU institutions, bodies, offices and agencies, the right to refer cases of maladministration to the European Ombudsman and the right to petition. Following an earlier commitment in Article I-50, the Charter confirms a right to good administration. Two further rights that echo provisions in Article I-10 are also set out: the right to move and reside freely within the European Union and the right to diplomatic and consular representation.

The sixth Title concerns justice and contains just four articles. The first confirms a right to effective remedy and free trial although, in anticipation of what follows in Title VII on implementation of the Charter, it restricts this to instances where an EU citizen's rights under EU law are violated. Fair and public hearings are guaranteed and there is an obligation to provide legal aid to ensure effective access to justice. The second article affirms the principle that a person charged is presumed innocent until proven guilty, and guarantees the right of defence. A third article focuses on the legality of offences and the proportionality of penalties. The final article confirms that individuals will not be tried or punished twice for the same offence.

To supporters of the Charter, the 50 articles containing the various rights of EU citizens and, in most instances, other residents in the European Union are a major step forward, symbolizing the European Union's political nature and its concern for core values. But for some it is a disappointing document in view of its restricted application. This is made clear in Title VII, which notes that the Charter is addressed to the EU institutions, bodies, offices, agencies and member states in the exercise of their respective competences. It is made clear that in the case of the latter, the Charter's provisions apply only when the member states are implementing EU law. It does not apply in other cases and does not constitute a power to overturn national rules. Hence, many rights – notably some of those in the Titles on dignity and solidarity – remain essentially declaratory, although the Charter arguably raises their political profile. Supporters of closer European integration are also likely to be disappointed by article II-111's statement that the Charter neither extends the application of EU law beyond the powers of the

European Union nor establishes any new powers or tasks for the Union. This is also reflected in Article II-112. The Charter is not, therefore, a blueprint for new EU activities, as many of its opponents maintain.

Nonetheless, some still see it as going too far. Employers' associations, for example, argue that it creates new social rights for workers. Others worry about the use that will be made of it by the Court of Justice to advance integration and social regulation. This is to read far more into the text than is actually there and to dismiss the restrictions found in Title VII.

These limiting revisions were included at the insistence of the UK government. It would have preferred that the Charter was merely a protocol, or had even been excluded, but once it became clear that constitutionalizing forces were insistent on including it as a full part of the Constitutional Treaty, the government became intent on ensuring that it should have only limited application and would not create new rights. It is widely accepted that the UK government was successful in achieving its goal. By integrating the Charter into the Constitutional Treaty, its provisions have been given legal and symbolic force, but this is limited to cases involving either the activities of the Union's institutions, bodies and agencies or the implementation of EU law by the member states. Moreover, an updated set of explanations on how the 1999–2000 convention envisaged that the Charter should be interpreted is included in a Declaration.

Equally, however, the Charter should not be regarded as a document that limits existing rights. Where individuals enjoy greater rights as a consequence of national constitutions or international agreements, for example the European Convention on Human Rights, these continue to apply. And it is made clear that no right in the Charter may be used to limit or undermine another right. Moreover, extra rights may come whenever the European Union signs up to the European Convention on Human Rights.

Part III

Generally less controversial, although perhaps more significant, than the Charter of Fundamental Rights is Part III, which is by far the longest and most detailed of the Constitutional Treaty's four Parts. Its content is signalled in Part I, but, as we have seen, the text is not wholly derivative but is, in fact, partly constitutive, setting out in its 322 articles, and often in considerable depth, the key principles, policy competences, external relation responsibilities and institutional framework and organization of the Union. This is reflected in its title: 'The policies and functioning of the Union'

It is divided into seven Titles, several of which contain a series of chapters and in some cases sections and subsections (see Box 6.2). The provisions we find here have, in the overwhelming majority of cases, been taken directly

Box 6.2 Part III: an outline

The policies and functioning of the Union

Title I	Provisions of general application	III-115 to III-122
Title II	Non-discrimination and citizenship	III-123 to III-129
Title III	Internal policies and action	III-130 to III-285
Chapter I	Internal market	III-130 to III-176
Chapter II	Economic and monetary policy	III-177 to III-202
Chapter III	Policies in other areas	III-203 to III-256
Chapter IV	Area of freedom, security and justice	III-257 to III-277
Chapter V	Areas where the Union may take coordinating, complementary or supporting action	III-278 to III-285
Title IV	Association of the Overseas Countries and Territories	III-286 to III-291
Title V	The Union's external action	III-292 to III-229
Chapter I	Provisions having general application	III-292 to III-293
Chapter II	Common foreign and security policy	III-294 to III-313
Chapter III	Common commercial policy	III-314 to III-315
Chapter IV	Cooperation with third countries and humanitarian aid	III-316 to III-321
Chapter V	Restrictive measures	III-322
Chapter VI	International agreements	III-323 to III-326
Chapter VII	The Union's relations with international organizations and third countries and Union delegations	III-327 to III-328
Chapter VIII	Implementation of the solidarity clause	III-329
Title VI	The functioning of the Union	III-330 to III-423
Chapter I	Provisions governing the institutions	III-330 to III-401
Chapter II	Financial provisions	III-402 to III-415
Chapter III	Enhanced cooperation	III-416 to III-423
Title VII	Common provisions	III-424 to III-436

from the existing treaties, albeit with numbers being amended and the provisions usually undergoing some textual changes to simplify the language and accommodate changes in the names of some institutions. The amendments to policy provisions rarely involve increases to the Union's competences. Rather they bring changes to the manner in which decisions will be made, normally through a shift to QMV and/or the ordinary legislative procedure. They also reflect the institutional arrangements laid down in Title IV of Part I.

The first Title contains seven provisions of 'general application' to the Union's activities; that is, principles, drawn from existing practice, which must be applied in all EU policies. Hence, among other things, the European Union must aim to eliminate inequalities, promote equality between men and women, encourage a high level of employment, provide adequate social protection and inclusion, and protect health, the environment and consumers. Equally important is combating discrimination based on sex, racial or ethnic origin, religion or belief, disability, age or sexual orientation. Animals are also to be well treated and 'services of a general economic interest' (essentially public services) maintained. Not surprisingly perhaps, the Title starts with a requirement that the European Union ensure consistency between its different policies and activities. Title II picks up on the idea of non-discrimination as an aspect of citizenship and describes the measures that may be taken in order to implement this.

Title III is by far the longest of the seven as it sets out in detail the various internal policy competences of the European Union and the instruments through which they can be exercised. However, the Title does not fully structure the policy areas according to the new forms of policy competence (e.g. exclusive, shared, complementary). Rather it presents most of them in a series of five chapters according to their centrality to the Union's activities. This was because of a shortage of time and a desire to avoid the difficult questions which would be thrown up by such a re-organization. It also reflects previous practice. However, there is a chapter detailing the areas where the European Union has supporting, coordinating or complementary action.

The first chapter on the internal market contains provisions governing the four basic freedoms – the free movement of good, services, capital and people – and the freedom of establishment, albeit in a re-ordered manner. These are set out in seven sections. Here the emphasis is on the removal of barriers to trade and movement, although there are a number of provisions allowing for limits on free movement to be adopted when war, security or public safety are threatened. A fifth section reiterates present provisions governing competition, the area where the Commission enjoys considerable powers as the independent arbiter on state aids and uncompetitive practices between undertakings. The following section contains one of the most controversial provisions of the Constitutional Treaty – at least from a UK perspective: Article III-171 on fiscal policy and tax harmonization. As has always been the case, decisions here are adopted by unanimity and apply only to indirect taxation – primarily turnover taxes and excise duties – as it affects the functioning of the internal market. As an amendment introduced by the Constitutional Treaty makes clear, their purpose is to prevent distortions to competition. The European Union does not have a competence to harmonize direct taxes, an assumption implicit in the UK debate.

The final section in Chapter I details how internal market legislation is to be adopted, normally through the ordinary legislative procedure with the Council acting by a qualified majority. An exception exists for three policy areas: fiscal policy, the free movement of people, and the social security rights and interests of migrant workers. In these areas, member states either retain a veto since unanimity is required in the Council (fiscal policy and the free movement of people), or can rely on an 'emergency brake' (migrant workers). The emergency brake permits a member state to refer a proposed measure to the European Council when it believes the measure will affect 'fundamental aspects of its social security system'. In such cases the European Council decides by unanimity how to proceed.

Chapter II covers economic and monetary union (EMU), and when the related Protocols are included it contains the most detailed set of institutional and policy provisions in the Constitutional Treaty. Thanks, however, to a paring down and updating of articles in the light of the final stage of EMU and the launch of the euro, the provisions have been rationalized. However, the chapter still opens with a statement of the activities that member states and the European Union are to pursue, essentially the coordination of member states' policies and the definition of common objectives. This is to be pursued 'in accordance with the principle of an open market economy with free competition'. The presence of such a principle has encouraged critics on the left, particularly in France, to view the Constitutional Treaty as reflecting Anglo-Saxon economic thinking. However, the principle has always been implicit in the existing treaties, although it was only included explicitly in 1993.

The role of the European Union regarding economic policy coordination is set out in the first of Chapter II's five sections. Broad policy guidelines are adopted by the European Council, with the Commission then monitoring member states' economic performances. Overall assessments are produced on an annual bases and form part of an approach to policy making known as the 'open method of coordination'. The emphasis here is not on compliance with legislative prescriptions, but on determining best practice and, in effect, shaming poorly performing member states into aligning national economic policy with the guidelines.

While most economic policy activities are to be pursued by all member states, the Constitutional Treaty's provisions regarding government deficits and monetary policy apply to member states to differing degrees, depending on whether they are part of the eurozone, are obliged to join or, like the UK, have an opt-out. Hence, the commitment to a single currency (the euro) and a single monetary policy does not apply. Nor do the sanctions in the associated Stability and Growth Pact which was adopted in 1997 but is now honoured as much in the breach as in the observance.

Provisions in the second section concern monetary policy and outline the roles of the European Central Bank and the European System of Central Banks. Further details are located in two Protocols. Additional institutional provisions regarding EMU are found in the third section, which focuses on the work of the Economic and Financial Committee and the comparatively limited role of the Commission in EMU. A fourth and new section relates specifically to those member states that are in the eurozone and permits them to adopt measures designed to strengthen the coordination and surveillance of budgetary discipline and to adopt additional economic policy guidelines. It also provides for meetings of the Euro Group of eurozone economic and finance ministers – which is governed by a dedicated protocol – and for common positions on EMU-related matters in international fora. The final section of Chapter II details the procedure by which member states outside the eurozone – the so-called 'Member States with a derogation' – may join, and also the extent to which the provisions of the Constitutional Treaty concerning EMU are applicable to them as they move towards membership. In a slight change to the existing rules, the Constitutional Treaty requires that any decision on entry is made on the basis of a recommendation of a qualified majority of the eurozone member states.

Title III's third chapter is loosely titled 'Policies in Other Areas' since it does not contain all remaining policy provisions. The first of its ten sections deals with employment, an area added by the Treaty of Amsterdam and one in which the Union's role is to assist in the coordination of member states' policies through the adoption of guidelines. The objectives are a high level of employment, the promotion of a skilled, trained and adaptable workforce, and labour markets responsive to market changes. The Union's engagement is non-legislative. Instead, the emphasis is on the open method of coordination, with an Employment Committee of member state appointees providing advice.

The second area covered is 'social policy', an unfortunate description for UK readers since it conjures up in the minds of many the notion that the European Union is involved in all areas of social welfare, including health and social services. The misconceptions are compounded by the existence of a Social Fund. The reality is somewhat different. Social policy in the EU context is generally restricted to matters concerning employment and working conditions. And the Social Fund supports measures designed to promote employment opportunities. Most legislation therefore concerns health and safety in the workplace and equal pay. But the European Union also promotes consultation between management and labour at the EU level, and there are areas, such as working conditions and social security, where the Commission is encouraged to promote cooperation between the member states through studies and consultations. Also included is social protection, for which there is a dedicated committee to monitor the social situation in the member states and promote experience and good practice. This all means that, as Article III-210(5) makes clear, a definition of the fundamentals and financing of national social security systems is very much in the hands of the member states. Much the same is true of health matters. Equally, member states are free to take more stringent protective measures.

Section 3 commits the European Union to develop and pursue action leading to a strengthening of its economic, social and, with the Constitutional Treaty, territorial cohesion. This provides the basis for the Union's regional policy for rural areas, areas affected by industrial transition, and island, cross-border and mountain regions. It also contains the legal basis for the European Regional Development Fund, one of the so-called Structural Funds which account for more than 30 per cent of budgetary expenditure. The other Structural Funds are the European Agricultural Guidance and Guarantee Fund, Guidance Section and the European Social Fund. A provision also exists for a Cohesion Fund directed at transport infrastructure. Their tasks, priority objectives and organization are determined by the Council acting unanimously and with the consent of the EP. The Constitutional Treaty provides, however, for an eventual move to majority voting. The ordinary legislative procedure is used for implementing measures.

Agriculture and fisheries are the focus of Section 4. Here, little has changed since the provisions for and objectives of the Common Agricultural Policy (CAP) were first drawn up in the 1950s. Some updating is introduced through the Constitutional Treaty but, more importantly, the decision-making process is changed. Policy under the CAP and the Common Fisheries Policy is now to be determined using the ordinary legislative procedure, thereby increasing the involvement of the EP and denying CAP financing its present protected status.

Section 5 sets out the objectives, principles and scope of the European Union's environment policy. The substance of the articles and principles underpinning policy remain unchanged although the wording has been amended in a number of instances. The same is true of the provisions contained in Section 6 on consumer protection and Section 8 on trans-European networks. In Section 7, on transport, the role of the EP has been increased slightly, and qualified majority voting in the Council now applies to all provisions except those allowing member states' derogations. The scope of the common transport policy remains the same: common rules on international transport; conditions governing non-resident carriers in a member state; measures to improve transport safety; and 'other appropriate measures'.

In Section 9, the Constitutional Treaty extends the scope of EU action with regard to research and technological development to include a reference to space. It also calls for the establishment of a 'European Research Area' in which researchers, knowledge and technology can circulate freely. This reflects an aim that the European Union has been pursuing since 2000.

In terms of substance, the existing provisions generally remain unchanged, although they go into more detail. And more of this is to be decided using the ordinary legislative procedure, such as the substance of a 'European space policy', which the Constitutional Treaty envisages involving joint initiatives and coordinated efforts in 'the exploration and exploitation of space'.

This brings us to the last section of Chapter III, that on energy. This is new, although the European Union has been addressing issues of energy supply and use for more than a decade. What the Constitutional Treaty does is provide EU action with a firm legal base for this. It also sets out its aims: the functioning of the energy market, secure energy supplies, energy efficiency and the development of new and renewable energy forms. Measures are to be adopted by the ordinary legislative procedure and hence by a qualified majority in the Council, although unanimity is required for primarily fiscal measures. Section 10 also makes it clear that no EU measure can affect the right of a member state to exploit its own energy resources and determine its own energy supply, provided it complies with EU environmental policy.

Chapter IV concerns the so-called area of freedom, security and justice. It brings together provisions that currently govern EU activities under Pillars I and III. As such, the 21 articles in this chapter, while corresponding to or drawing heavily on existing provisions, are in many cases new, at least in form. In terms of substance, the status quo is maintained in a variety of ways, although the Constitutional Treaty does introduce a number of institutional and policy changes, some of which reflect existing practice – notably the role of the European Council in setting strategic guidelines. Prominent among the changes are the envisaged evaluation of the extent to which member states live up to their obligations with regard to the area of freedom, security and justice and the role of national parliaments in monitoring compliance with the principle of subsidiarity. UK opt-outs are defined in Protocols.

Set out in Section 1 are the general provisions of the area: respect of both fundamental rights and the different legal systems and traditions of the member states. They also explain the Union's goals: ensuring the absence of internal border controls and framing a common policy on asylum, immigration and external border control. This is to be fair towards third-country nationals and stateless persons. It is also designed to ensure a high level of security and hence involves police and judicial cooperation as well as measures to prevent and combat crime, racism and xenophobia and, if necessary, the approximation of criminal laws.

Section 2 focuses on border checks, asylum and immigration and sets out the specific areas where the European Union may adopt measures. In general, following changes made by the Constitutional Treaty, qualified majority voting and the ordinary legislative procedure are to be used. The Constitutional Treaty is also responsible for a new provision on solidarity and burden-sharing in the implementation of policy. Section 3 is concerned with judicial cooperation in civil matters and, for the first time in the Union's treaty base, establishes the accepted principle that such cooperation should be based on the mutual recognition of judgements. The approximation of member states' laws using the ordinary legislative procedure is also provided for, although unanimity is required where family law is concerned.

Similarly, Section 4 confirms the principle of mutual recognition of judgements, but this time in the area of judicial cooperation in criminal matters, an area not covered by the UK opt-out. It also allows for the approximation of member states' laws and the adoption of measures using qualified majority voting and the ordinary legislative procedure. However, an 'emergency brake' allows a member state which maintains that a proposed measure affects 'fundamental aspects' of its criminal justice system to refer the matter to the European Council. A similar provision exists for other measures to be pursued under Section 4, such as minimum rules concerning the definition of criminal offences and the possible approximation of national criminal laws.

The remainder of the section includes a dedicated provision on cooperation in crime prevention – an area where the harmonization of member states' laws is ruled out – and rules governing the operation of Eurojust, the EU body established in 2002 to improve the effectiveness of national bodies dealing with the investigation and prosecution of serious cross-border and organized crime. What is new with the Constitutional Treaty is that the European Parliament and national parliaments now have a role in monitoring Eurojust's activities. Also, its activities will now be determined using the ordinary legislative procedure. Unanimity and EP consent is required, however, for the suggested creation of the office of the European Public Prosecutor. Its remit would be limited to 'investigating, prosecuting and bringing to justice' perpetrators of offences against the Union's financial interests, although the European Council, by unanimity, may in the future extend its powers over crimes having a cross-border dimension. The strong support for such an office among many of the member states may in due course be sufficient to overcome the scepticism of the UK government and others.

The final section of Chapter IV deals with police cooperation, which was previously dealt with in the intergovernmental Pillar III and consequently involved the member states agreeing measures by unanimity in the Council. Under the Constitutional Treaty, there is a switch to qualified majority voting and the ordinary legislative procedure. Unanimity and simple consultation of the EP is retained, however, for any measure concerning operational cooperation between national police, customs and other law enforcement authorities. The aim of EU action is the prevention, detection and investigation of criminal offences. To assist the European Union in its endeavours regarding cross-border crimes covered by an EU policy, there is Europol, whose mission is set out in Article III-276. This draws on the Treaty on European Union as well as on the 1995 Europol Convention.

This brings us to the final chapter of Title III which deals with the Union's coordinating, complementary and supporting policies. Here the Constitutional Treaty extends the remit of EU action to include 'physical and mental health', although the Constitutional Treaty underlines that the member states have primary responsibility for their own health policies. The second section consists of a single article on industry, which emphasizes open and competitive markets and so should not be seen as a precursor for interventionist industrial policies. Moreover, it now excludes harmonization of national laws. A similar provision has always featured in the article on culture, which appears in Section 3. Here the role of the European Union is essentially awareness promotion, and this has not been changed by the Constitutional Treaty, although it does now allow for 'incentive measures'.

What follows in Section 4 is a new provision on tourism, which envisages the European Union promoting the competitiveness of businesses. Once again, harmonization measures are excluded, as they are in the next section which covers education, youth, sport and vocational training. Much of the content of the two articles – which focus on facilitating cooperation and exchanges – is drawn directly from existing treaty provisions, although the attention paid to sport is new. Also new are the articles on civil protection and administrative cooperation that appear, respectively, in Sections 6 and 7. The first of these calls on the European Union to encourage cooperation between the member states to improve the effectiveness of systems designed to prevent or protect against natural and man-made disasters. The second draws on the Twinning programme, which the European Union has been running with candidate countries, and seeks to promote the exchange of information and civil servants to assist in the development of member states' administrative capacities for implementing EU law.

Having detailed the internal policies, Title IV switches attention to the European Union's external relations. However, the focus is not immediately on the common foreign and security policy or on the Union's treaty-making power, but on the Union's relations with those non-European countries and territories (including Greenland, New Caledonia and the Falkland Islands) that have special relations with Denmark, France, the Netherlands and the United Kingdom. Historically, these have always been accorded a special 'association' status and their own dedicated treaty provisions. The Constitutional Treaty maintains the tradition.

Title V deals with the more substantial elements of the European Union's external policies, namely the common foreign and security policy, the common commercial policy, development cooperation and relations with international organizations. In doing so, it covers the Union's involvement in foreign, security and defence issues, the Union's power to conclude agreements with non-member countries, and implementation of the solidarity clause. It begins with provisions of general application and in its first article brings together the overarching objectives of EU external action and the principles that underpin it. It also asserts the need for consistency and cooperation between the Union's institutions. The European Council's role in identifying the strategic interests and objectives of the European Union is then set out, as are the opportunities for the Union Minister for Foreign Affairs and the Commission to submit joint proposals.

A second chapter contains various provisions relating to the common foreign and security policy (CFSP), stressing member state support for the CFSP, the role of the European Union and its institutions and how operational action is to be pursued. The majority of the provisions are in substance the same as, or draw on, those in the existing treaties, except that they now accommodate the role and responsibilities of the Union Minister for Foreign Affairs and there is a new provision governing the establishment of the European External Action Service. Section 2 focuses on the common security and defence policy (CSDP). It brings together provisions contained in the Treaty on European Union and amends them in the light of policy developments since the Treaty of Nice. The Constitutional Treaty therefore provides a better reflection of where the European Union is in developing the CSDP. Among the changes are, first, those extending the so-called Petersburg Tasks to include joint disarmament operations, military assistance and advice, conflict prevention, post-conflict stabilization and the combating of terrorism. Second, Article III-310 also allows for individual tasks to be implemented by a group of member states that are willing and have the necessary capacity to do so. This reflects current arrangements based on so-called 'battle groups'.

A third change involves the establishment of the European Defence Agency, whose task is to identify operational requirements and encourage improvements in the military capabilities of the member states. Fourth, there are the provisions for 'permanent structured cooperation', which allow a qualified majority of member states to authorize the development of closer cooperation by those member states which have the will and the necessary military capabilities. The final section of Chapter II contains details of how the CFSP is to be funded – partly through the EU budget and partly through direct payments by member states. Unlike in the case of the EU budget generally, funding therefore remains in the hands of the member states, with only a marginal consultative role for the EP.

The third chapter on the European Union's external action, dealing with the common commercial policy, follows existing treaty provisions but increases the Union's commitment to the development of world trade and includes a new objective of progressively abolishing restrictions on foreign direct investment. There is also a new goal of lowering customs and other barriers. In terms of process, the Constitutional Treaty belatedly increases the involvement of the EP in the adoption of the policy. The ordinary legislative procedure is to be used and the EP must now approve trade agreements with non-member states.

With the policy competences and responsibilities of the European Union established, Title VI deals with how the Union is to function. Its initial focus is on the five institutions listed in Part I – the European Parliament, the European Council, the Council of Ministers, the European Commission and the Court of Justice – as well as the European Central Bank and the Court of Auditors. For each institution, there are provisions detailing composition, responsibilities, powers and procedures. After doing much the same for the Union's advisory bodies – the Committee of the Regions and the Economic and Social Committee – and the European Investment Bank, the Constitutional Treaty sets out the provisions common to all the institutions and bodies. These specify both the rules governing decision making in the European Union and the enforcement of decisions as well as the principles – openness, efficiency and transparency – underpinning these activities. The title then turns to the Union's finances: the principle of a five-year multiannual framework; how the annual budget is to be determined, implemented and discharged; and how the European Union is to combat fraud. Finally, Title VI sets out the mechanism by which enhanced cooperation can be activated.

Title VII contains a set of common provisions, all drawn from the existing treaties, dealing with matters such as the position of the outermost regions of the European Union, property ownership in the Union, staff regulations, statistics, the Union's contractual liability, languages, privileges and immunities. This brings to an end the most solid and indigestible part of the Constitutional Treaty. What it shows is that it is basically a restatement of what is already there. Hence, for some, it is all very timid. However, the Union's policy provisions are partially restructured to fit the Constitutional Treaty's changes and, in some cases, developed and extended.

Part IV

The last of the Constitutional Treaty's Parts – Part IV General and Final Provisions – reminds us that, despite the more than 400 articles in which the text talks almost consistently of a constitution, the document before us is in fact a treaty. This is not only reflected in the language used – the term 'constitution' is used only three times whereas the term 'this treaty' is used on 28 occasions – but also in the nature of the provisions. They deal, as Box 6.3 shows, with the sort of issues normally found in treaties. Despite seeming to be lost, sandwiched as they are between Part III and the series of Protocols, Annexes and Declarations, they are important and, despite their relative brevity, some are politically significant.

A number of the articles have direct equivalents in the existing treaties, notably where issues of geographical scope, the status of Protocols and Annexes, revision, duration, ratification and the authenticity of texts and translations are concerned. That said, there are a number of new articles in this 'housekeeping' section of the Constitutional Treaty. These concern the repeal of the existing treaties, succession and legal continuity, and simplified revision procedures. The last have important implications.

The opening article repeals the treaties on which the European Union is currently based: the Treaty establishing the European Community, the Treaty on European Union and the various accession treaties, etc. It also provides for continuing those elements of the latter which are still needed. Equally, when making it clear that the new Union is the legal successor to the old Community and Union, it provides for recognizing their output and acquis. If this is new, articles giving full status to Protocols, confirming the Treaty's application to the existing 25 member states, establishing that it is concluded for an unlimited period, and listing the 21 languages in which authentic versions of the text exist are virtually identical to the existing texts. Provision is also made for the Treaty to be translated into any other languages (e.g. Catalan) that enjoy official status in a member state.

Box 6.3 Part IV: an outline

General and final provisions	
Repeal of earlier treaties	IV-437
Succession and legal continuity	IV-438
Transitional provisions relating to certain institutions	IV-439
Scope	IV-440
Regional unions	IV-441
Protocols and annexes	IV-442
Ordinary revision procedure	IV-443
Simplified revision procedure	IV-444
Simplified revision procedure concerning internal Union policies and action	IV-445
Duration	IV-446
Ratification and entry into force	IV-447
Authentic texts and translation	IV-448

As before, ratification and revision normally require unanimity among the member states. However, while the ordinary revision process remains as now, albeit with the addition of a Convention, two new simpler revision procedures are added. One allows changes to be made in certain circumstances to domestic, but not external, policies by Council unanimity. The other allows the European Council to approve, by a qualified majority, further shifts to decision making by QMV and the ordinary legislative procedure in areas covered by Part III, except those having military implications. For some, these allow greater adaptability. Others think they either go too far and deny member states their rights, or not far enough because the ordinary revision procedure still requires unanimity. The fact that it does require unanimity again shows that the Constitutional Treaty remains a treaty at heart.

Protocols, annexes and declarations

Although all this is already long enough, there are further attachments to the Constitutional Treaty. These actually take up more space in the printed volume than Parts I-IV proper, even though they are not included in the general numbering. They are of varying status, ranging from the binding Protocols to advisory Declarations. Nonetheless they can all be of significance. And, taken as a whole, they underline the treaty nature and origins of the Constitutional Treaty.

The most important, weighty and binding of these are the 36 *Protocols* (listed in Box 6.4) which are attached to the document to avoid overloading it. Some of these are not much more than one paragraph; others are long documents divided into many Titles and articles. Most of them are revised versions of protocols attached to the Treaty establishing the European Community and the Treaty on European Union. There are three groups of these, beginning with the statutes of institutions (i.e. the Court of Justice, the ECB and the EIB). The second group covers a number of processes of governance and economic integration. The final group contains Protocols related to national concerns, which were either added on accession or agreed later as either opt-outs or special exemptions.

However, some new protocols have been introduced to provide more detailed guidance on innovations in the Constitutional Treaty. The first two deal with the precise role of national parliaments in the new European Union and the guidelines for applying subsidiarity. There are also provisions on transitional arrangements relating to the Union's institutions, the Eurogroup, permanent structured cooperation under the common security and defence policy, and the European Atomic Energy Community. Protocol 33 lists the treaties which the Constitutional Treaty repeals.

Box 6.4 Protocols: an overview

Protocols annexed to the Treaty establishing a Constitution for Europe

1. Protocol on the role of national parliaments in the European Union
2. Protocol on the application of the principles of subsidiarity and proportionality
3. Protocol on the Statute of the Court of Justice of the European Union
4. Protocol on the Statute of the European System of Central Banks and of the European Central Bank
5. Protocol on the Statute of the European Investment Bank
6. Protocol on the location of the seats of the institutions and of certain bodies, offices, agencies and departments of the European Union
7. Protocol on the privileges and immunities of the European Union
8. Protocol on the Treaties and Acts of Accession of the Kingdom of Denmark, Ireland and the United Kingdom of Great Britain and Northern Ireland, of the Hellenic Republic, of the Kingdom of Spain and the Portuguese Republic, and of the Republic of Austria, the Republic of Finland and the Kingdom of Sweden
9. Protocol on the Treaty and the Act of Accession of the Czech Republic, the Republic of Estonia, the Republic of Cyprus, the Republic of Latvia, the Republic of Lithuania, the Republic of Hungary, the Republic of Malta, the Republic of Poland, the Republic of Slovenia and the Slovak Republic
10. Protocol on the excessive deficit procedure
11. Protocol on the convergence criteria
12. Protocol on the Euro Group
13. Protocol on certain provisions relating to the United Kingdom of Great Britain and Northern Ireland as regards economic and monetary union
14. Protocol on certain provisions relating to Denmark as regards economic and monetary union
15. Protocol on certain tasks of the National Bank of Denmark
16. Protocol on the Pacific Financial Community franc system
17. Protocol on the Schengen acquis integrated into the framework of the European Union
18. Protocol on the application of certain aspects of Article III-130 of the Constitution to the United Kingdom and to Ireland
19. Protocol on the position of the United Kingdom and Ireland on policies in respect of border controls, asylum and immigration, judicial cooperation in civil matters and on police cooperation
20. Protocol on the position of Denmark
21. Protocol on external relations of the Member States with regard to the crossing of external borders
22. Protocol on asylum for nationals of Member States
23. Protocol on permanent structured cooperation established by Article I-41(6) and Article III-312 of the Constitution
24. Protocol on Article I-41(2) of the Constitution
25. Protocol concerning imports into the European Union of petroleum products refined in the Netherlands Antilles

Box 6.4 Continued

26 Protocol on the acquisition of property in Denmark
27 Protocol on the system of public broadcasting in the Member States
28 Protocol concerning Article III-214 of the Constitution
29 Protocol on economic, social and territorial cohesion
30 Protocol on special arrangements for Greenland
31 Protocol on Article 40.3.3 of the Constitution of Ireland
32 Protocol relating to Article I-9(2) of the Constitution on the accession of the Union to the European Convention on the Protection of Human Rights and Fundamental Freedoms
33 Protocol on the Acts and Treaties which have supplemented or amended the Treaty establishing the European Community and the Treaty on European Union
34 Protocol on the transitional provisions relating to the institutions and bodies of the Union
35 Protocol on the financial consequences of the expiry of the Treaty establishing the European Coal and Steel Community and on the Research Fund for Coal and Steel
36 Protocol amending the Treaty establishing the European Atomic Energy Community

Some Protocols also have interpretative political declarations attached to them. An example is the national statements on the incorporation of the Accession Treaty governing the 2004 enlargement.

At the end of the Protocols are two *Annexes*, left over from the Treaty establishing the European Community. These deal with products covered by Article III-226 and overseas territories covered by the Association provisions of Title IV in Part III. They are still needed because such trade and territories continue.

Declarations, of which there are 50, do not, as we have seen, have the same legal standing as Protocols. Most are mercifully brief but some – like Declaration 12, which contains explanations on the provisions of the Charter of Fundamental Rights – can be quite long. They are recognized but non-binding interpretations. They are actually classed, in true treaty style, as decisions of the Final Act of the IGC negotiations and can be either declarations adopted by the IGC, and thus apply to all, or declarations submitted by individual states.

The first category falls into two types: generally agreed interpretative texts on specific articles of the Constitutional Treaty and accepted national views on aspects of the various Protocols. Significant is Declaration 30, on what should be done if the Constitutional Treaty is not painlessly ratified. The second category consists of national statements about specific elements of the treaties, such as those by the United Kingdom and others on what they understand by the term 'nationals'. Hence they do need to be borne in mind in assessing the Constitutional Treaty and the significance of its contents. But, of course, to the public at large they are incomprehensible complications, so it is unlikely these final elements of the document will play much part when MPs and voters come to consider the ratification of the overall package that is the Constitutional Treaty.

7 Coming to a decision

In deciding what to think about the Constitutional Treaty, we clearly cannot just restrict ourselves to Part I. It is a package and needs to be understood as such. We hope we have shown that, partly because of the relatively open way in which it was drawn up, even if it is a complex package, it is still comprehensible if taken seriously. Certainly as a single, albeit longish, text, it is an improvement on the present treaty base, being more approachable than the existing 20 plus treaties. It also makes an attempt to spell out the principles and values underlying what the European Union has become. No doubt the text lacks a final polish and suffers from having the weaknesses of both sides of its dual nature, treaty and constitution. Yet it is no harder reading than the treaties or much UK legislation.

The Constitutional Treaty also offers simpler structures and procedures. There is only one European Union with rationalized competences, finance, institutions, instruments and voting procedures, as well as a new concern for democracy. And there are some improvements which remedy some of the weaknesses of Nice and may make it easier to cope with the stresses of enlargement to 30 states. Yet there is large continuity with the past, in terms of powers, politics and process. There is neither a large-scale transfer of authority nor a fundamental rebalancing of power between states and institutions. If anything, the document increases the ambiguous tension of the existing Union by strengthening both parties.

The outcome is a subtle, and not always consistent, compromise rationalization of the status quo. This makes it an imperfect and unspectacular document, neither working miracles nor likely to create chaos and tyranny. Indeed, it does not always answer the questions we might ask of it. This makes it difficult to explain to the people it seeks, so far unsuccessfully, to win over. And it needs to win these people over because the Constitutional Treaty cannot enter into force until it is ratified, which often means referenda – and these can raise issues beyond the text itself and unleash other political forces. So, statistically, it is likely to be rejected in one or more of the 25 states involved. Yet, though legally this would mean it would fail, the political reality is that many will wish to persevere with it, given the fallible nature of the Nice settlement and the total impossibility of coming up with a solution which will satisfy all the contending forces.

Ratification: the rules of the game

Before the Constitutional Treaty can enter into force, it must be ratified. That is to say that formal documents – 'instruments of ratification' – must be submitted to the Italian government signifying that the member state in question has duly and properly approved the Constitutional Treaty. The Italians act as a depositary because it was in Rome that the major EU treaties have been signed. This is probably not something that would happen if the document were a pure constitution.

There are rules for this in the Constitutional Treaty. However, because member states seem to regard it as an amendment to the existing treaties rather than a completely new start, ratification is actually governed more by Articles 48 and 52 of the existing TEU than the almost identical rules proposed in Article IV-447. Both require that each of the so-called 'High Contracting Parties' – the member states – ratify the 'Treaty' and then deposit their instruments. Only once they have all done this can the Constitutional Treaty enter into force. The expectation – or aspiration – is for the process to be completed by 1 November 2006. But if a member state is late in completing, then entry into force will occur on the first day of the second month after completion.

Neither treaty specifies how ratification should actually be carried out across Europe. There will be no one-day Europe-wide referendum, even though many – notably in the Convention – would have liked to see this. Again, had the document been just a constitution this might have been possible. But its dual nature helped to rule this out. Instead it is made clear that states decide on ratification procedures for themselves, 'in accordance', as the texts say, 'with their constitutional requirements'. In the United Kingdom this requires only a government statement countersigned by the Queen. In reality things are different and, although ratification technically means the act of legal approval, the resulting political process is wider.

Obtaining approval in 25 instances, each with their own legal rules and political concerns, is a larger challenge than the European Union has yet had to face in treaty ratification, irrespective of the precise problems posed by the Constitutional Treaty. Some member states must first adapt their own constitutions to remove incompatibilities. Thus the French Parliament's two chambers met in a 'Congress' at the end of February 2005 to approve constitutional amendments after a ruling from the Constitutional Council that these were necessary. Only then could the ratification bill be tabled when the Council ruled that there was no problem.

However, the key legal difference among member states is whether ratification is left wholly to parliaments or not. In some countries, like Germany and Portugal, national constitutions either make no provision for referenda or circumscribe their use to such an extent that they cannot presently be used to approve the Constitutional Treaty. So, either the constitution has to be changed, as in Portugal, or parliament alone takes the decision. In some cases, a simple parliamentary majority suffices. In others, particularly where the member state's constitution needs to be amended, a larger majority – often two-thirds – is necessary. Where a parliament consists of two chambers, both are normally required to endorse the Constitutional Treaty.

Even in those member states which have decided to call a referendum, parliaments also take part in the process. In Spain, the Cortes debated the Constitutional Treaty well after the successful referendum in February 2005. In the United Kingdom, conversely, parliamentary debate will precede the actual vote. And, although an unprecedented number of member states are holding referenda, their status can vary. In some countries they are a constitutional requirement; in others, it is up to the government to call them. In some countries, such as the Netherlands, the referendum is, nominally, only advisory; elsewhere they can be binding. The technical rules on such votes can also vary: some countries require a quota before a referendum decision becomes valid; others do not. Rules on publicity, funding and campaigning are also nationally determined, as is the sensitive question of what the actual question should be.

There are three reasons why so many member states are laying the Constitutional Treaty before their population. First, some member states felt that the proposals were sufficiently far ranging and changed their country's relations with the Union to such an extent that popular approval was necessary. However, Finland and other countries did not accept this. Second, other states, like Spain, believed that the Constitutional Treaty ought to be celebrated by citizens because of its virtues. Third, there was a Europe-wide movement for using referenda led by the Initiative and Referendum Institute, which believes most decisions should be made in this way. This lay behind the Vote 2004 campaign in the United Kingdom, which was largely aligned with opposition to the Constitutional Treaty. However, this movement could not persuade all member states to follow the direct democracy path, although efforts persist in Finland, Greece and Sweden.

With member states proceeding according to their own rules, the timetable of debates and referenda remains essentially uncoordinated, although a coordinated strategy on 'communicating Europe' as part of the ratification process was discussed. In most cases, the timing of ratification is determined by domestic political considerations and procedural requirements, although states like Italy deliberately sought to be among the first to ratify. Others, like the United Kingdom, hung back, possibly in the hope that others might reject the Constitutional Treaty and thus remove the need for a debate and vote. Alternatively, delay can allow a member state to benefit from any momentum of ratification elsewhere. In all this, the continuing importance of national differences within the European Union clearly emerges.

The challenge of ratification outside the United Kingdom

The variety of legal rules is, of course, only part of the problem. As differences in national appreciations of the Constitutional Treaty and uncertainties about both timing and question show, this is a highly political matter. Although, on paper, all countries are supposed to be voting on the Constitutional Treaty and its contents, experience shows that voters are often motivated by other issues. And these can often be contradictory, thanks to the play of national politics. Very often a referendum gives the electorate the opportunity to express their opinion of the government or the economic situation. Equally, other European issues can affect votes – the admission of Turkey, the Bolkestein directive, the style of a country's membership or the overall nature of the European Union. Such variety, combined with the way they widen the political process to new actors and interests, makes referenda diverse and unpredictable.

While the United Kingdom decided to go down the referendum path well before the final text was officially signed, it has been slower than most in engaging the process. Elsewhere ratification started quite early. Initially, there appeared to be much support for the Constitutional Treaty, even though it was clear that popular understanding of the document was limited and many people were not particularly interested. Most states wish to resolve the issue relatively soon. If all goes well, most countries will have come to a decision by the end of 2005.

Some, in fact, have been very prompt. The Lithuanian parliament endorsed the Constitutional Treaty on 11 November 2004, within two weeks of it being signed (see Table 7.1). This ruined the Berlusconi government's hopes that Italy would be first to ratify. With the Hungarian parliament ratifying the following month and the Slovenian parliament voting in favour in early February, the best the Berlusconi government could hope for was that Italy would be the first of the original six member states to complete ratification. With the Senate taking its time to complete its scrutiny, Italy was also overtaken by Spanish approval in a referendum held on 20 February 2005 (see Table 7.2) that pioneered innovative campaigning methods by co-

Table 7.1 Parliamentary ratification: timetable and progress

	As of 11 July 2005		*Yes*	*No*	*Absten-tions*	*Absen-tees*	
Austria	Nationalrat	11.05.05	182	1	0	0	
	Bundesrat	26.05.05	59	3	0	0	
Belgium	Chambre	19.05.05	118	18	1	13	
	Sénat	28.04.05	54	9	1	7	
Cyprus	House of Reps.	30.06.05	30	19	1	6	
Czech Republic							*
Denmark							*
Estonia							
Finland							
France	Congrès (Joint)	28.02.05	730	66	96	15	*
Germany	Bundestag	12.05.05	569	23	2	7	
	Bundesrat	27.05.05	66	0	3	0	
Greece	Voulis	19.04.05	268	17	15	0	
Hungary	Az Orsàg Hàza	20.12.04	322	12	8	44	
Ireland							*
Italy	Camera	25.01.05	436	28	5	61	
	Senato	06.04.05	217	16	0	82	
Latvia	Saeima	02.06.05	71	5	6	18	
Lithuania	Seimas	11.11.04	84	4	3	50	
Luxembourg	1st reading	28.06.05	55	0	0	5	*
Malta	House of Reps.	07.07.05	65	0	0	0	
Netherlands							*
Poland							*
Portugal							*
Slovakia	Narodna Rada	11.05.05	116	27	4	3	
Slovenia	Drzavni zbor	01.02.05	79	4	7	0	
Spain	Congreso	28.04.05	311	19	0	20	*
	Senado	18.05.05	225	6	1	27	
Sweden							
United Kingdom							*

Note
* Also holding a referendum (see Table 7.2).

opting footballers, Big Brother contestants and cola manufacturers. While it won the expected big majority, turnout was low and many Spaniards voted not on what was in the text but on their general support for the European Union. Nonetheless, the process of ratifying the Constitutional Treaty got off to a good start. The EP also endorsed the text in mid-January 2005, a political gesture that pleased supporters of the Constitutional Treaty.

Yet commentators have long pointed out that the process is unlikely to be universally smooth. In some member states rejection has always been viewed as a distinct possibility. This is true of Denmark, which initially rejected the TEU in 1992 and has since seen close votes on the Treaty of Amsterdam

Table 7.2 Ratification by referendum: timetable and progress

As of 11 July 2005		*Yes* %	*No* %	*Spoilt* %	*Turnout* %
Spain	20.02.05	76.73	17.24	6.03	42.32
France	29.05.05	44.18	53.30	2.51	69.34
Netherlands	01.06.05	38.17	61.07	0.76	63.30
Luxembourg	10.07.05	54.86	42.19	2.95	90.44
Denmark	(27.09.05)				
Ireland	(10.05)				
Portugal	(12.05)				
Poland	(05)				
Czech Republic	(06.06)				
United Kingdom	(06)				

Note
These figures differ from those often used because they come from the total votes cast and not just from those which were valid. Dates in brackets were possibilities, now suspended.

(approved) and adoption of the euro (rejected). Early Eurobarometer opinion polls indicated that those opposed to a European constitution (41 per cent) outnumbered those in favour (37 per cent), but by late 2004 – by which time an agreement had been reached between governing parties and the opposition Social Democrats on maintaining the existing opt-out from judicial cooperation in the Union – support for the Constitutional Treaty had risen significantly, to 54 per cent, with only 17 per cent indicating that they would vote 'no'. Bearing in mind that less than one-third of the electorate have made up their minds which way they will vote, the outcomes of past referenda and the existence of a well-organized eurosceptic movement, the actual vote – due in late 2005 – could be closer than this.

Similarly, in Poland the outcome of the referendum – foreseen to take place at the same time as the presidential election in late 2005 – is expected to be much closer than the 2004 Eurobarometer polls suggest. These showed overwhelming support (62 per cent and 73 per cent) for a European Constitution, yet the government's failure to obtain a reference to 'God' in the Preamble, coupled with a sense that the size and importance of the country has not been fully recognized in the new system of majority voting, could make the task of selling the Constitutional Treaty very difficult. The government's difficulties are compounded by its own instability and the evident scepticism in some quarters – both outside and within parliament – about what the European Union has to offer Poles. Views may be changing in the light of generally positive experiences of membership so far, but there is still a problem of voter apathy. If turnout is less than 50 per cent, then a positive vote could be ineffective.

In France and the Netherlands – where referenda are due in May and June 2005 – the outcome is even less certain. In France, where memories of the near failure of the referendum on the TEU in 1992 remain relatively fresh, vocal opposition has come from politicians and commentators on the far right and the far left as well as from within both the ruling centre-right party and, especially, the opposition Socialists. Indeed, the latter have had to endure bitter debate on the Constitutional Treaty despite the clear membership vote in December 2004 in favour of supporting a 'yes' vote.

Public opinion polls initially revealed support for the Constitutional Treaty, the autumn 2004 Eurobarometer suggesting 70 per cent in favour. But then, again, French voters had supposedly been clearly in favour of the TEU prior to the 1992 vote, but the gap closed dramatically under pressure from the far left and the sovereignist right. Polls in late 2004 and early 2005 revealed a reversal of views as opposition became fashionable. There were also fears of a high abstention rate. By late March the 'no' camp scored as high as 55 per cent. It profited, on the one hand, from the government's unpopularity, its unsuccessful economic policy and its slowness to launch its campaign. On the other hand, it also drew on unease about the general development of the European Union, the reformist agenda of the Barroso Commission and, most significantly, the decision to begin accession negotiations with Turkey. In an attempt to counter the last of these, the proposed amendments to the French constitution necessary for ratification included a new clause providing for a referendum on the accession of Turkey and other states (albeit not Bulgaria, Croatia and Romania) to the Union. Concessions on domestic issues were also made.

How people would vote in the Netherlands, in what was the first-ever nationwide referendum in Dutch history, was a matter of intense speculation given the rise in euroscepticism in the country and the poor standing of the government. Eurobarometer polls in 2004 suggested a seemingly unassailable majority of over 70 per cent for a constitution for the Union, and this in a country traditionally associated with support for euro-federalism. By early 2005, however, the situation had changed, with opinion polls indicating majorities against ratification due to concerns over immigration and, again, Turkish accession, as well unease at the course of integration generally. Calling off the vote in the event of a French 'no' was even mooted.

In the Czech Republic, where voters may have to wait until 2006 – either with the June general election or at some other time – before they have their say on the Constitutional Treaty, opinion polls indicate that a 'yes' vote is the likely outcome. Overcoming the euroscepticism that was evident in the results of the 2004 EP elections and is being promoted by, among others, the country's pamphleteering President, Vaclav Klaus, will be a major challenge for the government. Moreover, a constitutional amendment is necessary before a referendum can take place. Divisions over its nature may encourage the governing parties, and the somewhat fractious Civic Democracy opposition, to proceed by parliamentary means, given that their electorates are strongly in favour.

Of the remaining member states where referenda will be held, Ireland will attract much attention given the popular rejection of the Treaty of Nice in 2001. Yet, here, the Constitutional Treaty is expected to be approved by the people, without much threat of a 'no' vote, primarily because the government can sell the text as the product of diplomatic skill and perseverance during the successful Irish Presidency of 2004. Moreover, the political establishment has learned the lesson of the Nice defeat and maintained an active communication campaign on European Union matters through its National Forum on Europe. However, awareness of the Constitutional Treaty's content remains low, and this has caused concern. Opposition is likely to be vocal, especially from those who see the development of the CDSP as threatening Irish neutrality.

In Luxembourg, popular support for the Constitutional Treaty is very high, and there appears to be little likelihood of it being rejected. Rejection is also unlikely in Portugal, where there is majority support among politicians and electorate. Plans to hold an early referendum in April 2005 – and capitalize on the appointment of José Manuel Barroso as President of the European Commission – were abandoned following the electoral upheaval which brought the Socialists to power and the Constitutional Court's dismissal of the proposed question. The new government then said that the referendum would be in October 2005, assuming the necessary constitutional amendment was in place.

This leaves us with the remaining 15 member states which have been, or will be, ratifying by parliamentary procedure alone. Few are expected to face problems even if pressure for referenda persists. In most cases, this expectation reflects the view that the changes to the European Union contained in the Constitutional Treaty are not so great as to merit a referendum. This was certainly the case in Finland and also in Slovenia. In Sweden, the government ruled out a referendum because the Constitutional Treaty does not affect the country's constitution. Added to this, the majority view in parliament was against a referendum. Similar arguments shaped the Latvian and Estonian governments' decision not to hold a referendum. Some consideration was given to ratification via a popular vote in Greece, but with no tradition of referenda on European matters, the government's preference for parliamentary ratification prevailed. This was also the case in Cyprus, the only one of the ten countries to accede to the Union in 2004 which did not hold a referendum on the question of accession.

Elsewhere, referenda were rejected for domestic reasons. The Belgian government initially envisaged one, but was forced to drop the idea in February 2005 because of fears that it would encourage both opposition to Turkish entry and linguistic divisions. The Italian government also toyed with a possible referendum but, as it became clear that this would exacerbate differences within the coalition, stuck with parliamentary ratification. In Austria, the main political parties and the government were even less enthusiastic, resisting various calls for a popular vote, although there was some support for an EU-wide referendum. Calls for a referendum in Slovakia were also rejected, the government fearing a low turnout would invalidate the outcome. A similar argument was behind the decision of the Hungarian government to proceed in parliament, despite popular support for a referendum.

By contrast, political parties in Germany did seriously consider holding a referendum – a July 2004 opinion poll showed over 80 per cent of the electorate in favour. However, doing this would require a constitutional amendment and, despite debates on this in late 2004, the government soon abandoned the idea because of lack of agreement with the Christian Democratic opposition about the form the amendment should take. So the parliamentary process started, with first readings in late February 2005. Completion was scheduled for 12 May to help the 'yes' camp in France and elsewhere.

In most cases where the national parliament will be responsible for ratification the Constitutional Treaty is expected to enjoy a smooth passage. If few governments enjoy commanding parliamentary majorities, there is a general consensus both inside parliament and beyond in favour of integration and the Constitutional Treaty. But some of the votes will be close. In Malta only a narrow majority in favour is likely, while in Sweden there are strong opposing voices, although the majority of seats are held by pro-EU parties. Thus there are still challenges ahead in continental Europe, many of them reflecting national concerns rather than the actual text. Few states, however, are faced with as many difficulties as in Britain.

The UK approach to ratification

The decision of Tony Blair to put the Constitutional Treaty to the people runs counter to established approaches to the ratification of EU treaties. In the past, the process has involved parliamentary scrutiny and a series of formal votes in both the House of Commons and the House of Lords. Technically, as we have implied, treaties are ratified by the Foreign Secretary, who acts on behalf of the Crown, thereby exercising the 'Royal Prerogative'. Parliament itself does not actually ratify. Rather, its function is to vote on a bill amending the 1972 European Communities Act, which gives effect in domestic law to the treaty changes envisaged. In the case of the Constitutional Treaty, a similar process will be used with one notable exception: the bill amending the 1972 European Communities Act will only enter into force once it has been approved in a referendum. Only then can the Foreign Secretary formally ratify.

The decision to hold a referendum was announced on 20 April 2004 and represented a volte-face by a government which had previously argued, like the Finns, that there was no compelling reason for the Constitutional Treaty to be referred to the people. There was, however, mounting domestic pressure for a referendum. Within parliament, opposition parties, notably the Conservatives and the Liberal Democrats, were demanding that the document be submitted to the people, and by early 2004 a private member's bill calling for a referendum was being debated. Outside, right-wing sections of the media, in particular, were calling for a referendum, as were a number of pressure and interest groups. In 2003 both the *Sun* and the *Daily Mail* ran campaigns in favour of a popular vote and the Vote 2004 campaign was launched. With the Conservative Party seeking to make it an issue in the 2005 general election, the government soon capitulated. However, it refused to name a date for the referendum, although it was clear it would be after the election.

Having opted for a referendum, the government resisted opposition calls to move swiftly to a vote, partly because the final text of the Constitutional Treaty would not be available until the early autumn. However, to facilitate debate, a provisional text of the document was submitted to parliament on 19 July 2004. Two months later the Foreign and Commonwealth Office published its *White Paper on the Treaty establishing a Constitution for Europe* as well as an on-line guide. Initial debates followed in both the House of Commons and the House of Lords, mainly occasioned by private members' bills. The text of the Constitutional Treaty as actually signed was published on 8 December. Shortly afterwards the FCO published an exhaustive commentary.

By then it had been announced that the referendum would take place in 2006. The ratification bill duly appeared in late January 2005 and set out the wording of the question to be put to the people: 'Should the United Kingdom approve the Treaty establishing a Constitution for the European Union?'. Although the bill received its second reading on 9 February, further debate was postponed until after the May general election. The third reading – needed prior to the referendum – would have to wait until later. Moreover, speculation that the referendum might not be held until autumn 2006 implied a third reading that year too.

Decisions, dilemmas and prospects for the United Kingdom

Although the referendum, whenever it comes, will formally be on adoption of the Constitutional Treaty – the Electoral Commission was quick to insist that it must be – the nature of the debate so far suggests that, as elsewhere in Europe, the electorate could in practice be voting on something else. In the United Kingdom it is unlikely to be domestic economic conditions or Turkey. More likely the vote will reflect attitudes to Blair, concerns regarding immigration and, especially, the far more existential question of whether the United Kingdom should remain in the European Union. Indeed, Liberal Democrat MP Menzies Cambell has argued that it will be impossible to get a debate on the contents of the Constitutional Treaty.

There are several reasons for this. The first reflects the dilemma faced by the Blair government. Having called a referendum for somewhat short-term domestic reasons unrelated to the content of the Constitutional Treaty, it now faces the challenge of obtaining a 'yes' vote from an electorate that, as we have noted, is generally ill-informed about, and increasingly hostile, towards the European Union. Hence people are likely to vote on their general perceptions of the Union. And the electorate has many other *arrière-pensées* about the Blair government which could well influence its decisions.

The second reason is the increased euroscepticism in the UK. This has been reflected in the rise of the United Kingdom Independence Party (UKIP), which clearly sees a 'no' vote as the gateway to secession. The party has had an impact on opinion, encouraging the Conservative leadership to adopt more eurosceptic positions on the European Union, such as renegotiating much of the United Kingdom's present commitments, notably the Common Fisheries Policy and social policies. Other Tories would go further and seek a fundamental reworking of UK involvement in the Union, and there seems little doubt that the press will treat the referendum as a vote on membership.

Third, most outside commentators, and even some UK MEPS, will see things in the light of the broader UK–EU relationship. Abroad, a conventional view is that if the French or Dutch reject the Constitutional Treaty, the Union has a problem, but if the British say 'no' it is they who have the problem. And some, like former Commissioner Mario Monti, have long been saying that this is an 'in or out' question and urging member states to commit to a second vote on continued membership if they turn the Constitutional Treaty down.

It is possible that the UK government will play the referendum in this way. Some argue that such is the backlog of doubt and ignorance that only by turning the vote into a plebiscite on membership – which is still supported by a majority – can the government get a positive vote. Conversely, some argue that this would be a double mistake. For, on the one hand, voters' unease about the Constitutional Treaty could see the government's bluff being called. On the other, many believe that the government must be positive and not seek to scare people into voting 'yes'.

Will this mean that the fundamental debate, which eurosceptics say the people have never been allowed, will take now place? The likelihood is a replaying of old arguments about what was said in the 1970s – not that this is particularly relevant for much of the electorate who were too young to vote then – and a focus on EU policies, even though these do not really change with the Constitutional Treaty. Above all, it will be on the virtues of membership. In other words, the referendum debate will be about more than ratification of the Constitutional Treaty.

Debate of any kind has actually been slow to take off, at least where government and supporters of UK membership have been concerned. Whereas opponents of the Constitutional Treaty have long been fund-raising, organizing and publicizing, the months immediately after the Constitutional Treaty was adopted were devoid of any significant official activity. The government did commission a communications campaign in early 2005, but this was to 'inform' only. The 'Britain in Europe' group's profile remained low and there were few government or Labour Party efforts to break what one *Financial Times* columnist referred to as the 'conspiracy of silence' over Europe. Speeches that were made tended to go unreported. Added to this, the Liberal Democrats, supportive trade unions and business intervened only occasionally, reluctant to commit themselves in the absence of active government engagement.

Opponents of the Constitutional Treaty meanwhile enjoyed a high profile, thanks in part to the sympathies of much of the press. Buoyed by their success in the 2004 EP elections, and not deterred by the UKIP–Kilroy Silk soap opera, three broad groups of opponents have launched largely uncoordinated campaigns. The first came from the centre-right of UK politics and comprised the Conservative Party and various Northern Ireland unionists as well as most of the tabloid press, notably the *Sun* and the *Daily Mail*, plus the two broadsheets of the right, *The Times* and the *Daily Telegraph*. Taking its lead from the statements of the Conservative Party leadership, this group rejects the Constitutional Treaty as unnecessary, as 'bad for Britain and bad for Europe' and sees little, if anything, of value in the text. Instead, they look for a renegotiation of the terms of UK membership and welcome all signs of similar thinking in other member states.

Second, the more extreme eurosceptics associated with UKIP and bodies such as the Campaign for an Independent Britain, the Democracy Movement and the Bruges Group have been advocating not only rejection of the

Constitutional Treaty but also UK withdrawal from the European Union, as do some Tory MPs. Third, there is a group drawn from the left of UK politics, including around 30 Labour MPs, trade unionists and organizations such as the Centre for a Social Europe, and the Greens. They claim, among other things, that the Constitutional Treaty would institutionalize privatization and neo-liberal economics and, by transferring powers to the European Union, undermine national governments. Here again, the argument is as much about the Union's policies and the perceived nature of the Constitutional Treaty as about its actual contents.

In the absence of meaningful public debate, significant sections of the public remained undecided about the Constitutional Treaty. The general perception is that opponents easily outnumber supporters, even though Eurobarometer polls in 2003 and 2004 reported that more than 40 per cent favoured a constitution for the Union and less than 25 per cent were opposed. Such findings were not reflected in other early polls. A survey conducted soon after the announcement of a referendum indicated that 55 per cent of people opposed 'Britain' signing up to an EU constitution.

The first surveys of public opinion conducted after the Constitutional Treaty was agreed also indicated a hostile majority. A first, in June 2004, suggested that 49 per cent would vote against and 23 per cent in favour. However, a second, conducted by The Foreign Policy Centre, found that only 35 per cent of voters had made up their mind how they intended to vote, and a later poll recorded that only 14 per cent believed they had enough information to make a considered decision. Of the 35 per cent that had made up their minds, 27 per cent were decidedly against the Constitutional Treaty while only 8 per cent supported it. That two-thirds of the voters were still undecided gave some hope to those campaigning in favour of the Constitutional Treaty. A few months later there were mixed signals. While Eurobarometer suggested that 49 per cent of the electorate supported the Constitutional Treaty, another poll showed opposition running at 69 per cent. However, when the referendum question was published, polls showed opinion either broadly balanced at around 40 per cent or in favour (36% v 29%).

As to the future, much of course depended on who won the General Election and what happened elsewhere. A Tory victory would have meant a rapid referendum and, presumably, a crushing rejection, opening the way for very difficult negotiations to decide whether the UK will have a place in the European Union. A Labour victory meant, on initial domestic expectations, further delay before a very tense and difficult referendum. And, again, a 'no' vote elsewhere was always likely to cause real problems. A French 'no' would complicate matters considerably as it would ensure that future French negotiation strategy would lean towards exactly those leftist ideas which eurosceptics detest. It might also encourage a Labour government to abandon a vote, but this would involve going back on a formal undertakings and implicitly supporting the arguments of whichever coalition helped to vote the Constitutional Treaty down.

The likelihood was that there would be a referendum, but when and in what circumstances remains unclear. The outcome seemed very uncertain, with much depending on the actual campaign, whenever that started. Some government voices suggested it will start immediately after the May election, perhaps as early as 8 May. This was not to be so.

In any case, it is possible that not all other member states will have ratified the Constitutional Treaty by the time the United Kingdom votes. As we have seen, there are doubts about the Czech Republic, France, the Netherlands and Poland. However, it is still theoretically possible that in the end most will ratify, even if by very small majorities. This means that the UK electorate's decision could yet be crucial and, if it were a 'no', it would leave both the United Kingdom and the European Union in uncharted waters.

Rejection?

That one or more member states might reject the Constitutional Treaty has always been a possibility. Its authors recognized this and made an attempt to deal with it. Thus Declaration 30 states that if two years after the document has been signed, and assuming at least 20 member states have ratified it, one or more member states 'have encountered difficulties in proceeding', then the matter will be referred to the European Council. It might seem odd to look to the Constitutional Treaty to solve a problem about its own ratification, but a declaration is actually a decision of the IGC, not part of the treaty, and, in any case, it only restates current practice. The European Council would inevitably meet in such a crisis, whether or not it was formally mandated to do so by a treaty, though what it would do in these circumstances we do not know.

There seem to be three common British assumptions about what the consequences of a UK, or other, 'no' vote would be: that it would bring the whole process to a halt; that it would allow for the European Union to start again on a new 'satisfactory' treaty; or that it would allow the United Kingdom to dictate its own terms for future relations. None of these are likely. Moreover, if the Constitutional Treaty is rejected, there is likely to be a major political, and possibly economic, crisis. Both could adversely affect the United Kingdom, even though it is outside the eurozone and might be seeking to weaken its ties with the European Union.

The rules of the game do not insist that ratification must cease if there is a 'no' vote. In any case, legally speaking, if the Constitutional Treaty is not ratified, then life will continue as usual with the existing treaties remaining in force. But it is possible – indeed probable, given the dissatisfaction with the Nice arrangements (shared by the Conservatives) – that, difficult though this may be, the more integration-minded member states would seek to implement the Constitutional Treaty, or at least aspects of it, by other means. Thought has already been given to how this might be achieved, both in the chancelleries of Europe and by think-tanks such as the UK Centre for European Reform. So a 'no' would not leave things as they were.

The other two assumptions are also problematic. As far as getting a 'satisfactory' new treaty is concerned, the ratification process has shown that opposition comes from irreconcilable positions. And we believe it is an illusion to imagine that the likes of French Socialist Henri Emmanuelli, who sees the Constitutional Treaty as embodying Anglo-Saxon neo-liberalism and weak institutions, would agree a new consolidated text with Conservative MP David Heathcoat-Amory, who wants a simple, free-trade document in which all decisions have to be ratified by national parliaments. In any case, the majority of opinion, as the European Convention showed, believes that the Constitutional Treaty has something to offer and should be maintained.

UKIP, Michael Howard and others believe a 'no' vote will allow the United Kingdom to carve out the deal that it wants, perhaps as the price for letting the others move forward. This too may not be so. To begin with, the UK stance, from the calling of a referendum onwards if not before, has been disliked by many. Being aware of the government's poor job of selling the text, they will have seen a 'no' coming and, noting the europhobe desperation to leave, could demand harsh terms. Historically, in its relations with member states and those outside, the European Union has demanded a balance of rights and obligations. And the other states may not think, as many in the UK do, that the Union needs the United Kingdom more than it needs the Union. Here, too, the complexion of the UK government would be crucial.

In any case, successful renegotiation would require an IGC to adopt the large scale opt-outs envisaged by the Tories, and the conclusion would require both agreement and ratification from all member states. If there were a lack of sympathy for the United Kingdom, these might not be forthcoming. Equally, if the UK referendum outcome were close and it were clear that its 'no' did not have full support, the government could find itself subject to domestic pressures which could limit its freedom of manoeuvre. So the bluff could be called and the United Kingdom could have to withdraw. It would have to do this in the knowledge that most other member states disapproved of it and would not be willing to make concessions. In fact, for those who want out, approving the Constitutional Treaty and then invoking Article I-60 on voluntary withdrawal would be easier and more certain. Despite what

UKIP says, this does not need an agreement or QMV. After two years a state can leave anyway, although it would have to sort out loose ends itself.

But what would the situation actually be following a rejection? Obviously much would depend on who is rejecting, why and how emphatically. A narrow rejection in a small state would probably lead, as with Denmark and Ireland in 1992 and 2001 respectively, to a request to think again. However, it is hard to see what could be offered to meet voters' concerns. If it was in a big member state, things would be more complicated.

Three kinds of possibilities have been canvassed so far. First, the Constitutional Treaty could be abandoned, leaving the Union to continue with the existing treaties. This seems unlikely. More plausible is the possibility of what Charles Grant of the Centre for European Reform calls a 'Nice Plus' situation in which elements of the document could be informally implemented by those member states in favour. This could include some of the institutional arrangements. By meeting at 24 ahead of formal meetings, the other states could leave the UK exposed.

Second, there could be a solution involving renegotiation. Thus, in the hope of gaining approval, a quick IGC might be held to eliminate any particularly contentious elements. Liberal Democrat MEP Andrew Duff has also suggested that a 'short, sharp IGC' could be called with the sole purpose of amending Article 48 TEU in order to allow the Constitutional Treaty to come into force before all member states have ratified it. A quid pro quo for this would be a special deal for the United Kingdom. There could also be a whole new negotiation, but this is unlikely as so much effort has already been expended on the present compromise and, as we have suggested, there is little chance that a generally acceptable new text could be agreed or gain popular consent. Even less convincing is the idea that an IGC could simply relabel the Constitutional Treaty as a treaty.

A third set of possibilities focuses on the member state or states that say 'no'. This could involve a second vote, which is often said to be impossible in the United Kingdom. However, if there were no satisfactory alternative on offer, then a further vote on the principle of membership might be feasible, even though this would mean having to accept the Constitutional Treaty. Another possibility would be to invite the rejecting member state to withdraw of its own volition and to promise that a favourable special deal would be agreed. This might be membership of the European Economic Area with observer status in the institutions – though the latter would also have to be offered to Norway and Iceland – or a bilateral deal such as that developed with the Swiss. Unfortunately, both of these require more acceptance of EU rules and requests than many appreciate. And having to accept decisions without having any voice in them would be hard for the UK to stomach.

Alternatively, the rejecting member state could be outflanked by such devices as intergovernmental deals, application of the enhanced cooperation arrangements or the creation of a linked hard core led by France and Germany in a series of policy areas. This is close to what Grant calls a messy core, something which would leave the United Kingdom marginalised within the Union. Even more radically, as Jo Shaw and others have noted, the other member states could themselves secede from the Union, leaving the United Kingdom with the rump and going on to implement the Constitutional Treaty in a new body.

How such changes might be legally achieved remains unclear. Not all seem valid under international law. In any case they could create immense confusion and division, especially if several states fail to ratify or decide to stick with the existing Union. So, although the Constitutional Treaty has been signed, its future remains uncertain and at the unavoidable mercy of member states' efforts to ratify it, notably in the UK.

All these things show that, no matter what the UK vision, there is support for the Constitutional Treaty elsewhere. People have invested in it and see it as a symbol of achievement and something which is vital for the future. And they are already planning for its rapid implementation as the establishment of the European Defence Agency and the nomination of Solana as the EU Minister for Foreign Affairs prove. Nor do they believe, as British eurosceptics do, that a UK 'no' trumps all else. So a 'no' vote, while rejecting the Constitutional Treaty (including its democratic possibilities and rights), will not ensure a 'yes' to anything else.

Postscript

The preceding discussion assumed what, at the time of the Constitutional Treaty's conception seemed the most likely outcome of ratification, that United Kingdom would be the lone objector. Events since have disproved this. Even though ten member states had ratified it by parliamentary means, as Table 7.1 shows, the French and Dutch 'no' votes clearly changed the dynamics of ratification in ways unforeseen when we wrote. Yet, although the whole process has now effectively been put on hold as the member states 'reflect' on what to do, the analyses we have offered remain relevant, notably to emerging attitudes to the United Kingdom after the budget fracas at the June 2005 Brussels European Council. Indeed, the document may have more of an afterlife than many expect, or wish.

The clear rejection of the Constitutional Treaty in France and its even more emphatic defeat in the Netherlands three days later (see Table 7.2) caused a real crisis. Even though the reasons for rejection seem to have been contradictory both within and between countries, and were often unrelated to the document itself, the momentum of ratification was broken and fundamental questions about the European Union and its future direction were posed. So, though there was much talk of going on with the process of ratification – whether to conform with Declaration 30 and international law or to respect the rights both of those states who had either approved or who had yet to decide – political realities dictated otherwise. In the United Kingdom most people thought it would be a costly nonsense to vote on something which was obviously dead. So, to the annoyance of France and Germany, the Blair government soon announced its decision to postpone moves towards a referendum pending an agreed EU decision about the Constitutional Treaty's future. Elsewhere, opinion was more affected by the emerging evidence of a knock-on effect which was eating into support for the document in countries like Denmark (which could mean further crippling defeats) and by the fact that going on could paralyse the life of the Union. Hence the European Council of 16–17 June decided there should be a period of 'reflection' before a decision would be taken on how to proceed sometime in the first half of 2006 The 'reflection' would entail a 'broad debate', which hopefully will be more meaningful than that which emerged as part of the 'Future of Europe' debate following the Treaty of Nice. So while Jan Peter Balkende of the Netherlands called for big debates both nationally, and at the European level, and the European Council nominally endorsed this, it gave the idea neither structure nor steer – beyond declaring that discussions should be wide ranging and involve citizens, civil society, social partners, national parliaments and political parties. The modalities would be left to the member states, showing how far the European Union is from being a superstate.

In the meantime, it would be up to the member states whether they would proceed with ratification or put it on hold. Most indicated that they would defer ratification to a later date, although the Luxembourg government insisted that it would continue with its referendum on 10 July. No formal decision was reached on extending the deadline for ratification although Prime Minister Juncker of Luxembourg hinted that the process might be completed by 2007. His Swedish counterpart indicated that it could take five years, if it is ever achieved. Nonetheless, technically speaking ratification continues and there was no thought of renegotiation or reopening the text.

Clearly the Constitutional Treaty has not lost all significance. It is still there and will obviously figure both in the debate called for by the European Council and in any renegotiation – whether of the brief statement of principles wished by many critics, or of a revised and full consolidation of the existing treaties – even if only as something to be avoided. In the meantime, some of its contents have already been anticipated and more may be, despite strictures about re-introducing the treaty through the 'back door' and using the corpse for 'body parts'. More significantly, the 85 per cent of its contents which come from the existing treaties will remain in effect. Indeed, it is not impossible that future negotiators and others, once they experience the bruising and uncertain political bargaining necessary for treaty revision, may come to feel that the Constitutional Treaty was not as bad as it was painted. Admittedly, as we have consistently pointed out, it is far from perfect, and some of its authors now accept that it went too far: in its name, its ambition and its range of changes. But it was a working compromise and getting a better one from the very diverse and rancorous 'no' camps will be far harder, as the June 2005 European Council showed. This is even more likely if the prophecies following the French 'non' and Dutch 'nee' of economic upset, rejection of enlargement and blocked decision making come true. Nonetheless, subsequent approval of the Constitutional Treaty in Cyprus, Malta and Luxembourg has encouraged further speculation about its future. So it remains worth knowing exactly what is in the Constitutional Treaty, why it is there and what it actually means. We hope that this book will still help people to engage with the real text rather than just its symbolic and catalytic roles.

Glossary

One of the criticisms of the Constitutional Treaty and its predecessors is that they are riddled with initials and jargon, or what has been called the 'Humpty Dumpty vocabulary of EU bureaucracy'. This is true but it is no different where domestic legislation in any specialized and complex field is concerned. Complex activities can require complex explanations and the best we can do is to try and explain those relating to the European Union, as we do here.

Accession The technical term for a state joining the European Union.

Acquis The sum total of EU law, obligations and aspirations, acceptance of which is a requirement for accession.

Amendment The process of making changes to the treaties or constitutions. The way this is done is seen as a symbol of the document's status.

Annexes Lists attached to the Constitutional Treaty that detail the agricultural products covered and the countries to which association applies.

Area of freedom, security and justice is used to describe the European Union's interest in justice and home affairs such as asylum, crime and migration. Decisions in this area are subject to special intergovernmental rules.

Articles The basic element of a treaty or constitution, equivalent to clauses. They can be grouped into Titles and Chapters or subdivided into paragraphs.

Benelux The economic union of Belgium, the Netherlands and Luxembourg, set up in 1944 and allowed to continue even though the European Union took over most of its functions.

Blocking minority The minimum number of member states or votes needed to prevent the adoption of EU legislation under QMV.

Brussels-ization The process of member states pursuing activities collectively in Brussels, whether or not formal EU procedures are used.

Case law Judgements made by courts which are regarded as a basic part of the law and the constitution and, in the European Union, the acquis.

Chapter A subdivision of a Title in an EU treaty. Can itself be subdivided into sections.

Charter of Fundamental Rights and Freedoms The document drawn up in 1999–2000 by a specially appointed Convention to list the rights of EU citizens. Proclaimed rather than legally enforced. It appears as Part II of the Constitutional Treaty.

Citizenship The status of membership of a political community. Enjoyed by individuals and carrying with it specific rights. Normally a national matter, EU citizenship came in 1993. Requires national citizenship, to which it is subordinate.

Civil society Term used to indicate grass roots social feelings but monopolized by interest groups to legitimize their influence in the European Union.

Co-decision The basic EU legislative procedure in which legislation has to be approved by both the Council and the EP. The Constitutional Treaty renames it the 'ordinary legislative procedure'

Codification The process by which laws or treaties are systematically brought together into one document.

Comitology The system of EU committees set up to aid the Commission and the Council in their policy making.

Common accord The form of agreement either between institutions or member states normally governing appointments.

Common provisions Rules in a treaty which apply to a number of sectors and actors, thus avoiding the need for repetition. Those in the Constitutional Treaty lay down what form legislation should take across all EU activities.

Community basis or method denotes a decision normally being taken by the EP and the Council jointly on a Commission proposal, with advisory bodies being consulted where relevant. Its use is odd given that the Constitutional Treaty does away with the European Community and fails to define the term.

Competence A French term used to describe the European Union's authority, or less accurately powers, to undertake specific activities.

Complementary A description of those powers that allow the European Union to legislate alongside the member states in specific fields.

Conciliation Part of the ordinary legislative procedure which brings together representatives of the EP and the Council to see if differences can be reconciled so that legislation can be adopted.

Conferral The underlying political basis of the European Union, now spelt out in the Constitutional Treaty, with member states jointly agreeing to delegate specific powers to the Union. Member states remain sovereign in all other respects.

Configuration The various forms in which the Council meets to discuss specific issues (e.g. agriculture or foreign affairs).

Consensus Both an undefined term used to describe how some decisions are to be made in the EU and a synonym for broad agreement. Similar to 'nem con' it is the normal decision-making mode in the European Council and is generally sought in the Council.

Consolidation A technical term for the updating, polishing and re-arranging of treaties.

Constitutional requirements Phrase used to indicate that it is up to the member states how they ratify changes in the treaties etc. In many member states this is laid down in the constitution; in the UK it is a matter of unwritten practice.

Constitutionalism A much-debated term, especially among academics, that usually means running public affairs in a manner consonant with a legitimate constitution and especially with those rules which constrain the exercise of power.

Constitutionalization The process of giving the existing EU treaties a more constitutional style.

Convention A body set up with a constitutional remit, as with the Philadelphia Convention of 1787. In the context of the European Union, conventions were used to draw up the Charter of Fundamental Rights and the *Draft Treaty establishing a Constitution for Europe.*

Cooperation Either a way of harmonious working in general or the taking of decisions on an inter-governmental basis.

COREPER The gathering of national ambassadors to the European Union who prepare meetings of the Council.

Court of First Instance A court set up in the 1980s to help take some of the burden off the Court of Justice. It has since become the EU's main court. The Constitutional Treaty refers to it as the General Court.

Decision can be either a general term for deciding something or a specific form of EU legal act.

Declaration Normally a subordinate text found at the end of a treaty expressing the intentions of the signatories, generally agreed or tabled by individual member states. The term is also used loosely to describe formal statements by the European Union

Degressively proportional A mathematical term describing the principle of seat allocation in the EP. It means that the smaller the state, the less the attention paid to population size as a factor in awarding seats. This allows very small member states to be given enough seats to enable them to be represented in committees and prevents very big member states from dominating.

Delegation The act of entrusting limited powers to the Commission and other bodies to undertake legislative and other action on behalf of the European Union, thus giving rise to comitology.

Democratic deficit Term used to describe the perceived lack of democracy in the procedures of the European Union.

Demos Greek term for people, as in democracy, the 'rule of the people'. It is often argued that there is no single 'European demos' to support the European Union; only many national 'demoi'.

Derogation A formal exemption from otherwise binding requirements.

Dialogue A requirement for formal contacts between institutions and non-EU bodies in order to enhance democracy.

Directive The current name for a 'framework law'. This is an EU act which lays down a principle but leaves it to national authorities to decide how this is best achieved in their situation.

Directly effective In EU law the fact that legislation acts on citizens and not just on states. Very often this means it does not need to be enacted in domestic law before having effect.

Directoire A term, derived from French history, used to suggest that the European Union is, or will be, run by a small group of larger member states.

Double hatting Term used to describe the proposed Union Minister for Foreign Affairs who will be a member of both the Council and the Commission.

Double majority The new requirement that EU decisions and acts be adopted in the Council not just by state votes but by percentages of states and populations.

Economic and Monetary Union The area of EU activity that includes management of the euro and the monetary policy of the eurozone.

Enhanced cooperation Also known as 'closer cooperation' or 'flexibility', this allows groups of states to pursue further integration, subject to various constraints. Variants have been in the treaties since 1999 but so far they have not been used..

Eurobarometer The standard European Commission sampling of public opinion on integration, appearing at least twice a year.

Eurogroup The ministerial council formed by Finance Ministers of member states which have adopted the euro.

Eurojust is a system of delegated national prosecutors, magistrates and police officers that facilitates cross-border judicial cooperation. There are also European Judicial Networks in civil, commercial and criminal matters.

European Atomic Energy Community The second Community, created in 1958 and usually known as Euratom, now largely subsumed into the mainstream European Union after nuclear power proved not to be the main impetus to integration. Its constitutive treaty remains in force but may be reviewed.

European Central Bank The directing element of the European System of Central Banks which runs EMU. Its key roles are to set interest rates and manage the euro.

European Coal and Steel Community The original community, set up in 1952. Its constituent treaty expired in 2002, although some of its provisions are still reflected in the Constitutional Treaty.

European Community The modernized name of the original European Economic Community. It symbolizes integration based on pooled sovereignty and the use of common institutions and processes. From 1992 onward it was contrasted with the European Union, which was seen as a more intergovernmental body.

European Convention on Human Rights The senior human rights agreement in the wider Europe, drawn up in 1949 by the Council of Europe and policed by a special court, the European Court of Human Rights, sitting in Strasbourg. Assuming the European Union signs up the convention, it will override the Charter of Fundamental Rights.

European Council The quarterly meetings of the heads of government and state – often known as 'summits' – which are meant to give overall direction to the European Union. Its role has been enhanced by the Constitutional Treaty.

Nonetheless, it does not produce legislative acts but signals its intentions in notes of its decisions or 'conclusions'.

European Court of Justice The generic term given to the EU judiciary, embracing not just the Court of Justice itself but also the Court of First Instance and specialized tribunals. It plays a key role in interpreting the treaties and is often, somewhat inaccurately, seen as a supporter of integration. Its seat is in Luxembourg.

European Investment Bank The long-established EU institution which funds development both inside the European Union and elsewhere.

European Parliament The directly elected parliament of the European Union, which represents the people and shares with the Council the right to act as legislator.

European Rapid Reaction Force The military formation, composed of national units, meant to give the European Union the ability to intervene promptly in implementing the common security and defence policy.

European social model denotes a belief that continental western Europe differs from the United States in its preference for social welfare, social rights and consultation over unrestrained competition.

European Union The entity established in 1993 that brought together the existing Communities and supplemented them with two intergovernmental Pillars. It is overhauled by the Constitutional Treaty and despite calls for change retains the name.

Europol A police coordinating office, based in The Hague, set up in 1991 to facilitate police cooperation across the European Union.

Eurosceptic A term originally used to describe thosc who had doubts about European integration but one that is now often used to describe outright opponents.

Eurozone The territory of those states using the euro as their currency. Subject both to special rules, such as the Stability and Growth Pact, and the decisions of the European Central Bank.

Exclusive Competences which can only be exercised in common through the European Union.

Federal In the UK debate symbolizes centralized government at the expense of local autonomy. For others, it is a way of preserving the interests of states inside a wider framework. For political scientists, the European Union, because it shares power among various levels of authority each with its own sphere of activity, is federal in spirit.

Final Act A report summarizing the results of an intergovernmental conference to which Declarations are attached.

Flexibility Used in a variety of EU contexts. In the Constitutional Treaty it describes a clause which allows the European Union to undertake activities that are not specifically mentioned if they are necessary to achieves existing objectives. It can also be used to describe a kind of variable geometry European Union in which some member states do not participate in a given area of activity, e.g. EMU.

Framework Term used to describe the inter-related institutional structures of the European Union, an outline plan for financing the European Union, a structure for programmatic activity, the European Union itself or the context of a policy or strategy.

Future of Europe debate Term used to describe the post-2001 process of thinking about institutional and treaty reorganization.

General and final provisions comprise that part of a treaty (e.g. Part IV of the Constitutional Treaty) which lays down rules for bringing it into effect, applying it and altering it.

Governance The wider processes of running organizations, whether businesses or countries. In the latter it is seen as involving not just government and laws but also social actors and informal politics. The European Union is formally committed to 'good governance'.

Heads of state occupy the top spot in the constitutional hierarchy of states and normally have the power to sign treaties. They are not always powerful, although the French President is an obvious exception, and tend to fulfil ceremonial roles, with effective power being with the head of government or prime minister.

Hierarchy of norms refers to the fact that certain rules in constitutions are more important than others and may thus need to be enacted in different ways.

High Contracting Parties A state's signatories to treaties in international law.

Implementation The business of applying rules, which in the European Union is done by national administrations.

Initiative means the right to propose action. Generally the Commission is empowered to present legislation, but other bodies can both invite it to consider acting and make reports of their own.

Institution An entity enjoying enhanced status and decision-making powers, as compared to advisory bodies or agencies.

Instruments are the various legal forms which European Union acts may take.

Integration means bringing things together or is the way of describing the European process of common action through the use of EU institutions and procedures.

Intergovernmental describes activities undertaken by states which decide, of their own volition, to cooperate, usually through their delegates and without use of supranational structures.

Intergovernmental conferences are the traditional mechanisms used to revise treaties. They involve representatives of the participating states and operate on several levels, including specialist advisory groups and ministerial meetings. In the European Union, meetings of the European Council conclude such conferences.

Interpretations are the decisions taken on what laws and treaties actually mean or imply. Usually adopted by the ECJ when uncertainties or conflicting views are referred to it.

Legal act A binding EU decision.

Legal continuity denotes the continuing efficacy of existing legislation even though treaties may have been repealed. It avoids unnecessary legal aggravation.

Legal personality allows the European Union to take binding and recognized international decisions and be accountable for them in relevant courts. Currently only enjoyed formally by the European Community, the Constitutional Treaty extends it to the European Union.

Legitimacy is the quality enjoyed by a political regime, or other body, which is recognized at a popular level as having the right to take binding decisions and have them obeyed. Some believe that the European Union does not presently have this.

Luxemburg compromise The informal agreement reached in 1966 that member states would not be overruled when they felt their vital interests were at stake. It has since been rendered largely obsolete by the use of qualified majority voting.

Mandating Binding instructions given to an EU institution or a conference delegate. A mandate can either mean the precise instructions given or a general authority to act.

Member state The formal status of those countries which have joined the European Union.

Multiannual financial framework A set of financial allocations, agreed by member states for a five-year period, which lays down ceilings and targets for EU spending. Annual budgets must keep within the envelopes set down in the framework.

North Atlantic Treaty Organization Defence body set up in 1949, during the Cold War, which now fulfils a wider role and embraces many former Communist states. The Constitutional Treaty recognizes that many member states rely on NATO for defence.

Objectives guide what the European Union does in pursuing its aims and implementing policies.

Ombudsman The EU official whose job is to receive complaints from citizens about maladministration, investigate them and report on them.

Opinion An EU legal act which is a non-binding view on a major issue.

Opt-in The right of a member state currently outside an area of EU activity to participate if it so wishes.

Opt-out describes a statutory right given to a member state not to take part in an EU activity, as with the UK opt-out from EMU.

Organ is sometimes used to describe an EU institution or a technical or advisory body. These are now known as 'offices' or 'agencies'.

Paragraph A subdivision of an article in a treaty.

Part The main subdivision of the Constitutional Treaty and treaties in general. It can be subdivided into Titles.

Participatory Form of democracy in which citizens are actively engaged in governance, as opposed to representative democracy.

Passerelle Controversial bridging procedure which allows the transfer of specific subjects from unanimity to qualified majority.

Philadelphia was the location for the 1787 Constitutional Convention that drew up the present US Constitution.

Pillar One of the three elements of the existing EU: the European Community, the common foreign and security policy, and justice and home affairs. Under the Constitutional Treaty the Pillar structure as such disappears but separate decision-making procedures still pertain.

Plenary A meeting of all members of a body such as a parliament or a convention.

Pluralist describes western states in which a variety of interests both exist and are given means of expression, without there being a monolithic and dominant group.

Pooling describes the way that member states are said to be sharing their sovereignty to make collective decisions within the European Union.

Praesidium Steering group of bodies, such as a convention or continental parties and parliaments.

Preamble The opening sentences of a treaty, following the list of signatories, which sets out the aims of those signing it and the main themes contained in it. It has symbolic importance and can be used in interpretations of EU law.

Prejudice Often appears in the phrase 'without prejudice', which means that a clause in a treaty is meant to have no implications for another part of the treaty even though this may appear to be in contradiction.

Presidency Currently the member state chairing the European Council and meetings of the Council. This rotates on a six-monthly basis. Under the Constitutional Treaty, the President of the European Council will be appointed for a two-and-a-half-year period. Rotating Presidencies will remain in an altered form in the Council.

Primacy The doctrine – sometimes known as supremacy – that in those areas where the European Union has competence, EU law takes precedence over conflicting national law. This was established by the Court of Justice and accepted by member states in the 1960s. It now appears in the Constitutional Treaty.

Proportionality The legal doctrine, enshrined in a Protocol, that EU acts should not use sledgehammers to crack nuts but should only use as much emphasis as the subject deserves.

Protocol Supplementary texts to a treaty which enjoy equal status but contain detailed material that is too bulky for inclusion. Required to provide detailed implementation of general provisos.

Provisions The rules laid down in a treaty.

Qualified majority voting Voting rules which reflect the different size of member states when decisions are taken. This is done through an allocation of votes roughly proportionate to size and tends to favour small states. The Constitutional Treaty will replace this complicated system with a double majority system.

Ratification The process of approving a treaty by the signatory states according to their own constitutional rules. This may involve parliamentary votes or a referendum.

Recommendation A legal instrument that involves non-binding advice about a course of action. Often aimed at an individual state.

Referendum A popular vote on a policy matter.

Region Larger sub-national territorial unit with its own administration and now recognized in the Committee of the Regions.

Regulation Currently the highest form of EU legislation which is generally binding and is immediately and fully applicable within member states without any domestic legislation being required. Will be known as a European law after ratification.

Repeal The act of formally abrogating existing treaties. The Constitutional Treaty repeals various treaties but provides for legal continuity.

Representative Form of democracy in which citizens elect others to engage in governance on their behalf without being mandated.

Rights Entitlement of individuals to proper forms of treatment. Rights are enshrined in the European Convention of Human Rights. Because rights are seen as the epitome of democratic polities, they have become a growing theme in the European Union, leading to the drafting of the Charter of Fundamental Rights.

Seat The headquarters of an EU institution, usually in Brussels or Luxembourg but can be scattered across member states. Having one is a fiercely defended privilege.

Section An element of a chapter and, as such, the lowest level of treaty subdivision.

Simplification is often used to describe the tidying up – or toiletage – of a treaty text. This is done once key decisions have been reached and can also involve institutional changes to make structures simpler.

Solidarity A term meaning practical fellow feeling with others. It is used in three different contexts in the treaties: in internal relations where the European Union seeks to respect and aid other states; in social affairs where it involves workers rights, social security and health; and among the Union's own member states.

Sovereignty describes the quality of being an autonomous and independent state, recognized as such by other states, and therefore with the exclusive right to exercise supreme authority over its territory. Sovereignty of both kinds is generally vested in a government: For some people it is indivisible and essential to national existence. Hence they want the European Union reorganized so as to give this full weight. Others believe that sovereignty is not absolute and can be pooled without harm. In the United Kingdom, the idea of parliamentary sovereignty, that is the ability of a majority in the Commons to make any laws it chooses except ones which bind its successors, makes it a sensitive concept, closely linked to national identity.

State A political entity possessing sovereignty, normally within a nation of which it is the organized political expression. The term is usually used to describe the totality of political and other relevant institutions in a nation, as distinct both from government as such and from civil society.

Statute A formal piece of UK legislation, entered up in the so-called Statute Book. In the European Union it means the detailed standing orders for bodies such as the ECB and the ECJ.

Subsidiarity A doctrine which argues that decisions be taken at the lowest possible level and not imposed from above. It was introduced to the European Union in

1992 to counter fears of unfettered centralization, and its application has since been extended. The Constitutional Treaty contains a policing role for national parliaments.

Summit Journalistic name for the European Council.

Superstate A pejorative term used by eurosceptics to describe the European Union, whether now or in the future. It is inaccurate since the European Union is not a state, does not have most of the powers of an ordinary state and lacks the ability to coerce its members.

Supranational A form of governance in which there are institutions and rules which take precedence over national decision making. However, such rules emerge from decisions of member states and only apply in specific fields, so it should not be taken to imply the extinction of nation states.

Team Presidency A grouping of three member states which, under the Constitutional Treaty, will share the task of chairing Council meetings (other than that for Foreign Affairs) over an 18-month period. This preserves the old rotating Presidency but within a more stable framework.

Title A subdivision of a treaty below a Part which can itself be divided into chapters.

Transitional describes provisions for moving from the existing treaties to the full operation of the Constitutional Treaty.

Transparency denotes a new concern for openness, clarity and approachability in the working of the European Union. Part of the attempt to make the Union less remote and both more comprehensible and more democratic by, *inter alia*, allowing access to official documents, the holding of public sessions and the use of one's own language in dealings with the Union. It can also refer to getting more readable and simpler instruments, processes and texts.

Treaty establishing the European Community The original 1957 Treaty of Rome which set up what was then known as the European Economic Community. As it was amended many times from the 1960s to the 1990s, the present text is much longer than the original version. The Constitutional Treaty repeals it but incorporates much of its contents.

Treaty of Amsterdam An amending treaty signed in 1997 which remedied some of the failings of the Treaty on European Union and began the constitutionalization process by consolidating the TEU and the TEC.

Treaty of Nice An amending treaty agreed in 2000 which was widely felt to be unsatisfactory in the changes it made to decision making.

Treaty on European Union The so-called Maastricht Treaty of 1992 which set up the old European Union as an umbrella body above and around the EC, bringing in the second and third Pillars. To be repealed and largely incorporated into the Constitutional Treaty.

Unanimity Mode of voting used in the European Council and the Council which requires the consent of all those participating, thus giving a member state which disagrees with the majority an effective veto. Abstentions are not counted. Defenders of sovereignty place stress on this as a means of preserving their own ways and powers. Supporters of integration see it as an obstacle to efficiency and progress.

Union Either a process of coming together or the structure envisaged by the Constitutional Treaty to replace the current European Union.

United Nations The international body bringing together most states in the world. Based on a charter which is the source of much international law. The Constitutional Treaty recognizes it as a framework which the European Union must respect.

Withdrawal A new facility, set out in Article I-60, for a member state to secede from the European Union of its own volition and largely on its own terms. This is not presently possible.

World Trade Organization International body, replacing the General Agreement on Tariffs and Trade, policing world commerce, including that of the European Union.

Finding out more

In a book of this length it is not possible to cover all of the Constitutional Treaty, let alone its context or the issues arising from it. This brief guide tries to point readers to other sources which provide the full text of the treaties, fill in gaps, provide useful background or offer different perspectives to those adopted here. As well as guiding readers towards copies of the complete text of the Constitutional Treaty, it also has readings on the present treaties, ratification, the process of reform, the Convention and its draft Treaty, the European Union, and United Kingdom relations with the European Union. There are also suggestions on how to stay up to date.

1 The text of the Constitutional Treaty

Treaty establishing a Constitution for Europe: Including the Protocols and Annexes, and Final Act with Declarations, Rome, 29 October 2004, Cm 6429, London, 8 December 2004 (also available via www.europe.gov.uk).

Treaty establishing a Constitution for Europe, to be found in the *Official Journal of the European Union,* C 310, 16 December 2004 (also available via europa.eu.int/eur-lex)

Treaty establishing a Constitution for Europe, European Parliament (London Office), 2004 (www.europarl.org.uk/constitution/constitutionmain.htm)

2 The Constitutional Treaty: appraisals and commentaries

Birkinshaw, P. 'A Constitution for the EU?' *European Public Law,* 10 (1) 2004, 57–84.

Bogdanor, V. 'The Eurosceptic Constitution', *E!Sharp,* September 2004, pp. 17–20.

Bonde, J-P. (ed.). *The EU Constitution: The Reader-Friendly Edition,* 21 December 2004 (via www.euabc.com).

Centre for European Reform. *The CER Guide to the EU's Constitutional Treaty* (London: Centre for European Reform, 2004). (www.cer.org.uk/pdf/policybrief_constitution_july04.pdf).

Cowgill A.W. and Cowgill, A.A. *The European Constitution in Perspective* (Stroud: British Management Data Foundation, 2004).

Devuyst, Y. *EU Decision-Making after the Treaty establishing a Constitution for Europe*

(Pittsburgh: University Center for International Studies, 2004) (via www.ucis.pitt.edu/cwes).

Duff, A. *The Constitution for Europe* (London: I B Tauris, 2005). Cf. also *The International Spectator*, 39 (3) 2004, 73–81.

European Citizen Action Service. *50 Questions and Answers on the Treaty establishing a Constitution for Europe* (Brussels: European Citizen Action Service, 2005) (via www.ecas.org).

Federal Trust. *EU Constitution Project Newsletter,* Special Issue, July 2004 (www.fedtrust.co.uk/uploads/constitution/News07_04.pdf).

Feus, K. (ed.). *The EU Charter of Fundamental Rights* (London: Federal Trust, 2000).

Foreign and Commonwealth Office, *White Paper on the Treaty establishing a Constitution for Europe,* Cm 6309, London, 9 September 2004 (also available via www.fco.gov.uk).

Foreign and Commonwealth Office. *Treaty establishing a Constitution for Europe: Commentary,* Cm 6459, London, 26 January 2005 (also available via www.europe.gov.uk).

Grevi, G. *Light and Shade of a Quasi-Constitution: An Assessment,* EPC Issue Paper 14, European Policy Centre, Brussels, 23 June 2004 (via www.theepc.be).

Laude, Y. 'The European Union Constitutional Treaty: An Analysis', *EIS: Europe Information,* Special Report, 7 July 2004.

MacCormick, N. *Who's Afraid of a European Constitution?* (Exeter: Societas - Imprint Academic, 2005).

Millar, V. *The Treaty establishing a Constitution for Europe: Part I,* House of Commons Library, Research Paper 4/66, 6 September 2004 (www.parliament.uk/commons/lib/research/rp2004/rp04-066.pdf).

O'Rourke, A., Donaghue J. and Dukes A. (eds). *Europe Re-United: A Constitutional Treaty* (Dublin: Institute of European Affairs, 2004).

Pernice, I. and Zemanek, J. (eds). *The Treaty Establishing a Constitution for Europe: Perspectives after the IGC of 2004* (Baden-Baden: Nomos, 2005).

Phinnemore, D. *The Treaty Establishing A Constitution For Europe: An Overview,* European Programme Briefing Note 04–01, Royal Institute of International Affairs, London, 2004 (www.riia.org/pdf/research/europe/BN-DPJun04.pdf).

Pinelli, C. 'The Powers of the European Parliament in the New Constitutional Treaty', *The International Spectator,* 39 (3) 2004, 82–90.

Smith, R. 'Constitutionalising the European Union', *UACES European Studies On-Line Essays* No. 3 (London: UACES, 2004) (www.uaces.org/E53Smith.pdf).

Winn, D. *An EU Constitution for Britain?* (London: Futuro, 2004).

3 The existing treaties

Church, C. and Phinnemore, D. *The Penguin Guide to the European Treaties* (London: Penguin, 2002).

Craig, P. 'Constitutions, Constitutionalism and the European Union', *European Law Review,* 7 (2) 2001, 125–50.

Euroconfidential. *The Rome, Maastricht, Amsterdam and Nice Treaties: Comparative Texts* (London: Europa, 2003).

Nelson, S. (ed.). *The Convoluted Treaties II: Treaty establishing the European Economic Community* (Oxford: Nelson and Pollard, 1993).
OOPEC. *Consolidated Treaties* (Luxembourg: OOPEC, 1997).
OOPEC. *Selected Instruments Taken from the Treaties* (Luxembourg: OOPEC, 2000).
Rudden, D. and Wyatt, D. *EU Treaties and Legislation* (Oxford: Oxford University Press, 2004).

4 Ratification

Eurobarometer: europa.eu.int/comm/public_opinion.
Gill, M., Atkinson, S. and Mortimore, R. *The Referendum Battle* (London: Foreign Policy Centre, 2004).
Grant, C. *What Happens if Britain Votes No? Ten Ways Out of a European Constitutional Crisis* (London: Centre for European Reform, 2005).
Hannan, D. *Voting on the Constitution: What should this country know about the consequences* (London: Politeia, 2004).
Hussain, N., Hudson, G.M. and Mortimore, R. *Referendums on the EU Constitutional Treaty: The State of Play*, European Programme Briefing Note 05-02, Royal Institute of International Affairs, London, 2005 (www.chathamhouse.org.uk/pdf/research/europe/BP-NHOct04.pdf).
Keohane, D. *A Guide to the Referenda on the EU Constitutional Treaty*, Briefing Note, Centre for European Reform, London, 2004 (www.cer.org.uk/pdf/briefing_referenda.pdf).
Roberts-Thompson, P. 'EU Treaty Referendums and the European Union', *Journal of European Integration*, 23 (2) 2001, 105–37.
Shaw, J. *What happens if the Constitutional Treaty is not ratified?* European Policy Brief, Issue 6 (London: Federal Trust, 2004) (www.fedtrust.co.uk/admin/uploads/PolicyBrief6.pdf).
Tosato, G.L. and Greco, E. 'The EU Constitutional Treaty: How to deal with the ratification bottleneck', *The International Spectator*, 39 (4) 2004, 7–24.
Wall, S. 'Perilous to say No', *The World Today*, 61 (3) 2004, 16–17.

5 Treaty reform

Beach, D. *The Dynamics of European Integration* (Basingstoke: Palgrave, 2005).
Chryssochoou, D.N., Tsinisizelis, M.J., Stavridis, S. and Ifantis, K. *Theory and Reform in the European Union*, 2nd edition (Manchester: Manchester University Press, 2003).
Devuyst, Y. 'Treaty Reform in the European Union: The Amsterdam Process', *Journal of European Public Policy*, 5 (4) 1998, 615–31.
Falkner, G. (ed.). 'EU Treaty Reform as a Three-Level Process', *Journal of European Public Policy*, Special Issue 9 (1) 2002.
Feus, K. (ed.). *A Simplified Treaty for the European Union?* (London: Federal Trust, 2001).
Galloway, D. *The Treaty of Nice and Beyond* (Sheffield: Sheffield Academic Press, 2001).

Griffiths, R.T. *Europe's First Constitution: The European Political Community, 1952–1954* (London: Federal Trust, 2000).

6 The European Convention

Allen, D. 'The Convention and the Draft Constitutional Treaty', in Cameron, F. (ed.) *The Future of Europe* (London: Routledge, 2003), 18–34.
Kiljunen, K. *The European Constitution in the Making* (Brussels: Centre for European Policy Studies, 2004).
Michalski, A. (ed.). *The Political Dynamics of Constitutional Reform: Reflections on the Convention on the Future of Europe* (The Hague: Netherlands Institute of International Relations, 2004).
Norman, P. *The Accidental Constitution: The Story of the European Convention* (Brussels: EuroComment, 2003).
Shaw, J., Magnette, P., Hoffmann, L. and Bausili, A.V. (eds). *The Convention on the Future of Europe: Working Towards an EU Constitution* (London: Federal Trust, 2003).
Stuart, G. *The Making of Europe's Constitution* (London: Fabian Society, 2003).

7 The European Convention's draft treaty

Cowgill, A.W. and Cowgill, A.A. *An Analysis of the Draft Treaty establishing a Constitution for Europe* (Stroud: British Management Data Foundation, 2003).
Eijsbouts. W.T. (ed.). *European Constitutional Law Review*, 1 (1) 2005. Special number on the Convention and the European Constitution.
European Convention. *Draft Treaty establishing a Constitution for Europe* (Luxembourg: OOPEC, 2003) (also via europa.eu.int).
Kokott, J. and Rüth, A. 'The European Convention and its Draft Treaty establishing a Constitution for Europe: Appropriate Answers to the Laeken Questions?', *Common Market Law Review*, 40 (6) 2003, 1315–46.
Prospect. *Draft EU Constitution* (London: Prospect, 2003).
Schwarze, J. 'Guest Editorial: The Convention's Draft Treaty establishing a Constitution for Europe', *Common Market Law Review*, 40 (5) 2003, 1037–46.
Witte, B. (ed.). *Ten Reflections on the Constitutional Treaty for Europe* (Florence: European University Institute, 2003).

8 The European Union

Bainbridge, T. *The Penguin Companion to European Union* (London: Penguin, 1998).
Blair, A. *The EU Since 1945* (London: Pearson/Longman, 2005).
Bomberg, E. and Stubbb, A. (eds). *The European Union: How Does it Work?* (Oxford: OUP, 2003).
Dinan, D. *Encyclopaedia of the European Union*, updated edition (Basingstoke: Palgrave, 2000).
Dinan, D. *Europe Recast: A History of the European Union* (Basingstoke: Palgrave, 2004).
Green, M.C. and Dinan D. (eds). *Developments in the European Union* (Basingstoke: Macmillan, 2004).

Hix, S. *The Political System of the European Union*, 2nd edition (Basingstoke: Macmillan, 2005).
McGowan, L. and Phinnemore, D. *A Dictionary of the European Union* (London: Europa, 2004).
Nugent, N. *The Government and Politics of the EU* (Basingstoke: Palgrave, 2003).
Pinder, J. *The EU: A Very Short Introduction* (Oxford: OUP, 2001).
Ramsey, A. *Eurojargon* (London: Europa, 2001).
Siedentop, L. *Democracy in Europe* (London: Penguin, 2000).
Wallace, H. and Wallace, W. (eds). *Policy-Making in the European Union*, 4th edition (Oxford: OUP, 2000).
Warleigh, A. *European Union: The Basics* (London: Routledge, 2004).

9 The United Kingdom and the European Union in general

Barendt, E. 'Is there a United Kingdom Constitution?', *Oxford Journal of Legal Studies*, 17 (1) 1997, 137–46).
Blair, A. *Dealing with Europe: Britain and the Negotiation of the Maastricht Treaty* (Aldershot: Ashgate, 1999).
Booker, C. and North, R. *The Great Deception* (London: Centurion, 2003).
Forster, A. *Euroscepticism in Contemporary British Politics* (London: Routledge, 2002).
Geddes, A. *Europe and British Politics* (Basingstoke: Palgrave, 2004).
Menon, A. 'Britain and the Convention on the Future of Europe', *International Affairs*, 79 (5) 2003, 963–78.
Stephens, P. 'Britain and Europe: An unforgettable Past and an unavoidable Future', *The Political Quarterly*, 76 (1) 2005, 12–21.
Young, J. *Britain and European Unity 1945–1999* (Basingstoke Macmillan, 2000).

10 Keeping up to date

Books and articles can soon get out of date, especially in such a fast-changing area as European Union reform. Thus following new developments is very necessary if proper judgements are to be made. There is a huge amount of information on the Union's own website – europa.eu.int – especially on the constitution homepage: europa.eu.int/constitution. And there is also a very informative weblog run by students in Geneva and Florence: blogs.unige.ch/droit/ceje/dotclear/index.php. In addition, analysis and commentary are available from a variety of other sources including the following:

Agence Europe: www.agenceeurope.com
Centre for European Reform: www.cer.org.uk
CIDEL: www.unizar.es/euroconstitucion/Home.htm
EU Business: www.eubusiness.com
Euroactiv: www.euroactiv.om
European Observer: www.euobserver.com
European Policy Centre: www.theepc.be

European Policy Institutes Network: www.epin.org
Federal Trust, EU Constitution Newsletter: www.fedtrust.co.uk/constitution_newsletter
Friends of Europe: www.friendsofeurope.org
Notre Europe: www.notre-europe.asso.fr

Index

Note: Entries in *italic* indicate mentions in the official text of Part I of the Constitutional Treaty as printed here. Specific articles of treaties other than Part I of the Constitutional Treaty are not indexed. The Glossary on pages 176–86 gives a full explanation of terms used in the book.